Ethnic minorities in English Law

Richard Jones and
Gnanapala Welhengama

with an introduction by Werner Menski

Gems No. 5

G E M S

Trentham Books and School of Oriental & African Studies

First published in 2000 by Trentham Books Limited
Trentham Books Limited
Westview House
734 London Road
Oakhill
Stoke on Trent
Staffordshire
England ST4 5NP

British Cataloguing in Publication Data
A catalogue record for this book is available from the British Library
ISBN 1 85856 138 8 (hb ISBN 1 85856 137 X)

Designed and typeset by Trentham Print Design Ltd., Chester and printed in
Great Britain by Bell & Bain Ltd., Glasgow

Ethnic Minority Studies at SOAS

is a series of monographs and collected papers that focus on current issues in the study of ethnic minorities in Britain and elsewhere in the world.

The series is edited by Dr. Werner F. Menski, Senior Lecturer in South Asian Laws at the School of Oriental and African Studies and the Chairman of GEMS, the Group for Ethnic Minority Studies at the School.

No. 1 Sanjiv Sachdeva
The primary purpose rule in British immigration law

No. 2 Werner Menski (ed.)
Coping with 1997: The reaction of the Hong Kong people to the transfer of power

No. 3 Claudia Mortimore
Immigration and adoption

No. 4 António Cruz
Shifting responsibility: Carriers' liability in the Member States of the European Union and North America

No. 5 Richard Jones and Gnanapala Welhengama
Ethnic minorities in English law

No. 6 Werner Menski (ed.)
South Asians and the dowry problem

Acknowledgments

We would in particular like to thank several colleagues for their help in the preparation of this text. Bill Douglas and Dr. Derek Clifford for reading the manuscript and making helpful comments, Ms. Wendy Neale at Liverpool University Law Library for her help in finding relevant materials. Professor Penny Pearce, Elizabeth Douglas, John Backwell and Gwen Backwell for providing encouragement. Dr. Menski at SOAS for his many helpful suggestions and for taking on the task of editing and publishing of this text. Any errors are of course ours.

We would also like to acknowledge the supportive role of the staff at Trentham Books and at Trentham Print Design Ltd. in the efficient production of the book.

Finally we would like to thank our families, Sanda, Chamene, Jean, Nicola and Paul for their continued support and encouragement.

Richard Jones
M.A (Nottingham); LL.B. (Lond)
Reader in Law and Information Technology,
Liverpool John Moores University

Gnanapala Welhengama
LL.M (Lond), LL.B; B.A. (Sri Lanka), Ph.D.
Attorney-at-Law of The Supreme Court of Sri Lanka,
formerly Tutor in Law, Sri Lanka Law College,
Research Fellow in Law, Liverpool John Moores University

List of Abbreviations

AC	Law Reports, Appeal Cases
AllER	All England Reports
CA	Court of Appeal
ch.	chapter
Ch	Chancery
Cl & F	Clark and Finnelly's Reports, HL, 1831-1846
CJ	Chief Justice
Cr App R	Criminal Appeal Reports
CRE	Commission for Racial Equality
CRiLR	Criminal Law Reports
CUKC	Citizen of the United Kingdom and Colonies
DHSS	Department of Health and Social Security
EAT	Employment Appeal Tribunal
ECHR	European Convention on Human Rights
EHRR	European Human Rights Reports
EOR	Equal Opportunities Reports
EU	European Union
Fam Law	Family Law
FLC	Family Law Cases
FLR	Family Law Reports
HC	House of Commons
HL	House of Lords
HLR	Housing Law Reports
IAT	Immigration Appeal Tribunal
ICR	Industrial Court/Cases Reports
ImmAR	Immigration Appeal Reports
IRLR	Industrial Relations Law Reports

J(J)	Judge(s)
KB	King's Bench
LC	Lord Chancellor
LGR	Local Government Reports
LJ	Lord Justice
LR	Law Reports
MR	Master of the Rolls
MTA	Manchester Transport Authority
NZLR	New Zealand Law Reports
P	Probate
PD	Probate Division
P&M	Pollock & Maitland, History of English law
QBD	Queen's Bench Division
s.	section
SC	Supreme Court
SI	Statutory Instrument
SOAS	School of Oriental and African Studies, University of London
Sol Jo	Solicitors Journal
TH	Thanet House
WASP	White Anglo-Saxon Protestant
WLR	Weekly Law Reports

Contents

Introduction

Ethnic minority studies in English law

Werner Menski

Compared to the sociological and political aspects of ethnic minority presence in Britain, the related legal issues have received only scant attention in law classrooms and in the literature. Ethnic minorities, often with poor English language skills and encumbered with the 'baggage' of their cultural and personal law, face and create many complex legal challenges but such conflict scenarios have interested only few legal academics (see in particular Pearl, 1972, 1986; Poulter, 1986, 1987, 1989 and 1998). One major reason for this lies in the dominant conceptualisations of 'law', apart from the fact that assimilationist assumptions about ethnic minorities in their relation to the law have prevented lawyers from studying 'the others' and their norm systems.

The authors of this study aim to provide a detailed examination of the approach of English law to some of the challenges posed by migrants and the subsequent generations of ethnic minority residents in Britain. Their book is not intended to be a full statement of the present law, but they illustrate how the reluctant acceptance of ethnic minorities has influenced the political processes and legislative structures of post-war British society. They also examine in depth how the judiciary has responded to the new legislation on 'race relations' and to the legal issues raised by the presence of new ethnic minority groups, particularly those of Asian and African-Caribbean origin. The responses of the judiciary show significant inconsistencies, judicial analysis in the cases tends to be shallow, and there is a notable lack of conceptual awareness to facilitate a comprehensive strategy for accommodating different norms and customs.

Reviewing the responses to ethnic minority presence in Britain within the conceptual context of legal pluralism, the authors also aim to rekindle debates on legal pluralism. Their conclusion expands the thesis that both the legislators and the judiciary have shown a remarkable lack of clarity in the application and exposition of their strategies for coping with social diversity and with new facts and circumstances arising in cases involving ethnic minority parties. By drawing together a number of important cases, especially from the field of employment and discrimination law, this study shows that the judicial strategies to handle diversity are at best unclear and at worst muddled.

Some explanation is required as to the terminology in this book. Following vigorous debate at the drafting stage, the term 'migrant' was used to identify those who actually came to Britain through immigration, in other words, first generation members of ethnic minority communities. 'Migrant' or 'immigrant' is a politically sensitive term and people from ethnic minority communities do not generally feel comfortable with it, as confirmed in Ursula Gregory v Lambeth City Council (Croydon Industrial Tribunal, unreported, cited in The Guardian, 22 February 1996). Nonetheless, 'migrant' is used to give a more expressive political assertion of identity for people of African-Caribbean and Asian origins. British readers may not be aware that the term 'migrant' has been widely used within the EU, with the tacit agreement or without any significant opposition from the leaders of Black, Asian and other ethnic minority organisations of the EU. In fact, a Migrants Forum has been in existence for some time, as a separate unit, within the structure of the EU. The purpose of this grouping has been to give political identity to people from different minority groups settled in the countries of the EU and to highlight the concerns of such groups within the European Union.

The term 'ethnic minorities' is used to include those who have settled in Britain or have been born in the UK to migrants. The term 'black' or 'Black', widely used since the 1950s, has served its historical obligations towards the people of African-Caribbean and Asian origin in their struggles during the past decades, but is no longer descriptive. For many who have suffered from white domination, and continue to suffer, 'Black' has become a focus of collective pride, particularly among African-Americans, African-Caribbeans and other people of African origin, not just in Britain but now also in sub-Saharan Africa. The use of 'black' for all ethnic minorities in Britain remains problematic for many reasons. In particular, the majority of Asians from the Indian sub-continent and of East African origin do not like to be identified as 'black' and, at any rate in Britain, refer to themselves as 'Asians' or 'South Asians'.

The general use of the term 'ethnic minorities' is also not without its difficulties as 'ethnicity' continues to be a widely debated concept and demonstrates only certain characteristics of minorities. Some minority groups such as the Jews and Muslims consider themselves 'religious groups' – and at least the former have promptly been recognised as an 'ethnic group' by a legal system which purports not to include religion among the criteria for defining a 'racial group'. As the book as a whole illustrates, this field of legal study continues to be marked by multiple confusions.

*****

This book asks more questions than it answers, reflecting the current state of our knowledge, torn between assimilation and pluralism. It remains impossible to tackle all the key questions about the interaction of ethnic minority communities and English law in any one study. We are still at an early stage in the development of a very complex analysis. The present study is a necessary stepping stone, describing and analysing areas in which significant tensions have arisen which remain unresolved. Cases in point are the English law on blasphemy and the precise definition of who falls under the label of 'racial group' for the purposes of the Race Relations Act, 1976.

This book was urgently needed, since there is so little legal literature available to students and others which is devoted to this significant area of law, affecting a large number of people. Without texts to base our analysis on, the area remains closed to academics and to students, the professionals of the future. The authors and myself are aware that far more could have been written here, but we did not want to delay publication – especially when Poulter (1998) appeared. Poulter's six case studies, focusing in turn on Jews, Gypsies, Muslims, Hindus, Sikhs and Rastafarians, contain some material that overlaps with our study but he seldom addressed the interaction of English law and ethnic minorities from a critical perspective. A very different perspective emerges here, as we re-examine the interactive patterns between ethnic minorities and English law from the perspective of the ethnic minorities themselves.

For example, in the chapter 'Rastafarians: Confrontation concerning dreadlocks and cannabis' (Poulter, 1998: 333-376), the chance to compare the law's favourable treatment of the Sikhs (in Poulter's chapter 8) who are said to have experienced 'tussles', not 'confrontations', with the denial of ethnic group status to the Rastas, is totally missed. While Dawkins v Department of the Environment [1993] IRLR 284 is discussed in some depth, Poulter focused much attention on drug abuse (which was not at all an issue in Dawkins), thus manifestly contrasting the law-abiding, Empire-supporting Sikhs with the ambiguous position of African-Caribbeans, particularly Rastafarians. Poulter duly welcomed the favourable treatment of the Sikhs by English law, but then proceeded to write that '[i]dentical treatment with the rest of the population is.... appropriate for Rastafarians in respect of the consumption of cannabis' (Poulter, 1998: 381). Thus, rather than highlighting the legal discrimination against Rastas in terms of 'ethnic' recognition, the element of 'special treatment' is employed to suggest that English law did nothing wrong when it denied Rastafarians legal recognition as a 'racial group' along the lines of Sikh, Jewish and Gypsy cases.

By failing to address the plainly differential treatment of Sikhs and Rastas in almost identical circumstances (pressure to cut long hair in order to get entry to a school or to obtain employment), and by not highlighting many other unsatisfactory legal positions, Poulter's study continuously avoided the real question: If certain ethnic minority groups (which may not even wish to be seen as such) are somehow treated as the 'darlings' of English law, while others continue to be excluded and criminalised, what has happened to the principle of tolerance and the officially heralded commitment to human rights? The field is thus still wide open for further research, which will have to address such troubling queries.

The present study aims to show that the legal treatment of ethnic minorities by English law has been inconsistent and haphazardly confusing for lawyers and scholars, and for members of ethnic minorities in Britain. The authors demonstrate how the entire field suffers from insufficient analytical depth on the part of judicial and other legal personnel, as well as academic commentators. They make a strong call for an open-minded re-assessment of the entire field, within the conceptual framework of strong legal pluralism, to work towards better understanding of a more inclusive system of legal regulation that does not insist on unilateral assimilation of the ethnic minorities into the official legal system. While we are not always sure about how explicitly multicultural legal rules may be operated in practice, in principle we envisage a system of socio-legal regulation in which a variety of culturally-rooted value systems receive official legal recognition instead of being ignored, dismissed, ridiculed, or even penalised by the law.

*****

Chapter 1 charts the 'white' protest reactions during the 1950s against the growing evidence of ethnic minority reconstruction 'on their own terms', as Roger Ballard (1994: 1-34) would eventually tell us in his brilliant analysis of desh pardesh, the reconstruction of South Asian life patterns in Britain. As it became evident that simple assimilationist expectations were not turning into social reality, fear of colonisation by the new migrants and their descendants set in. Fifty years later, the 'white' majority is struggling to come to terms with the changes brought about by post-war non-white migration. The role of religion as an ethnic signifier, especially although not only for Muslims, is duly highlighted. The English legal system has reacted to these challenges in a basically defensive form, seeking to exclude as many non-white people as possible through immigration controls, while expecting those who came and chose to stay in Britain to 'do as the Romans do'.

Chapter 2 focuses on the concept of 'racial group' under the provisions of the Race Relations Act, 1976 and continues the story of inconsistent and even irrational judicial approaches to this complex problem. While it appears that the Sikhs and the Jews have managed to obtain legal recognition, Gypsies are less well protected and the picture for Muslims, Hindus and the smaller groups is abysmal. The 1990s have been a decade of growing despair. The case of the Pushtuns or Pathans illustrates that either way, as Muslims or as local tribesmen, they have been denied official legal recognition. Other communities from around the world remain unprotected from discrimination despite the smokescreen of the Race Relations Act, 1976.

Section 3 of the 1976 Act deprives members of most ethnic minority groups in Britain of the chance to claim discrimination on 'racial grounds' under other provisions of the Race Relations Act, 1976. Evidently the seemingly inclusive precedent of Mandla v Dowell Lee in 1983, with its liberal, culture-focused interpretation of what it means to be an 'ethnic group' in Britain, has not been followed through in subsequent case law. While Sikhs should now be protected from discrimination based on challenges to their desire to keep long, uncut hair, the present authors find that this is not so. Rastafarians, at any rate, do not have the same protection as Sikhs, nor do other groups.

This status quo is dangerous and not good for race relations, since it highlights the direct discrimination between those few groups which have found recognition as 'racial groups', the Jews, Sikhs and Gypsies (the latter only if they continue to pursue an itinerant lifestyle), and the rest. There are also some cases which indicate that the Japanese in Britain and 'whites' themselves have been implicitly recognised as members of a 'racial group' under the 1976 Act (Hutley, 1998). Such cases need to be researched in depth to provide a fuller picture than is currently available. Another research job for the future is to analyse the precise interpretation of s. 3(2) of the Race Relations Act, 1976, which seems to suggest that the internal diversity of any one ethnic group should not be an impediment to official legal recognition as a 'racial group'.

The widespread assumption in the 'ethnic press' and within the communities that the persistent refusal of legal recognition is no coincidence but evidence of systematic official discrimination, is hard to deny in light of the legal evidence. While earlier GEMS studies concerned immigration-related questions (Sachdeva, 1993; Mortimore, 1994; Cruz, 1995), the present study makes no attempt to analyse the recent developments surrounding the important 'race and crime' debates in Britain and the disproportionate incarceration of ethnic minority people. This, too, is on the agenda for future studies.

In chapter 3, the authors put the spotlight on the English judiciary and examine how judges have been involved in commenting on Britain's immigration and race relations laws. There is much evidence of judicial reservations about making special legal provisions for ethnic minorities and of hostile comments about curtailing the common law's traditional concept of freedom to discriminate. Many judges support special legal treatment of migrants through legal controls of immigration and apply this in a manner which has generated concern among immigration lawyers, who find themselves opposing violations of human rights by the very legal system that trained them in principles of basic justice. A scattering of evidence suggests that not all is bad, but far more common is resentment of ethnic minorities who refuse to assimilate and seem to ask for special favours from the law. One outcome is 'ethnic' training for judges, few of whom are themselves members of ethnic minority communities. Whether or not this is effective, it is fitting that such leading figures should receive continuing education about new developments in society, in this case about ethnic minority cultures and customs which relate to the work that judges do.

Chapter 4 opens with a theoretical analysis of legal pluralism, arguing that a pluralist approach would serve Britain well as an instrument of future legal reconstruction. A wide range of family law cases provides yet another picture of haphazard and incomplete legal recognition of ethnic minority concepts and practices within a generally restrictive and occasionally hostile framework. The section on polygamous marriages shows particularly well, however, that outright hostility is not really a viable strategy. The growing evidence of active reconstruction of family law practices by ethnic minorities in Britain, not only Muslims, taking place largely within the 'extra-legal' unofficial sphere, can no longer be overlooked by legislators and judges, nor by those who analyse legal developments in modern multicultural Britain.

Chapters 5-7 explore examples from existing legislation and case law supporting the book's thesis that the English legal system is not doing enough to accommodate the needs and perceptions of the various ethnic minority communities. Chapter 5 focuses on parents and children, a difficult and complex area of the law in which there have been many new developments, crystallised in the Children Act, 1989. While we would like to believe that the 1989 Act appears committed to cultural pluralism when it comes to making decisions about children's lives, analysis of the legislation and the case law confirms that the value system of the majority tends to prevail. Since almost all superior judges come from white Christian backgrounds, this does not surprise, but there are other reasons, too. Take for example cases on mixed-race placement or inter-racial adoption, where the judges have tended to emphasise stability and recognition of the status quo over specific socio-cultural concerns from an ethnic minority perspective. In some cases, this is justified on the basis of the facts, but we see that ideological positions about same-race placements, in particular, have interfered in the judicial thought processes. The general assumption that ethnic minority standards are somehow lower than 'our own' reinforces the claims to legitimacy of the official legal system in imposing rules and policies that are perceived to be appropriate. There is little evidence that multicultural realities and the concerns of ethnic minority parents are being fully recognised.

The situation is still worse regarding English law on blasphemy, the subject of chapter 6. The 'Satanic affair' is discussed in the context of Muslim and English legal concepts and the resulting conflicts are highlighted. English law can be flexible when it wishes, as shown by R v R [1992] AC 599. Such flexibility was clearly not exercised when Muslim petitioners approached the English and even the European judicial fora. Significantly, Poulter (1998: 391) also refers to R v R to claim that the English common law is 'capable of evolving in the light of changing social, economic and cultural developments', but the evidence presented here tells a story of unwillingness to listen to ethnic minority arguments. The fact that the claimants were Muslims, and the subject matter was religion, and therefore concerned the position of Islam in England, has undoubtedly complicated the judicial task. Small wonder that sensitivity over matters of religious doctrine and orthodoxy has increased (see Asian Times 25 August 1998).

Chapter 7 returns to the Sikhs and raises further important questions over what is reasonable and legally acceptable in today's multicultural Britain, where so many rule systems compete for official legal recognition. While the focus appears to be on facial hair and turbans, and thus questions of adherence to religious and cultural traditions, the case law on employment and discrimination also brings out concerns about public health standards and the ever-present expectation that migrants – and especially their descendants – should comply with the general rules and norms of modern British society. British Sikhs are now concerned about the effects of proposed European harmonisations of rules which would mean that certain legal exemptions for turbaned Sikh building workers may not be acceptable under European law. Clearly, recourse to European law and to international human rights standards does not guarantee adequate recognition of ethnic minority concerns.

The main thesis of the present study, that legislators and the judiciary in England have shown a lack of clarity and goodwill in the application and exposition of multicultural elements in modern English law, could also have been explored through analysing processes of discrimination in employment law for others than the Sikhs, and changing evidence of ethnic minority self-employment in Britain today. Such developments are certainly closely linked. Self-employment used to be prominently through the retail trade, with now proverbial Patels owning corner-shops and newsagents. Close local observation suggests new patterns of self-employment for Asian taxi drivers and other service sector activities. To what extent legal processes have influenced particular kinds of ethnic minority economic activity remains under-researched. For example, we do not appear to know why many Muslims have now entered various forms of self-employment. Is this related to the desire to be able to pray during the working day in an appropriate atmosphere, to take Friday as a day of rest, and to arrange the home life, as it were, around customary patterns of behaviour? There are many pointers to the fact that ethnic minorities in Britain today are engaged, as Ballard (1994) observed, in reconstructing their lives on their own terms and as 'skilled cultural navigators'.

If one accepts a pluralist position – Griffiths (1986) defined this as 'strong' legal pluralism – and does not dismiss such social evidence as extra-legal and irrelevant for legal analysis, it becomes urgent to re-assess how such observable and recorded social change among ethnic minorities impacts on the law. The simplistic assumptions of legal centralism are shown to be false by the skilled legal navigation undertaken by British Muslims and other minorities. The persistent marginalisation of ethnic minorities and their concerns – most obviously through immigration laws which do not respect transnational family links, but also through the suffering of people like the Lawrence family, who have to live with the burdensome knowledge that British justice means no justice for them – has caused multiple reactions. The more or less subconscious withdrawal of many ethnic minority citizens from state-sponsored and majority-dominated legal processes should not just alarm those who would allege violations of basic rights in the ethnic minority sphere. Rather, it should alert lawyers and legal scholars to the negative effects of persistent official alienation of ethnic minorities. Coupled with pressure to assimilate and a concomitant refusal to acknowledge claims for recognition of ethnic differences, this is an unhealthy base for harmonious relations.

Recent attempts to introduce the concept of 'visible minorities' instead of 'ethnic minorities' disclose uncomfortable majority reactions to the powerful and pluralising forces of ethnicity and echoes the racialised foundations of post-war discourses about ethnic minorities. The law has always been good at creating fictions, but it will not be able to define away ethnicity and its many pluralist consequences. The legal establishment is uncomfortable with increasing evidence of 'ethnic resurgence' and the hardening arguments about respecting cultural pluralism in the legal sphere. However, being afraid of ethnicity and defining it away is not an option open to the law, because the people concerned will not follow suit, since they are proud of who they are.

Surreptitious attempts to de-culture the debates about legal recognition of ethnic minority patterns of life suggest that we are moving in circles of confusion. Little progress has been made in the past twenty years or so in the field of ethnic minority legal studies in Britain – in stark contrast with the vigorous development of British immigration law and anti-discrimination law. These now separate legal fields seem to have prospered because they have accepted the challenge of legally sponsored racism. As far as the general law is concerned, I see much evidence of regression, greater hostility towards legally pluralist claims during the 1990s than in the late 1960s and early 1970s. The old assimilationist assumptions, continually fed by new discourses on globalisation and idealistic formulations about uniform and binding international human rights standards, are still unrealistic. English judges will, for all we know, continue to resist being 'pluralised' through certain forms of 'ethnic training'. The picture does not look bright at present and a lot of work remains to be done.

Chapter 1

Ethnic minorities and immigration

This chapter provides a factual review of the immigration process of Asians and African-Caribbeans to the UK, concentrating particularly on the last 40 years. The responses of the indigenous community to the resulting demographic changes and the consequent debate among policy makers are briefly analysed. We believe that the extreme attitudes of some people in the so-called 'host community' were mirrored in the early political and judicial responses to migrants and continue to have important negative repercussions in the law and in society today.

1.1 The immigration process

A small number of black people lived in the UK by the time of Queen Elizabeth I (Hiro, 1971: 3; see generally Fryer, 1984). A significant number of Jews and Gypsies, various Eastern Europeans and many Irish people were also resident in the UK before the 20th century (Dummett, 1973). The threat of the imminent presence of more people from different ethnic groups, fuelled by the large-scale immigration of 'people of colour' after 1945, raised apprehensions in the indigenous population. The trend towards numerically significant immigration of non-white peoples had already begun during the First World War (see now Spencer, 1997). Some people from India, the Caribbean islands and Africa were recruited to work in various army units, the chemical industry, munitions factories and related industries. Such recruitment was mirrored in the Second World War and such workers formed the basis of the immigration surge of the 1950s and hence of Britain's new ethnic minorities. Former servicemen came in search of work and settled in the UK to fill vacancies

1

in London Transport, the health service, cotton mills and other areas of manual work generally undesired by white workers (details in Hiro, 1971). Until 1948, 'their numbers were too small to arouse much concern and the issue was seen as primarily a matter of Commonwealth policy' (Banton, 1985: 29).

The immigration to Britain of people from African-Caribbean and Indian sub-continental backgrounds gathered momentum between 1946 and 1951, when 460,000 people from the New Commonwealth, mainly the Caribbean islands and the Indian sub-continent, came to Britain, lured by the relatively high economic prosperity (Anwar, 1979: 3; Rich, 1990: 181; Shaw, 1988). Immigration flattened in the early years of the 1950s, with 2,000 persons in 1952, 10,000 in 1953-4, 24,473 in 1955 and 26,441 in 1956 (Rich, 1990: 181). Figures then increased dramatically between 1957 and 1960, when the average number of migrants per year was over 200,000 or 0.5 per cent of the population (Cashmore and Troyna, 1990: 56). Between 1961-62 numbers again rose, as African-Caribbeans and Asians tried to beat the impending immigration regime of the Commonwealth Immigrants Act, 1962. In these two years alone, 98,000 persons migrated to Britain from the Caribbean islands.[1] The new regime, introduced by the 1962 Act and developed in subsequent legislative enactments on immigration in 1968, 1971 and 1988, had the effect of significantly reducing immigration by restricting immigration rights to dependants and refugees. At the same time, as the most recent study on this period (Spencer, 1997) confirms, this also led to the establishment of fully settled migrant communities, the subsequent development of Britain's new multiculturalism, and a significant shift towards Asian, rather than African or African-Caribbean migration.

1.2 Population effects

It is generally assumed that migrant communities now account for just over three million people, or 5.5 per cent of the total population.[2] We provide some further details in Figure 1 below. While Muslims claim anything between one and two million adherents to their faith in Britain, Jews, Hindus and Sikhs each have populations well in excess of 300,000.[3] Indians, Pakistanis and Bangladeshis constitute 1.7 per cent of the population or 34 per cent of the migrant population as a whole. Black Caribbeans, Black Africans, and 'Black Others' together constitute 1.8

Figure 1: 1991 Census Figures (LBS/SAS HMSO 1991)

	Total persons: White	Total persons: Black Caribbean	Total persons: Black African	Total persons: Other black	Total persons: Indian	Total persons: Pakistani	Ethnic %
England	44,144,339	495,682	206,918	172,282	823,821	449,646	6.19
Wales	2,793,522	3,348	2,671	3,473	6,384	5,717	1.47
Scotland	4,935,933	934	2,773	2,646	10,050	21,192	1.25
Total	51,873,794	499,964	212,362	178,401	840,255	1,018,656	5.49
%		0.91	0.39	0.33	1.53	1.86	

	Total persons: Bangladeshi	Total persons: Chinese	Total persons: Other Asian	Total persons: Other ethnic groups	Total persons: Total population	Totals ethnic minority
England	157,881	141,661	189,253	273,721	47,055,204	2,910,865
Wales	3,820	4,801	3,677	7,660	2,835,073	41,551
Scotland	1,134	10,476	4,604	8,825	4,998,567	62,634
Total	162,835	156,938	319,773	290,206	54,888,844	3,015,050
%	0.30	0.29	0.58	0.53		

per cent of the population or 36 per cent of the ethnic minority population (Social Trends, 1998: 34). By the year 2000, the number of persons from the ethnic minorities is expected to have risen to 5.9 per cent or 1 out of every 17 (The Independent, 28 January 1993).

It is well-known that new migrants have tended to concentrate in and around major British cities and conurbations. Today, large sections of the Asian and African-Caribbean communities are located in inner and outer London, particularly Brent, Newham, Tower Hamlets and Hackney (for details on the 1960s see Lee, 1973). Greater London as a whole is now home to one third of all Asians and half of all African-Caribbeans in Britain. Other large communities are found in the conurbations of Birmingham and Manchester (Rex and Tomlinson, 1979: 105; Brown, 1984: 55). Settlements of East African Indians and Sikhs are mainly found in the Midlands, particularly Leicester, Birmingham, Nottingham, and Derby (Brown, 1984: 54-55). Twenty per cent of the population in Greater London now constitutes African-Caribbeans, Indians, Pakistanis and Bangladeshis; in the West Midlands they represent more than 8 per cent, whereas Wales, Scotland, the North and the South West have no more than 1 per cent, concentrated in a few small local concentrations. The demographic composition shows that Britain is both culturally and ethnically pluralist (see already Anwar, 1979: Preface). Crick (1995: 168, 174-180) speaks of a 'multi-national State or Union of different nations with different cultures and different histories'. Some writers have argued that Britain has been pluralist for a considerable time (Lynch, 1989: 29). Marquand (1995) points out that Britain has been multi-national since 1707, the year in which the UK was established, bringing together Scots, Welsh, Irish and English. The 1965 White Paper, Immigration from the Commonwealth, stated that even if not one additional black person were to arrive in Britain, it was no longer and would never again be a white society (see Dummett and Dummett, 1982). Spencer (1997) argues that Britain really only became a multi-racial society after 1945, when more significant numbers of non-white people came to Britain. According to Crick (1995: 168), Britain is now more like Belgium, Canada, or Czechoslovakia (as it was) than Italy or France – but even these countries have now begun to reconsider their views on their ethnic composition.

Does the ethnic composition of a state necessarily impact upon the development and operation of its domestic laws? In addition to the perceived need to frame legislation to prevent discrimination, challenges will be posed by those who wish to express their own values and norms within a legal system that may not recognise or even be hostile to such 'ethnic minority norms'. We shall have much to say about these issues. However, before any thinking about legal adjustment processes started, the migrants were faced with historic prejudices held by the British against 'black' people. We present some evidence of these unpleasant attitudes here to contextualise the continuing unwillingness to recognise new migrants and their descendants fully as equals.

1.3 'Awful hands', 'wide, flat noses', and 'flabby mouths'

Jordan (1982: 42) reports that, traditionally, many indigenous white people felt uncomfortable in the presence of Black and Asian people:

> Englishmen found the peoples of Africa very different from them-selves; 'Negroes' looked different to Englishmen; their religion was un-Christian; their manner of living was anything but English; they seemed to be a particularly libidinous sort of people.

Negative perceptions were evident when navigators, slave traders and soldiers first confronted Africans (see Fryer, 1984). English travellers and adventurers were not only astonished by their colour but drew unfavour-able cultural comparisons. The traveller Robert Baker described in a poem the strangers he saw in Africa in the 1560s (cited by Jordan, 1982: 43):

> And entering in [a river], we see
> a number of blacke soules,
> whose likelinesse seem'd men to be,
> but all as blacke as coles.
> Their Captain comes to me
> as naked as my naile,
> Not having witte or honestie
> to cover once his taile.

Blacks were looked upon with disdain and the word 'black' came to be used to mean 'dirty, ugly and contemptible'. Jordan (1982: 44) suggests that no other colour except white conveys so much emotional impact and refers to the Oxford English Dictionary, which gives the meaning of black before the sixteenth century as including:

...deeply stained with dirt; soiled, dirty, foul... Having dark or deadly purposes, malignant; pertaining to or involving death, deadly; baneful, disastrous, sinister... Foul, iniquitous, atrocious, horrible, wicked... Indicating disgrace, censure, liability to punishment, etc.

Such ingrained attitudes, analysed in detail by Jordan (1982) and others, have hounded black people throughout history. Slave trade and the exploitation of African-Caribbeans and, later, Asians in the colonies have contributed to these myths. Further mythologies developed to justify the unchristianlike ways they were treated. Blacks were said to originate from monkeys and Orang Utans, or thought to be merely two-legged animals. They were regularly referred to as the missing link between animals and humans, some sort of strange hybrid, probably the offspring of a dangerous liaison (Cohen, 1988). They were also branded as great eaters and no less drinkers, lecherous and thievish, and addicted to unclean habits (Walvin, 1982: 61; Barker, 1978). That black people were inferior was typical of 18th century thinking and views about the promiscuity of blacks and their similarity to animals spread with little concern for verification. Similar perceptions continued into the 20th century. For example, writing from the 1950s still asserts that blacks came from primitive jungle societies, or had tails, or were cannibals (Rich, 1990: 175).

So when blacks came to the UK after the Second World War, they were often treated with contempt by indigenous whites, as illustrated in the 'Empire Windrush' anniversary documentaries on television in 1998. The Spectator warned that their presence would lead to the creation of Black ghettos similar to those American pre-war towns (Rich, 1990: 189) and African-Caribbean lifestyle was seen as a gangland culture of drugs, prostitution and criminal activity (Rich, 1990: 175). An anti-immigration campaigner, John Sanders (cited in Dummett, 1973: 139), took a typical stance:

> The Afro-Asians are feckless peoples with cultures different from our own. By our standards they are barbarous. No one really bothers about the Irish. They don't peddle dope, they don't kill chickens in the kitchens. This civilization of the North Sea and of Kipling's five nations is in danger of destruction through this flood coming in. It must be stopped.

The native British were obviously unable to understand, still less accept, the behavioural patterns of the new migrants. Their standard of civilisation, argued Lord Altrincham, was far below that of the British (House of Lords Debates, Vol. 156, cols. 995-7, 21 June 1948). The gap of civilisation between them was likened to that of head hunters to noble Lords. Blacks were described as having 'awful hands', 'wide, flat noses', and 'flabby mouths'. One female university student is quoted by Banton (1959: 140-141):

> Niggers have awful hands, – it makes me shudder to think of one touching me. If I had to meet one I should try and avoid all physical contact with him. I wouldn't dance with one, and I would try not to shake hands. I think I have got a phobia... I can't bear to think of a nigger kissing me – and his wide, flat nose.

Blacks and Asians were accused of failing to cover their windows, of being noisy and of being involved in commercial prostitution (Banton, 1959: 172). One landlord wondered whether his black lodger was eating raw meat. Another complained that 'they' were killing chickens in the kitchen. A white woman who saw a Jamaican drinking water from a public fountain protested that 'children have to drink after you' (Banton, 1959: 160). Lord Elton, an influential political figure and anti-migrant campaigner, was willing to disseminate degrading rumours. He considered Asians unable to become 'masters of the arts of toilets' (Elton, 1965: 14) and said he had heard that Leamington white ladies found it 'virtually impossible' to find beds in maternity hospitals for first confinement, because the beds were full of pregnant migrant women (Elton, 1965: 31). He claimed that fifteen Pakistanis were living in a single derelict house, 'eating grapes, whose pips were spat on the floor' (Elton, 1965: 14). Enoch Powell, another prominent anti-migrant politician, claimed that a middle-aged, decent, ordinary working man told him: 'If I had the money to go, I wouldn't stay in this country, because, in fifteen or twenty years' time the black man will have the whip hand over the white man' (cited in Berkeley, 1977: 129). Elton (1965: 10-15) concluded that ethnic minorities were a formidable social problem and harbingers of the gravest social crisis since the industrial revolution. Asian and African ethnic minorities were seen by politicians as a threat to law and order and to the racial character of the English.

Politicians, particularly on the right of both the Conservative Party and the Labour Party, spread the myth that new migrants would carry a threat of division, violence and bloodshed of American dimensions, adding a powerful weapon to the armoury of anarchy (Berkeley, 1977: 19). The 'problem' thus became more than just an immigration issue and attention turned to employment, housing and welfare benefits, aggravated as immigration increased. The perception of some observers was that the numbers shot up 'as fast as the green pawpaw tree' (cited in Banton, 1959: 157). The arrival of blacks and Asians in large numbers was seen as an unarmed invasion (Elton, 1965: 63-64), and the 'race problem' was born (Gordon and Rosenberg, 1983, ch. 1). New migrant labourers occupied low-paid employment and tended, due to their weak bargaining position, to be more co-operative with the management, working under harsh conditions without complaint. So they were blamed for reductions in wages and increases in unemployment. One local trade union member considered joining the newly formed British branch of the Ku-Klux-Klan because, he said, 'I am not one of those who maintain that all blacks should be murdered, but I firmly believe they should be sent back home' (Banton, 1959: 167).

The settlement of new ethnic minorities in inner cities caused property values to fall. Powell argued that the English neighbourhood had changed beyond recognition (Berkeley, 1977: 134). The people who looked 'foreign', speak 'strange' or smell 'funny' became, in political discourse, 'the enemy within' (Samuel, 1989: xiv) and were referred to as 'coloureds', 'Blacks', 'Pakis', 'Nigger', 'Nig-nog',[4] and 'coons' (James, 1989: 234). As discriminatory practices against the newcomers became more blatant, the Race Relations Act, 1965 was introduced, amended in 1968 and 1976, making discrimination on the basis of race, nationality or ethnic or national origins unlawful.

1.4 'Kill the Paki bastards'

Racial tensions peaked in the late 1950s. White residents in inner cities attacked members of the new ethnic minorities, and racial attacks became a regular part of their day-to-day lives (Sivanandan 1991: 9). In summer 1958, a group of white residents surrounded a group of blacks at a pub in Nottingham, and they were reported to have produced knives and stabbed six whites (Banton, 1959: 171). This was the spark for the Notting Hill riots. During July and August of 1958, unprecedented violence erupted against blacks. The riots spread, encompassing Notting Hill, Kensal New Town, Paddington and Maida Vale. 'Nigger hunting' and 'nigger baiting' was pursued in earnest, directed by the Mosleyites and the White Defence League, neo-fascist groups originating in 1932, when Sir Oswald Mosley created the British Union of Fascists, or Blackshirts. Blacks were molested, humiliated and beaten up by 'Teddy Boys' who, armed with knives, behaved as self-appointed guardians of the peace (Ramdin, 1987: ch. 7). Normally detested by the public, these Teddy Boys were acclaimed as local heroes for their courageous stand against the 'coloureds', in contrast to the government's perceived inaction over black immigration. The resulting prosecutions were used by anti-immigrant campaigners to 'prove' that ethnic minorities had become a law and order problem. Mr. Justice Salmon, who tried several race riot cases thought otherwise. When sentencing nine white 'Teddy Boys' to prison, he declared that their behaviour had filled the whole nation with horror, indignation and disgust (Sivanandan, 1991: 10).

1.5 'Keep the Niggers out'

As early as 1948, the Ministry of Labour had argued that West Indians were unfit to live in the UK and there was a general government consensus that mass immigration had to be opposed (Rich, 1990: 164). Immigration control, a contentious issue in the cabinet between 1950 and 1954, was by 1955 seen as the only solution (Solomos, 1992: 10; Saggar, 1992: ch. 5). Politicians and the electorate had begun to consider the effects of migrants on housing, employment, the health service and crime. Demands for tougher action from the government gradually increased (Solomos, 1992: 10). Right-wing Conservatives, in particular, were eager to point out biological and cultural differences (Banton, 1985: 34). Conservatives Cyril Osborne, Lord Salisbury and Norman Pannell launched a vigorous campaign in the early 1950s, urging the reduction or even halting of non-white immigration (Dummett, 1994: 339). Organisations devoted to such aims surfaced, among them the Union Movement, a revival of the Mosleyite movement of the pre-war British Union of Fascists, A. K. Chesterton's League of Empire Loyalists, Colin Jordan's White Defence League, John Bean's National Labour Party, and Andrew Fountain's British National Party (for details see Sivanandan, 1991: 9).

In 1955 the Central Council of the Conservative Party passed a resolution calling for strict immigration control (Cashmore and Troyna, 1990: 57) and the government succumbed to domestic pressure. Sir Alec

Douglas Home presented a secret Cabinet Memo in 1955, urging speedy action to keep out migrants of a bad type, implying those from the New Commonwealth. Later, he brought a proposal for reparation for new migrants who wished to go back home (Spencer, 1997: ch. 3). He even suggested that immigration officers could use discriminatory measures, without giving rise to publicity, to curtail the immigration of 'coloured' people. The minutes of the Cabinet meeting of 3 November 1955 reveal that Cabinet members were now worried about 'colonial immigration'. Released under the 30 year rule on 2 January 1986, they record that if migrants from India and Pakistan were allowed to continue coming unchecked, 'there is a real danger that over the years there would be a significant change in the racial character of the English people' (Carter, Harris and Joshi, 1987, cited in Miles, 1993: 150).

The government faced a dilemma over how to impose strict immigration controls without damaging Britain's relationship with the New Commonwealth, but in 1958 a number of factors came together and were used to legitimise restrictions of Commonwealth immigration. Firstly the riots of 1958 had a significant impact on British politicians and public opinion (Cashmore and Troyna, 1990: 55; Ramdin, 1987: ch. 7). Secondly, the government's loyalty to the Commonwealth was beginning to fade as more and more countries became independent. Thirdly, by the late 1950s, the UK had entered a recession. Pressures on employment, housing and state benefits were becoming more apparent. Finally, in the late 1950s immigration from the Indian subcontinent increased, while less people now came from the Caribbean. The newcomers were still seen as competitors for scarce resources, especially housing and employment (Banton, 1985: 35).

The background for a strict regime of immigration control being laid out, many politicians openly began to discuss tougher measures. A backbench MP suggested the open-door policy for Commonwealth migrants to be abandoned as soon as possible (House of Commons Debates, Hansard, 3 April 1958, cols. 1415 ff.). Cyril Osborne MP, a prominent member of the anti-immigration camp, objected with particular vigour to the presence of blacks and Asians and was reported as saying that 'this is a white man's country and I want it to remain so' (Daily Mail, 7 February 1961, cited in Sachdeva, 1993: 19).

At its annual conference in October 1961, much to the delight of the delegates, the Conservative Party promised legislation to curb New Commonwealth immigration and the Commonwealth Immigrants Bill received Royal Assent in April 1962. Justifying the introduction of the Bill, Home Secretary R. A. Butler said that it was necessary, taking into account the economic situation of the country, to curtail this seemingly endless immigration (House of Commons Debates, 16 November 1961, vol. 649, col. 687). Members of the opposition attacked the Bill, arguing that the government had surrendered to racism, 'to satisfy those who viewed the issue largely on racial and ethnic grounds' (Evans 1983: 63). The Commonwealth Immigrants Act, 1962 came into force in July 1962, abolishing free entry for New Commonwealth migrants and subjecting all persons to immigration controls. For the first time in British history, the Home Secretary was given powers to deport Commonwealth citizens.

This approach to black and Asian immigration was in stark contrast to the treatment of white migrants from the old Dominions of Canada, Australia and New Zealand, the Irish Republic and Eastern Europe. Post-war Labour and Conservative governments had launched specific programmes, including the European Volunteer Workers Scheme (EVWS), to take many Eastern Europeans into the British labour market. Between 1948-50, 2,341 Austrian women were recruited for the textile industry under the Blue Danube scheme. The 'North Sea Project' brought 9,713 German women to Britain for domestic work. During 1949-51, 1,655 Italian women were recruited, and Belgian and Italian labourers were brought to work mainly in the building industry (Miles, 1993: 156-7). In addition, thousands of Polish nationals were given residential status. The Polish Resettlement Act, 1947 introduced various projects supporting Polish migrants in education, health, housing and general welfare matters. Mrs. Leach Manning, MP for Epping, in the debate on the Polish Resettlement Bill, expressed her satisfaction with Eastern European labourers, indicating that they would integrate into the majority population, unlike black and brown migrants (House of Commons Debates, Hansard, 1946-7, vol. 433, col. 399). Sachdeva (1993: 17) pointed out that the official efforts made to alleviate the problems of Polish migrants were considerable and 'stand in sharp contrast to the position of succeeding migrant groups'. Generally speaking, British immigration control had become more political than economic (Sachdeva, 1993: 35) and therefore promoted a racialisation of immigration in British politics (Miles, 1993: ch. 6).

After 1962, several legislative steps strengthened the immigration control mechanisms for non-white migrants from Africa, the Caribbean and the subcontinent, encouraged in part by right-wing politicians. Peter Griffiths, long associated with the anti-immigration campaign, stood for the Smethwick constituency in the 1964 general election on a wholly racial agenda. His slogan 'If you want a Nigger neighbour, vote for Labour' is said to have won him the seat. In 1965, Sir Cyril Osborne put forward a motion which called for the banning of all future immigration, except for those whose parents or grandparents were born in Britain (Dummett and Nicol, 1990: 195). In the same year, the Labour government issued a White Paper on Immigration from the Commonwealth, asserting that the control regime introduced by the Commonwealth Immigrants Act, 1962 would remain in place. Part two of the White Paper included details on future control mechanisms, about reductions of work-vouchers, the introduction of an eligibility test and medical examinations for dependent relatives. Paras 25 and 26 contain details about the most controversial proposal, repatriation, later known as the 'Little England Policy'. The Labour government, exercising powers conferred by the 1962 Act, reduced the work-voucher scheme in 1965 and further restricted entry rights for dependants.

1.6 'Thousands of Indians sitting on the doorstep'

In 1967 the immigration debate lurched into a further crisis as British passport holders of South Asian descent became increasingly subject to discrimination at the hands of East African countries, particularly Kenya. Oppressive africanisation policies drove more and more East African Asians to Britain during the early 1960s – at its height some 750 Asians were arriving in Britain daily, most of them legally entitled to enter as holders of British passports by virtue of the status of Citizen of the United Kingdom and Colonies (CUKC). The tabloids and certain right-wing MPs started a vociferous campaign against these newcomers. Cyril Osborne wrote in the Daily Telegraph that 'it will not be long before there will be more coloured than white people in Britain. English people will become strangers in their own land' (cited in Bevan, 1986: 80). Enoch Powell, now as opposition front bench spokesman, gave leadership to the campaign, stirring racial hatred among the native population. He warned the nation on 9 February 1968 that 200,000 Indians in Kenya were ready to come here and the Daily Mirror reported 'uncontrolled floods of Asian migrants from Kenya' waiting in the queue (Sivanandan, 1991: 24). Speaking in a BBC Panorama programme on 12 February 1968, Powell said that 'another quarter of a million Kenyan Asians could be added to the existing migrant population' (Dummett and Nicol, 1990: 201). His speech on 20 April 1968 in Birmingham (cited in Berkeley, 1977: 131 and 136) became famous, but cost him his place in the Cabinet:

> We must be mad, literally mad as a nation to be permitting the annual inflow of some 50,000 dependants, who are for the most part the materials of the future growth of the migrant-descended population. It is like watching a nation busily engaged in heaping up its own funeral pyre, so insane are we that we actually permit unmarried persons to immigrate for the purpose of founding a family with spouses and fiancées whom they have never seen. As I look ahead, I am filled with forbidding. Like the Roman, I seem to see the 'River Tiber foaming with much blood'. That tragic and intractable pheno-menon which we watch with horror on the other side of the Atlantic... is coming upon us here by our own volition and our own neglect.

Powell and Duncan Sandys went on to raise the mass arrival of the Kenyan Asians at the Conservative Party Conference later that year. The comments from Sandys were something of a surprise, for he was the Minister who had given certain assurances to the Kenyan Asians when he signed the independence agreement with Kenya's leaders. The figures quoted by Powell were far from true. Government data showed that the number of Kenyan Asians entering was 6,149 in 1965, 6,489 in 1966, and 13,600 in 1967. At most the government expected that some 20,000 Kenyan Asians might enter in 1968 (Evans, 1983: 95) but it was willing to ignore its own figures. As one commentator stated, 'what Powell says today, the Tories say tomorrow and Labour legislates on the day after' (Sivanandan, 1991: 24).

Most of the East African Asians were British citizens and therefore entitled to come to the UK with virtually no hindrance. While Kenya's independence was being discussed, it had been agreed and confirmed that Asians with British passports issued by the High Commission were legally entitled to come to the UK. Although this position had been contested by Duncan Sandys as Commonwealth Secretary during the discussions before independence, the then Colonial Secretary, Reginald Maulding, stated in the debate of the 1968 Commonwealth Immigrants Bill, as cited by Evans (1983: 66):

> When (the Kenyan Asians) were given those rights it was our intention that they should be able to come to this country when they wanted to do so. We knew it at the time. They knew it and in many cases they have acted and taken decisions on this knowledge.

Home Secretary James Callaghan complained of the difficulty of granting residential status to Kenyan Asians. Parliament was asked to pass, within a twenty-four hour sitting, new legislation restricting the entry of the Kenyan Asians, so as to stop the arrival of 'thousands of Indians sitting on the doorstep'. When challenged, Callaghan angrily remarked that he was not going to tolerate this bloody liberalism any more (Crossman, 1976: 200, cited in Dummett and Nicol, 1990: 195). The former Labour minister Richard Crossman revealed that even liberal politicians such as Roy Jenkins wished to stop Kenyan Asians from coming to the UK. He wrote in his Diaries (Crossman, 1976: 526):

> Soon after we came back from the recess Roy Jenkins had come to see me in my Privy Council Office to tell me that he might urgently need a slot for legislation to deal with the problem of Kenya Asians with British passports. There are some 200,000 of them who are now threatened as a result of the Black-Africa policy... It's quite clear we couldn't allow some 50,000 Asians from Kenya to pour into Britain each year. On the other hand it's doubtful whether we have any legal or constitutional right to deny entry to these people from Kenya since they have British passports.

Crossman also, with a heavy heart, supported what he called 'this appalling violation of our deepest principles' under pressure of his electorate in the Midlands, where racial hatred towards new ethnic minorities was becoming a powerful force (Crossman, 1976: 200-202). Responding to public opinion and surrendering to the right-wing agenda, the Labour government introduced the Commonwealth Immigrants Act, 1968 in March. Proceedings went through the Commons in three days, 'in a Parliamentary atmosphere reminiscent of emergency measures passed under the shadow of war' (Evans, 1983: 65). The Act had the effect of treating Kenyan Asians with valid British passports as 'aliens', allowing only those who had ancestral connections with the UK to enter freely. The Commonwealth link had become irrelevant for migration purposes. Would-be migrants now had to prove that at least one parent or grandparent was born, adopted, naturalised, or registered as a citizen of the UK. The strategy worked, more or less instantly curtailing the immigration of East African Asians.

The UK was subject to much domestic and international community criticism. The Sunday Times of 27 February 1968 called it 'probably the most shameful measure' enacted by the Labour government. The International Commission of Jurists reported in their Bulletin that 350,000 individuals who had no other citizenship than that of the UK now found themselves without a right to remain in the country where they lived. It condemned the Act as a flagrant violation of international law and the human rights of UK citizens who happened to live elsewhere.[5] The European Commission on Human Rights later held, in the East African Asians case [1981] 3 EHRR 76, that the Act was racially motivated and therefore discriminatory and that the Act violated Articles 3 and 8 of the European Convention on Human Rights.

1.7 'The enemy within'

Migrant communities became seen as the 'enemy within', led by Conservative right-wing thinkers like John Casey, Alfred Sherman and Roger Scruton. Confusion over national identity, unemployment, housing shortage and increasing inner city violence were blamed upon the presence of ethnic minorities, an alien malaise afflicting British society (see Solomos, Findlay, Jones and Gilroy, 1982: 26). Ethnic minorities were branded as scroungers (Gordon and Rosenberg, 1983: 3) and it was even said in court that 'this dangerously overcrowded island' was being flooded by 'migrants from desperate lands' (per Lord Diplock in Dockers' Labour Club v Race Relations Board [1974] 3 WLR 533 HL). New Right philosophers argued that the new ethnic minorities were not just foreigners, but hostile aliens, representing a significant threat to national unity and integrity. In the view of some critics, they might all be fifth columnists. The speeches and statements of Enoch Powell, Norman Tebbit, Peter Griffiths, Sir Cyril Osborne, Lord Elton, Sir Gerald Nabaro, Ronald Bell, and Duncan Sandys were given extensive media coverage (see Dummett and Nicol, 1990: 195-204). Tabloids regularly published articles on migrants, such as 'Visa curb for immigrant fiddlers', 'Clampdown on illegal immigrants', 'Asian flood swamps airport', '3000 Asians flood Britain' (see Gordon and Rosenberg, 1983: 9).

Against this background, violence and racial attacks against Blacks and Asians increased. In the 1970s 'Paki-bashing' became a national sport among racially motivated individuals. Individuals were abused and attacked, their property damaged, women and children terrorised (Sivanandan, 1991: 24). Writer Hanif Kureishi (1989: 272) described his experience as follows:

> As Powell's speeches appeared in the papers, graffiti in support of him appeared in the London streets. Racists gained confidence. People insulted me in the street. Someone in a cafe refused to eat at the same table with me. The parents of a girl I was in love with told her she'd get a bad reputation by going out with darkies. Parents of my friends, both lower-middle class and working-class, often told me they were Powell supporters. Sometimes I heard them talking, heatedly, violently, about race, about 'the Pakis'...I was identified with these loathed aliens...The word 'Pakistani' had been made into an insult.

In 1967 Enoch Powell openly advocated a policy of repatriation, arguing that, rather than allowing migrants' families into Britain, the migrants should be reunited with their families by being returned home (Dummett and Nicol, 1990: 196). He maintained that Britain as a nation was declining and slowly destroying itself. Now the threat came not from the traditional European enemies but from this 'enemy within' (Solomos, 1992: 23; Samuel, 1989, Introduction) and in particular the blacks and Asians who appeared not to be integrating into the indigenous population. Powell also argued that migrants should be repatriated at the expense of the government to preserve the status quo, otherwise there would be continued ethnic conflicts between the native population and ethnic minorities. In June 1969 he suggested the establishment of a Ministry of Repatriation to get rid of ethnic minorities. His speeches were enthusiastically reported by the tabloid press and he was praised as a national hero for speaking out against migrants (see Searle, 1989; Troyna, 1981).

In 1969, Home Secretary James Callaghan introduced further immigration restrictions, aimed particularly at husbands and fiancés.

Henceforth, before travelling to the UK, an entry clearance certificate would have to be obtained. The simple rule was that no husband of a woman settled in Britain would have the automatic right to join her (Evans, 1983: ch. 3). In 1971 the Conservative party came to power promising that it would further curtail black and Asian immigration. They were particularly concerned about the primary migration of workers. The 1962 and 1968 Acts were proving incapable of controlling the influx of migrants and Parliament finally enacted the Immigration Act, 1971 to introduce stricter rules. Migration for work, according to the 1971 Act, would now be possible only through a work permit, valid for twelve months. Just like aliens, citizens of Commonwealth countries could now only gain entry to the UK after obtaining an entry clearance certificate at the port of entry. Additionally, the immigration rules under the Act applied the concept of 'patriality'. Patrials would be entitled to have the right of abode in the UK without hindrance, which meant that this new residence status was offered only to those Commonwealth citizens with a grandparent born in the UK. Popularly called the 'grandparent clause', it tended to help white individuals living in former colonies and discriminated indirectly against non-whites – not many Blacks or Asians could produce a grandparent born in the UK. Consequently, a large number of wives and children who sought to enter Britain were refused (Sondhi, 1987).

1.8 The British character

Soon after she became leader of the opposition in 1975, Margaret Thatcher moved her party away from the traditional compromise politics and developed a neo-conservatism later identified as Thatcherism. She vigorously entered the immigration debate, describing new migrants as 'dole cheaters' and 'undesirable elements' (Samuel, 1989, Introduction). She identified some of Britain's social problems as the result of migrant populations, especially misuse of the welfare system, mugging, inner-city crimes, and the spread of alien cultures. Speculating that by the end of the century there might be four million or more immigrants from the New Commonwealth, she warned:

> That is an awful lot, I think it means that people are really rather afraid that this country might be rather swamped by people with a different culture. The British character has done so much for

democracy, for law, and done so much throughout the world, that if there is any fear that it might be swamped, people are going to react and be rather hostile to those coming in....We are a British nation with British characteristics. Every nation can take some minorities, and in many ways they add to the richness and variety of this country. But the moment a minority threatens to become a big one, people get frightened.[6]

This is the rhetoric of Powellism, which now gained new ideological ground in social and political discourses. Thatcher's impact was to be greater than that of the Powellites. Her followers argued that 'black immigration had broken down the social order established during the Victorian period and was therefore a threat to the way of life of the majority population' (Casey, 1982). They identified 'migrant diseases such as tuberculosis',[7] ophthalmic ailments, leprosy, muggers, rapists, murderers, 'pimps' and 'ponces'. The New Right saw the migrants' alien culture as imposing itself on the British way of life, undermining the purity of the British nation and traditions. Norman Tebbit, a standard-bearer of Thatcherism, expressed fear that ethnic minorities would superimpose their culture and languages upon the host community (Solomos, 1989: 228). He asserted that British people did not wish to live in a multicultural and multiracial society (Evening Standard, 21 December 1989, cited in Solomos, 1989: 228). Enoch Powell's repatriation argument was resurrected, advocating voluntary repatriation of a proportion of the migrants and their descendants, or the retrospective withdrawal of the rights of black migrants to citizenship and the creation of a status analogous to the position of 'guest workers' in Europe. In 1997, Tebbit was still developing the one-nation theme at the Conservative Party Conference:

> Youngsters of all races born here should be taught that British history is their history, or they will forever be foreigners holding British passports and this kingdom will become a Yugoslavia. (Financial Times, 7 October 1997)

The Conservative MP for Daveyhulme, Randolph Churchill, asserted on Manchester Radio in April 1995 that 'selfish migrants' were flocking to Britain in 'banana boats' simply for economic reasons. He was frightened to see that 'more and more hungry mouths and bellies' were coming in search of the good life in the UK (Today, 29 April 1995). As reported in

The Sunday Times 30 May 1993, Churchill had complained that the annual immigration 'is equivalent to a town the size of Grantham' and alleged that 'the population of many of our Northern cities is now well over 50% immigrants'. Churchill's critics argue that such inflated figures are concocted for political reasons. Others, like Keith Vaz, MP for Leicester East, dismiss him as 'simply mouthing the empty rhetoric of Powellism' (The Sunday Times, 30 May 1993).[8]

The uprisings in Liverpool and Brixton in the 1970s again provoked cries of alarm over accommodating large migrant communities. Politicians argued that such 'subversions' were un-British and anti-British. Enoch Powell asked in Parliament in which town or city the Home Secretary expected the next pitched battle against the police (Solomos, Findlay, Jones and Gilroy, 1982: 31). Even The Financial Times 11 July 1981, under the heading, 'Outbreak of an alien disease', took this line:

> Like an epidemic of some alien disease, to which the body politic has no immunity, street riots have erupted in different parts of England during the past ten days... It is in a way all the more disturbing that there are so many conflicting explanations of the past week's violence. Riots in different towns seem to have been sparked off by rather different factors: in Southall by racial fear and racial hatred; in Liverpool perhaps by a tradition of lawlessness and rivalry between police and idle, frustrated youngsters; in Manchester apparently by imitation of their Liverpool neighbours; and perhaps worst of all, in parts of London, ...appears to be pure criminality and greed. (Also cited in Solomos, Findlay, Jones and Gilroy, 1982: 31).

Instead of identifying and addressing the real factors for the escalation of inner city disturbances, politicians resurrected anti-immigrant arguments. Improvement of race relations was again linked to restrictions on immigration. Considered a moderate, Secretary of State Douglas Hurd, in a 1987 Parliamentary debate, expressed his concern (as cited in Skellington and Morris, 1992: 51):

> It would not be in the interests of the ethnic minorities themselves if there were a prospect of further mass inward movement. That prospect would increase social tensions, particularly in our cities. That is why we say that firm immigration control is essential if we are to have good community relations.

Earlier, the Conservative government's legislative responses had been swift, wide-ranging and exclusionary. The British Nationality Act, 1981, which came into force on 1 January 1983, effectively excluded British Overseas Citizens of Asian origin from the right of abode in the UK. This Act also changed the existing law which allowed those born in the UK to claim British citizenship under the ius soli principle, irrespective of the parents' citizenship. The previous immigration laws had retained the principle that even if the migrant parents were deported on the ground that they were illegal migrants, their British-born children could not be deported. The 1981 Act aimed to deprive the children of ethnic minorities of British citizenship: unless one of their parents held British citizenship at the material time or was settled here, a child born in the UK would no longer have automatic rights to British citizenship. The Act caused much alarm and anxiety among minority communities, and was seen as a move towards the Powellite doctrine that the accident of the place of birth should give no claim to citizenship. The Act also failed to comply with international human rights guaranteed by the Universal Declaration of Human Rights of 1948 (Evans, 1983: 79). Changes to the immigration policy clearly indicated the British government's decision to sever its traditional liberal contacts with the New Commonwealth. Visa requirements were imposed in 1985 on citizens of Sri Lanka, extended in 1986 to citizens of Bangladesh, Ghana, India, Nigeria and Pakistan. Many countries have since been added to this list and in most cases entry clearance has to be obtained before departure to Britain. The Immigration Act, 1988 amended the 1971 Act further by some specific rules which targeted Asian migrants. During the 1990s, restrictions on asylum seekers became most prominent and the latest addition is the Asylum and Immigration Act of 1996, which came into force in July 1996.

1.9 Backlashes

The British National Front (see Fielding, 1981; Taylor, 1982; Walker, 1971) was a powerful force in the body politic of Britain during the 1970s. The 1980s saw their influence weaken as their policies were taken up by Thatcherite neo-Conservatives. To revive their fortune in the political arena, right-wing racists resorted to physical violence (Solomos, 1989: chapters 7-8) and second generation blacks and Asians now became subject to racial abuse and attack. Metropolitan Police Commissioner Peter Imbert's 1989 and 1990 reports confirmed that racially motivated attacks against ethnic minorities were increasing (details in Skellington and Morris, 1992: 63). The Annual Reports of the Home Affairs Committee also admitted that racial tensions were worsening every year.[9] According to government figures, in England and Wales the annual number of such incidents was roughly 7,000 (Gordon, 1989: 23). In 1991 the Runnymede Trust reported in their Race and Immigration Bulletin No. 248, at p. 7, that the number of such attacks in 1988 was 4,383, rising to 6,359 in 1990. By 1993-94 the figure had risen to 9,762,[10] although some estimate the actual number as high as 70,000 (Gordon, 1989: 23).

Several attacks stand out for their brutality. On 2 August 1992, Ruhullah Aramesh was beaten to death by a group of white youths shouting 'Kill the Paki'. Rohit Duggal was stabbed to death on 11 July 1992 in Greenwich, where racial attacks have increased by 87% since 1991 (Mazzel and Frewin, 1992: 17). In August 1992, Mohammed Sarwar and Siddik Dada were brutally murdered, a month after a 16 year-old Asian boy was killed in Eltham, South East London. Charlton Mosque was attacked by arsonists on 26 August 1992 and the suspects were said to be white youths.[11] Black teenager, Stephen Lawrence, was stabbed to death in 1993 while he was waiting at a bus stop in London, allegedly by a gang of white youths. The notable delay by the police to apprehend those responsible and their subsequent acquittal led in 1998 to the Home Secretary establishing an inquiry into the police investigation but the murderers are still free men. In April 1998, the government laid a Crime and Disorder Bill before Parliament and the Crime and Disorder Act, 1998 now contains the definition of a racially aggravated offence in S.28(1).

The effect of the scenario of racially motivated attacks has become that African-Caribbeans and Asians, in Peter Herbert's words, 'feel under siege in every walk of British life, from the court room to the cricket pitch'. Based on the Annual Report of the CRE for 1994, he adds that 'this is not some idle or over-sensitive perception but the hard reality based upon overwhelming evidence' (Herbert, 1995: 1139).[12] The rise in the rate of race-fuelled crimes and racial harassment was affirmed by a MORI survey conducted in Manchester, published by the Manchester Evening News, 14 February 1996. It was found that during 1995 alone, 21,428 ethnic minority individuals had suffered racially motivated harassment and attack in the city, but that 81 per cent did not report the incident to the police. The United Nations Committee on the Elimination of Racial Discrimination has also confirmed in its report on the UK in 1996 that many people who died in police custody were from ethnic minority backgrounds and the report severely criticises Britain's record on race relations (The Guardian, 15 March 1996). A recently completed Home Office study on entry into the criminal justice system concluded that ethnic minority individuals of African-Caribbean and Asian origin are more likely than whites to be arrested by the police, jailed by magistrates and sent to the Crown Court for trials than whites. This study, which confirms familiar patterns of disparity, was based on a sample of 4,000 people arrested between 1993-94 at police stations in Manchester, Leicester, Croydon and Hackney in London, Gateshead, Cardiff and Birmingham (The Times, 21 August 1998). Such figures appear to suggest patterns of systematic discrimination which have puzzled many academics but, as Peter Herbert indicated, are a matter of first-hand knowledge, if not direct experience, to non-white people in Britain.

In 1993, racial attacks turned into full-scale racial riots particularly around London. In Tower Hamlets, where at least 36% of the total population is of ethnic minority background, racial riots in 1993 revealed deep-rooted mistrust, fear and hatred towards ethnic minority communities. The British National Party, established by John Tyndall out of the ashes of the National Front in 1982, called for the compulsory repatriation of blacks and Asians and is alleged to have supported racial violence in Tower Hamlets by encouraging rioters (The Guardian, 18 September 1993). White residents complained of preferential treatment for Asians in housing, employment and service. Others were content to repeat the traditional fears of blacks, complaining for example that they were bringing cockroaches to the island. Liberal council members were accused of encouraging racial conflicts. The West Midlands Police now believe that there is evidence that Ku-Klux Klan groups operate in inner cities.[13]

Members of minority communities are now prepared to challenge the status quo, particularly second-generation British Muslims, while young Hindus and Sikhs have managed to avoid major confrontations with native whites. For the British Muslim community in Britain, which is viewed as 'the land of kufr' (disbelief), this has not always been the case. They have been willing – some would argue, forced – to adopt a more aggressive stance to fight for their rights while searching for an identity (see Appignanesi and Maitland, 1989; Nielsen, 1987, Eade, 1990: 503). Even some Muslim scholars call for Muslims to come out of their shells to 'explore the virtues of fundamentalism' (Akhtar, 1989: 96). There is strong evidence, in particular in areas such as Birmingham, Bradford and East London, to suggest that radical Muslim movements are gradually gaining ground. Unlike their parents, some Muslims, educated in British schools and in a Western liberal environment, are now determined to fight prejudice (Lewis, 1994: 18-24; Anwar, 1979). It is said that youngsters are deserting bars and pubs for mosques and religious classes (Modood, 1990: 156). Shabbir Akhtar (1989: 114) observes about Muslims that:

> Their sons and daughters are different. They know their rights; and, paradoxically, the very society that has taught them the language of political demand and request has often denied them the rights they have asked for.

The problem arises when these confident British-born citizens wish to be both British and Muslim. Muslims want to integrate but not to assimilate: they want to compromise on matters of fashion but not of principle.

A Muslim organisation, Muslim Wise, cited in Scantlebury (1995: 433), has proclaimed:

> Behind the sensational headlines hiding the Muslim community from full view is a growing, powerful movement that both 'Muslim leaders' and myopic race industry moguls are ignoring at their peril. The movement to have Muslims recognised as a distinct group of people to whom religion is more important than racial origins is grassroot and slowly but surely gaining momentum by the prayer time. It is a movement that will outlive the Blasphemy Laws in this country and, of course, the Commission for Racial Equality, insha'Allah.

The major grievance of British Muslims is that there has been a 'relentless campaign to reduce Muslim citizens of this country to the status of a disparaged minority' (Nielsen, 1991: 468; see also Solomos, 1993: 223). Thus, the general perception among the Muslim community is of a continuation of the historical hatred towards Muslims by the imperial West. Muslim opposition to the establishment was aggressively demonstrated by the Bradford Muslim Council of Mosques, particularly the Muslims belonging to the Barelvi tradition, in the 'Rushdie affair', in which the elements of Muslims fundamentalism and militancy were displayed in public (Samad, 1992: 507; Modood, 1990: 143-60, see also below, ch. 6). After their failure to persuade British politicians to ban the Satanic Verses, some radical Muslim leaders, in particular Dr. Kalim Siddiqui,[14] called for a 'symbolic breaking of the law and manipulation of the political process' (Ahktar, 1989: 112), demonstrating Muslim determination to go to any lengths to win their claims. Muslims see the fight against the tide of secularisation as part of their historic duty (Parker-Jenkins, 1991: 569) and are increasingly asserting their presence for a number of reasons.

In February 1996, parents and the local leaders of the Muslim community in Birmingham threatened that unless the authorities allowed a Muslim Imam to conduct religious education classes in Birchfield Primary School, they would not send their children to multi-religious classes. The local education authority ultimately agreed to this request, or, as the tabloids put it, surrendered to Muslim fundamentalism. This is not the first time an education authority has chosen to accede to Muslim requests. Following a campaign of some 18 months, Ray Honeyford, a Bradford headteacher of an inner city school with a large number of Muslim children, was compelled to retire following allegations that he had contributed racially motivated articles to the Salisbury Review and local papers, criticising Islam and Pakistani society, challenging multiculturalism and questioning the wisdom of accommodating the special needs of Muslim parents and Muslim children (Lewis, 1994: 2).

Direct Muslim challenges to the establishment were clearly demonstrated in 1991 when Muslims held a meeting in London to launch the Muslim Manifesto, which openly called for a Muslim Parliament (Majlis) in Britain, open only to members of the Muslim community.[15] It passed a resolution calling for the adoption of Muslim personal laws, which had been refused in the 1980s. The most controversial section of the Manifesto, 'General guidelines for the life of the Muslim individual in Britain', requires Muslim individuals to live according to the guidelines laid down by Islam and to obey the Prophet Muhammad. The two first paragraphs proclaim (cited by Nielsen, 1991: 469):

(1) Islam allows Muslims to accept protection of life, property, and liberty from non-Muslim rulers and their political systems. Muslims placed in this situation may also pay taxes and other dues to a non-Muslim state.

(2) Muslims living under the protection of a non-Muslim State must obey the laws of that State, so long as such obedience does not conflict with their commitment to Islam and the Ummah.

The third paragraph, cited below, is more controversial and deals with the obligations of Muslim individuals and law and order issues. It covers sensitive areas such as abortion, homosexuality, gambling, sale and consumption of alcohol, and usury. Responsibility for maintaining law and order covering the above areas is solely a right of the British government and is ultimately in the hands of the English courts. Nevertheless the Muslim Manifesto indirectly challenges this by reminding Muslims:

(3) Muslims can neither agree with nor condone any part of a legal and social agenda which so flagrantly violates the law of nature as well as God.

In a subsequent session of the Muslim Parliament, Dr. Kalim Siddiqui, the self-proclaimed leader of this assembly, said he might lead the Muslim community to civil disobedience if necessary (The Independent, 19 March 1992). At the press conference announcing the Parliament, he warned that the Muslim Parliament would not hesitate to operate as a separate government for Muslims in Britain (Akhtar, 1989: 115).

Such statements may provide a serious challenge to the establishment, as well as creating problems of law and order. Unsurprisingly, the British media began to attack the ulterior motives of the British Muslim community, questioning other migrants' loyalty as well. The Daily Express of 16 July 1990 sarcastically called it 'inflaming the passion for the love of Allah' (see Nielsen, 1991: 469). However, the British Muslims' campaign for recognition of their religious way of life is gaining momentum. Meanwhile, campaigns against ethnic minorities continue as well. Nobody knows what the future holds.

Notes to chapter 1

1 These figures are based on assumptions and 'official guesswork'. Before July 1962, according to Lord Elton (1965: 25-28), there were no official statistics.

2 Full statistics on the 1991 Census are now found in the various HMSO publications on the Census. For recent Labour Force Survey data see Jones, 1993.

3 The British Sikh Federation in its 1994 report stated that there are well over 400,000 Sikhs living in the UK. This figure has not been confirmed by any independent sources.

4 This derogatory term was (and still is) used to refer to Negroes by many, even by newspaper editors. For example, the deputy editor of the Sunday Telegraph was quoted, in the Spectator's Diary of 2 June 1984, as saying: 'I have always found the nickname of nig-nog applied to blacks a friendly one, or at the worst no more derisory than frog, pom, paddy, and so on'. See Patterson, 1984-85 for details.

5 See International Commission of Jurists, Bulletin No. 34, 1968: 36-37.

6 The Guardian, 31 Jan 1978. Compare this statement with Powell's speech at a gathering in Croydon on 4 October 1976. He prophesied: 'I have stated my conviction that physical and violent conflict must sooner or later supervene where an indigenous population sees no end to the occupation of its heartland by aliens with whom they do not identify themselves and who do not identify themselves with them'. See details in Berkeley, 1977: 16.

7 Particularly Asians in Birmingham, Bradford and Wolverhampton were identified with TB. Quoting one of the officials of the Birmingham Chest Clinic, The Daily Telegraph of 26 July 1964 reported that tuberculosis among Asians in Birmingham alone cost more than £60,000 a year. The Times 20 January 1965 reported sarcastically that the country's best investment so far seemed to be 'Pakistanis with TB'. These sources are cited in Elton, 1965: 8 and 43.

8 Haymas, C., C. Lloyd and S. Wavell (1993): 'Immigration: The false figures behind Churchill's outburst', in The Sunday Times 30 May 1993.

9 For details see: Racial attacks and harassment: The government reply to the Third Report from the Home Affairs Committee Session, 1993-4, House of Commons 71, London: HMSO 1994: 4.

10 Id.

11 See details in 'Racial violence: Taking stock', in CARF (Campaign against Racism and Fascism), No. 10 (September 1992), p. 3.

12 See further Holland, 1995; CRE, 1987; Ford, 1992; Harris, 1994.

13 For details see Campaign Against Racism and Facism (CARF) No. 10 (September 1992), p. 16.

14 This charismatic Muslim leader died in South Africa on 18 April 1996 while he was attending a seminar on Muslims. Dr. Siddiqui was a radical pro-Iranian leader, instru-mental in setting up the Muslim Parliament in 1991, earlier the Muslim Institute in 1972. See the obituary by J. S. Nielsen, 'Kalim Siddiqui', in The Independent, 20 April 1996.

15 They appointed a speaker, four deputy speakers, and a house leader. The Westminster-style Parliament planned to select 200 members as representatives. Members of the Parliament would be elected through 40 Muslim Manifesto Forums. Kalim Siddiqui alleged that it was the media which called the Muslim Majlis a Parliament (The Guardian, 29 October 1991).

Chapter 2

Ethnic or racial groups?

The immigration and race relations scenario generated a number of legislative responses designed to curb discrimination against members of ethnic minorities. Discriminatory practices, both direct and indirect, were seen to be increasing during the 1950s, particularly in housing, education, employment and the service sectors. Black and Asian civil rights movements campaigned during the 1960s for legislation prohibiting discriminatory practices on the grounds of colour, race and ethnicity. This culminated in the enactment of the Race Relations Act, 1965, subsequently amended in 1968 and the Race Relations Act, 1976, which remains the current law.

The terms 'racial group' or 'ethnic group' carry associations with social and human rights. Normally these terms refer to a particular group that is subject to the jurisdiction of a state. Ethnic communities are based upon unifying and spontaneous (as opposed to artificial or planned) factors essentially beyond the control of group members. They may develop separate identities to respond to the society surrounding them and survive as a group rather than as individuals. Biological factors may be less important than unanimity of cultural practices, religious beliefs and feelings of solidarity, and above all the desire to be identified as a separate group in social intercourse. Lord Fraser's test in the important Mandla case has partly considered the relevance of those sociological factors in interpreting the term 'racial group'.

The human rights dimension is also significant. Denial of the right to claim separate ethnic or racial identity is really a refusal to accommodate some human rights, whether or not such rights are guaranteed by domestic or international human rights documents. Deprivation of such rights is no more than subjecting a particular group of people to degrading and inhuman treatment, thereby prohibiting most of the basic rights to which they are laying claim as a separate group. The detailed debate on this wider issue has only just begun.

This chapter is concerned less with English race relations legislation than with how the English judiciary has approached the task of interpreting and applying the legislation centred around the concept of 'racial group'. We illustrate and elaborate here our argument that the English judiciary have been inconsistent and irrational in their understanding of ethnicity.

2.1 Race and ethnicity

There is little consensus on meanings of 'race' and 'ethnicity'. Race may alternatively suggest an awareness and consciousness of individuals relating to a specific primordial group, or belonging to a particular group of individuals living in a defined geographical area and closely connected with each other over a long period. E. Ellis Cashmore, an expert witness in the instructive case of Dawkins v Crown Suppliers (judgment of the South Industrial Tribunal, 28 March 1989), where the issue was whether Rastafarians are a 'racial group' (see the debate in Banton, 1989 and Cashmore, 1989), traces the English usage of 'race' to the 16th century. By the beginning of the 19th century, 'race' specified the outward appearances of specific human groups (Cashmore, 1984a: 214). For example, colour as well as facial features and hair are said to mark external boundaries. Descent from a common origin enables members to qualify as a particular racial group. Once membership is determined, it is assumed that no one can change this group identity, race being governed by natural and biological factors. In consequence racial groups have been identified by colours which are supposed to describe the outward appearance of each racial group (Banton, 1985: 3).

Why 'race' rather than the less emotive term 'ethnicity'? J. P. Humphrey, the first Director of the Human Rights Division of the UN and one of the chief architects of the Universal Declaration of Human Rights 1948, argued that as 'ethnic' includes other factors such as religion and language, it was better to retain 'race', a narrower and less wide-ranging concept, and maintained that there was nothing pejorative about the word 'race' (Humphrey, 1989: 50). Before and after the First World War, in the minority treaties and in other League of Nations documents, the term had been used to cover ethnic and cultural characteristics. Often, 'race' and 'nation' were used synonymously.

Particularly in the context of debates about the 'new minorities', however, there is a significant body of opinion wishing to avoid 'race'. The misuse of the term by the Nazis hastened the decline in its use. More recently, Banton and Harwood (1975) pointed out that, as a way of categorising people, 'race' is based upon a delusion. And a prominent Professor of Zoology, L. C. Dunn (1950: 249-250) agreed:

...the word race as generally used has no clear or exact meaning at all, and through frequent misuse has acquired unpleasant and distressing connotations. Many people become confused when the direct question is put to them as it is in some official documents. To what race do you belong?... The existence of that question is evidence of past misuse... Owing to its bad connotations and the absence of such an objective list, doubts have been expressed whether there is any valid and useful meaning of the word at all which would justify its retention in our vocabulary.

Capotorti (1967, para 196) distinguishes the 'non-scientific basis of racial categorisation and the more inclusive meaning of 'ethnic' as a reference to cultural, historical and biological characteristics, as opposed to 'racial', which refers only to inherited characteristics'. As a result 'race' has been widely replaced by 'ethnic' (Capotorti, 1967: 34). But 'ethnic' is not without its own difficulties. The term is often thought elusive, decorative, descriptive, mystical and frequently romanticised (Wirsing, 1981: 5). It derives from the Greek ethnos or ethnikos, the adjective of ethnos (Cashmore, 1984a: 85) and normally refers to a category of people or nation possessing some degree of coherence and solidarity, being aware of their common origins and cultural interests. An ethnic group is not a mere aggregate of people or a sector of a population, but a self-conscious collection of people united, or closely related, by shared experiences (Claydon, 1975: 26). 'Ethnic group' has been defined by Morris (1968: 167) as 'a distinct category of the population in a larger society whose culture is usually different from its own, whose members are, or feel themselves or are thought to be, bound together by common ties of race, nationality, or culture'. This distinction stresses the cultural aspects of ethnic communities while referring to attachment by reason of common ties specific only to group members. Subjective criteria such as sentimental factors are considered paramount. Ellis Cashmore (1984a: 85) wrote that 'ethnic group' stands for the creative response of a people 'who feel somehow marginal to the mainstream of society', which also gives emphasis to subjective criteria.

Some scholars see 'ethnic group' as a pressure group fighting for survival in competitive modern societies (Roosens, 1989: 15), whereas sociologists emphasise their cultural aspects. 'Culture' and 'ethnic group' were often used interchangeably. Adding a new dimension to these conceptual arguments, Gordon (1964: 26) stated that 'race, religion, and national origins are the competing models of ethnicity and around these factors 'ethnicity' is established'.

Is 'ethnic' a sub-category of 'race' or a synonymous term? Different racial groups are often interchangeably qualified by the term 'ethnic'. Seligman (1949: 607) wrote that, 'in its strict meaning the word ethnic denotes race: but when applied to communities in the above sense it is loosely used'.

2.2 National identity

Britain comprises the English, Scots, Welsh, Irish, Jutes, Celts, Romans, Angles, Saxons, Danes, Flemish, Britons, Huguenots, Norse and Norman French but was, until the mid-20th century, considered a relatively homogeneous society. As one commentator put it, 'the national hearts beat as one and the people of this island commonly speak English in communicating their feelings' (Gilroy, 1987: 46). This is identified as 'Britishness' or 'Englishness'. Yet it fails to provide definite criteria by which to judge and determine who is 'British' (Parry, 1957: 5). It was too vague, even before the arrival of migrants, so that 'the majority of the 'we' are very confused about whether their identity is British or English' (Crick, 1995: 167; see further Goulbourne, 1991: 22).

Three criteria began to emerge. Firstly a 'race' primarily from common European stock, 'white' people of the Christian religion. Secondly a common language, English. Finally one sought to determine citizenship through the principle of ius soli, the birthright as a result of being born in a particular territory, allegiance to the Union and loyalty to the Monarch.

The early presence of manifestly non-English individuals in Britain and later large-scale immigration posed challenges to such criteria. In the view of some self-appointed defenders of traditional Britishness, such as Norman Tebbit, the national identity was bruised by large waves of immigrants (Goulbourne, 1991: 29). Politicians were puzzled about how to respond and most fell back on biological criteria. Leah Manning, MP stressed in the debate on the Polish Resettlement Bill that the British are 'a mongrel race' which could absorb 'a great body of men' (HC Debate, Hansard 12 February 1947: col. 399). She was certainly not thinking of Black men then. Another MP, David Renton (HC Debate, Hansard, 7 July 1948: cols. 476-477), stressed that the British race was different from other races living in the UK. Even though there were numerous racial groups in Britain and the British Empire, only one group could be identified as fully British.

By emphasising that Britishness comprises common biological roots, a common language and an allegiance to the Crown, parliamentarians could exclude certain migrants. Caribbean and Indian migrants to Britain during and after the Second World War could be failed on language. Caribbean migrants brought a hybrid of Patois and English. Asians spoke Hindi, Urdu, Panjabi, Gujarati, Tamil and many other languages, rather than English. Allegiance has been questioned by Norman Tebbit's 'cricket test', reiterated by the Wisden Cricket Magazine (Daily Telegraph, 21 April 1990; Henderson, 1995), during the Gulf War and in the Rushdie affair, where Muslims were accused of lacking loyalty to Britain.

Ethnic minorities have variously been identified or identified themselves as coming from particular geographical areas. Terms such as Indians, Pakistanis, Bangladeshis, Afro-Caribbeans, Turks, Panjabis, Arabs and Chinese are in common use. A common racial or ethnic identity is expressed by terms like Sylhetis, Yorubas or Tamils. Many Indians mark their identity from a religious perspective, signified by Sikh, Hindu and Muslim labels.

The challenge during the 1960s was to devise workable definitions within the new demographic context (for details see Mercer, 1990; Hall, 1991; Miller, 1995). It was assumed that, unlike the United States, migrants to Britain did not easily shed their cultural baggage. In the United States, new migrants were welcome provided they were prepared to be identified with the American nation, respect the America flag and constitution. The 'melting pot' strategy of reshaping in the context of American identity (Parekh, 1995: 263) meant that American laws had less confusion about who belongs and who does not.

A redefinition of British identity was needed (Miller, 1995: 154), for political as well as legislative reasons. However, attempts to reflect and capture the new diversities have not been successful. Legislation, when it arrived, was primarily designed to reduce immigration, so was exclusionary in nature, designed to implement deportation, expulsion, and restriction. The artificial nature of the terms 'patrial', 'citizen', and 'British Overseas Citizen' deliberately excluded new ethnic minority groups from the concept of British identity (Marquand, 1995: 188; Dummett and Nicol, 1990). From this perspective, it helped to reject ethnic minorities from the mainstream rather than finding a solution to the definitional debate about identity.

Some of these definitional terms were subjected to interpretation by the English judiciary. One of the main criticisms appeared to be that these terms might confer legal rights or, as Lord Denning stated (see below) 'precious rights', upon the many Indian and Caribbean migrants. His Lordship, criticising the logic and rationale of 'patrial', remarked in R v Secretary of State for the Home Department, ex parte Phansopkar and ex parte Begum [1976] 1 QB 606, at p. 615:

> In 1971 the Parliament of the UK invented a new word. It made a new man. It called him 'patrial'. Not a patriot, but a patrial. Parliament made him one of us and made us one of them. We are all now patrials. We are no longer, in the eye of the law, Englishmen, Scotsmen or Welshmen. We are just patrials. Parliament gave this man a fine set of clothes. It vested him with a new right. It called it the 'right of abode in the United Kingdom'. It is the most precious right that anyone can have. At least I so regard it. It is declared in simple but expressive words. Every patrial 'shall be free to live in, and to come and go into and from, the United Kingdom without let or hindrance'; section 1(1) of the Immigration Act 1971. At the same time, Parliament made it very easy for many an immigrant to become a patrial and get this precious right. Those of us who were born here and live here get it automatically. Those coming from overseas get it by being registered as a citizen of the United Kingdom and Colonies.

Referring to the certificates of registration issued by the Home Office to Mr. Phansopkar, his Lordship said, at p. 616:

> And here is the important point. Not only does he himself, on registration, become a patrial and entitled to the right of abode here, but also his wife does automatically. Even though she is living in far off India or Bangladesh. Even though she has never been to England

and cannot speak a word of English. She, too, becomes a patrial and entitled to the right of abode here. So she has the right to come into the United Kingdom without let or hindrance: bringing, no doubt, her babies with her. The only thing in her way is that she has to prove that she is his wife or, I suppose, one of his wives, if by their law, such is permitted.

In Phansopkar, Lord Denning reiterated his anger about the way in which this 'precious right' was accorded to migrants from the Indian sub-continent. His Lordship noted, at p. 617:

...the husband became entitled to a most valuable right. He himself thenceforward had 'the right of abode in the United Kingdom'. His right was equal to the right of abode of one of us. You and I and our families have been born here and lived here from time immemorial. Yet Mr. Phansopkar, from the moment he was registered, had just as much right here as we have. And not only he. His wife also obtained at the very moment the self-same right. She had never been to England. She could not speak English. She could not read or write... And, as such, as soon as her husband, by registration, gained the right of abode in the United Kingdom, she acquired the selfsame right of abode.

Britishness could no longer be fixed or definite but became a developing and evolving concept (Parekh, 1995: 255). What criteria should be used to define Britishness? Are the 'British' to be defined as white-British and Black-British? Are all groups who claim separate racial and ethnic identities to be recognised in terms of ethnicity or race? In Northern Joint Police Board v Power [1997] IRLR 610, the employment appeal tribunal held that while England, Scotland, Wales and Northern Ireland are pro-perly categorised as Britain, and the people as British, the English are a 'racial group' for the purposes of S.3(1) of the Race Relations Act, 1976.

2.3 Legislation

The existence of separate groups raised the possibility of discrimination on the basis of colour, ethnicity, racial or national backgrounds. The common law imposed little restriction for those who wished to discriminate (Lester and Bindman, 1972). Discrimination was not con-sidered an illegal practice in pre-war British society. In fact, discrimination in domestic and social life by employers and in the service sector was considered not only legal but appropriate. In Scala Ballroom [Wolverhampton] v Ratcliffe and others [1958] 3 All ER 220, CA a colour bar was upheld provided it could be shown to be in the interest of the business. The commonly held view regarding the civil liberties of individuals was that there were adequate remedies available at common law – Mr. Justice Paul said in R v Hunt (The Times, 26 November 1958, cited in Macdonald, 1969: 7):

> Everyone, irrespective of the colour of his skin, is entitled to walk through the streets in peace with their heads erect and free from fear. That is a right which these courts will always unfailingly uphold.

The judiciary were therefore reluctant to develop the common law of discrimination unless there were infringements of civil liberties (Macdonald, 1969: 4-5). Some evidence of an attempt to limit discrimination was apparent in the earlier case of Constantine v Imperial Hotels, [1944] 1 KB 693, where a hotelier was ordered to pay only five guineas as nominal damages to a famous former West Indian cricketer, Sir Learie Constantine, for refusing to accommodate him, allegedly on the ground of colour. A claim for substantial damages was refused. This case is the exception rather than the rule. The common law was clearly inadequate (Lester and Bindman, 1972). The uncertainty, the cost of individual litigation and ineffective remedies mitigated against its use to suppress the growing number of discriminatory practices (Macdonald, 1969: 6).

Legislation was needed and it came in the various Race Relations Acts, now the Act of 1976. At the heart of such legislative intervention lay the assumption that separate groups could be defined, isolated and as such protected from discrimination. Section 3 of the 1976 Act provides the following definition of a 'racial group':

> 3. – Meaning of 'racial grounds', 'racial group', etc.
>
> (1) In this Act, unless the context otherwise requires –
>
> 'racial grounds' means any of the following grounds, namely colour, race, nationality or ethnic or national origins;
>
> 'racial group' means a group of persons defined by reference to colour, race, nationality or ethnic or national origins, and reference to a person's racial group refer to any racial group into which he falls.

(2) The fact that a racial group comprises two or more distinct racial groups does not prevent it from constituting a particular racial group for the purposes of this Act.

(3) In this Act -

(a) references to discrimination refer to any discrimination falling within section 1 or 2; and

(b) references to racial discrimination refer to any discrimination falling within section 1,

and related expressions shall be construed accordingly.

(4) A comparison of the case of a particular racial group with that of a person not of that group under section 1(1) must be such that the relevant circumstances in the one case are the same, or not materially different, in the other.

Case law relating to Jews, Sikhs and Gypsies has centred on whether they may be defined as a separate racial, ethnic or national group. An early commentator (Macdonald, 1969: 13) warned perceptively that '[t]he objective categorisation of people into different racial or ethnic groups involves making racist assumptions, and is an almost impossible task'.

We now discuss the main relevant cases under s. 3 of the 1976 Act and highlight the unsuccessful attempts by the judiciary to develop a coherent theory of 'racial group'. We analyse how particular groups have fared under the law, starting with the Sikhs, Jews and Gypsies, who have all been relatively successful in gaining acceptance of their particular claims, while the Rastafarians, Muslims, Hindus and others continue to battle against the law's inability, or unwillingness, to produce definite criteria for the legal recognition of ethnic groups under English law. This state of affairs tells us much about the present inadequate position in the law, where a person from one ethnic group will be protected by the 1976 Act, while a person from another group, in almost identical circumstances, cannot seek legal protection against discrimination.

2.4 Sikhs as a 'racial group'

Sikhs migrated to the UK mainly from the Panjab and then during the 1960s and 1970s also from East African countries (Aurora, 1967). They are a difficult group to categorise within s. 3 of the 1976 Act, having diverse origins and lacking common denominators which are unique to them, as opposed to other South Asians from the same region. One question was to what extent the lack of a common biological origin would prevent Sikhs from being categorised as a separate racial group.

There is no evidence from parliamentary debates that the legislators wanted to identify the term 'racial group' only in the biological context. In fact, some MPs expressed the view that factors such as race, colour, nationality or ethnic characteristics should be taken into consideration and some contributors to the debates argued that political and geographical grounds as well as biological aspects could help create the identity of a racial group (see HC Debates, Hansard 1975-76, vol. 1, col. 114). Some support for this view came from the judiciary. Lord Simon in London Borough of Ealing v Race Relations Board [1972] 1 All ER 105, HL at p. 115, pronounced that "racial' is not a term of art, either legal or scientific' saying that, 'I apprehend that anthropologists would dispute how far the word 'race' is biologically at all relevant to the species amusingly called Homo Sapiens'.

The legal position of Sikhs under the 1976 Act fell to be determined in Mandla v Dowell Lee [1982] 3 All ER 1108, CA. Mr. Seva Singh Mandla, a Sikh father, instituted legal proceedings against the Headmaster of Park Grove School in Birmingham, alleging that his son had not been admitted to that school on grounds of racial discrimination – thus violating s. 1(1)(b) of the Race Relations Act, 1976. Section 1 of the 1976 Act provides as follows:

1. – Racial discrimination

(1) A person discriminates against another in any circumstances relevant for the purposes of any provision of this Act if –

(a) on racial grounds he treats that other less favourably than he treats or would treat other persons; or

(b) he applies to that other a requirement or condition which he applies or would apply equally to persons not of the same racial group as that other but –

(i) which is such that the proportion of persons of the same racial group as that other who can comply with it is considerably smaller than the proportion of persons not of that racial group who can comply with it; and

    (ii) which he cannot show to be justifiable irrespective of the colour, race, nationality or ethnic or national origins of the person to whom it is applied; and

    (iii) which is to the detriment of that other because he cannot comply with it.

(2) It is hereby declared that, for the purposes of this Act, segregating a person from other persons on racial grounds is treating him less favourably than they are treated.

As a Sikh, Mr. Mandla could seek legal protection against racial discrimination on the grounds of race, colour or ethnicity only if Sikhs were treated as members of a racial group under s.3(1) of the Race Relations Act, 1976. The complaint was dismissed by the County Court on 10 December 1980. Mr. Mandla, a solicitor by profession, appealed and sought the assistance of the Commission for Racial Equality. In the Court of Appeal (reported as Mandla v Dowell Lee [1982] 3 All ER 1108, CA), Lord Denning MR, Oliver and Kerr LJJ unanimously refused to accept that Sikhs are a racial group as defined by the Race Relations Act 1976. The reasoning of Lord Denning centred around the definition of 'ethnic' as 'racial'. He stated at p. 1111:

> The word 'ethnic' is derived from the Greek word... which meant simply 'nation'. It was used by the 72 Palestinian Jews who translated the Old Testament from Hebrew into Greek (in the Septuagint). They used it to denote the non-Israelitish nations, that is, the Gentiles... When the word 'ethnic' was first used in England, it was used to denote peoples who were not Christians or Jewish. This was the meaning attached to it in the great Oxford English Dictionary itself in 1890.

> But in 1934 in the Concise Oxford Dictionary it was given an entirely different meaning. It was given as: 'pertaining to race, ethnological'. And 'ethnological' was given as meaning: 'corresponding to a division of races'. That is the meaning which I, acquiring my vocabulary in 1934, have always myself attached to the word 'ethnic'. It is, to my mind, the correct meaning. It means 'pertaining to race'.

His Lordship took great pains to find a meaning for the term 'ethnic group' in a biological context. Lord Denning's position was that the 'group' must be distinguished from other groups by some definable and permanent characteristics and he therefore refused to admit that Sikhs could qualify as a 'racial group' distinct from other South Asians. His Lordship referred, at p. 1113, to expert evidence by Roger Ballard, then a lecturer in race relations at Leeds University, who had submitted a report to the effect that:

> Sikhs, most obviously, are not a race in biological terms. Their origins are extremely diverse, probably more diverse than us English... I think they are a classic example of an ethnic group because of their distinctive cultural traditions... We are busy coining lots of new words here. I think ethnicity is the proper word to coin...'.

Having heard other evidence, Lord Denning found that his concept of 'race' and the facts pertaining to the Sikhs as an 'ethnic group' could not be harmonised. Thus he held, at p. 114:

> On all this evidence, it is plain to me that the Sikhs, as a group, cannot be distinguished from others in the Punjab by reference to any racial characteristic whatever. They are only to be distinguished by their religion and culture. That is not an ethnic difference at all.

Having agreed with the decision of the lower court that Sikhs are not a racial group, Lord Denning went on, at p. 1114:

> They cannot be defined by reference to their ethnic or national origins. No doubt they are a distinct community, just as many other religious and cultural communities. But that is not good enough. It does not enable them to complain of discrimination against them.

> You must remember that it is perfectly lawful to discriminate against groups of people to whom you object, as long as they are not a racial group. You can discriminate against the Moonies or the skinheads or any other group which you dislike or to which you take objection. No matter whether your objection to them is reasonable or unreasonable, you can discriminate against them, without being in breach of the law.

> No doubt the Sikhs are very different from some of those groups. They are a fine community upholding the highest standards, but they are not a 'racial group'. So it is not unlawful to discriminate against them. Even though the discrimination may be unfair or unreasonable, there is nothing unlawful in it.

The Court of Appeal decision in Mandla was, however, soon reversed by the House of Lords in Mandla v Dowell Lee [1983] 1 All ER 1062, HL. Sikhs as a group defined by reference to colour, race, nationality or national origin were seen to be as indistinguishable from many other groups, especially those living, like most Sikhs, in the Panjab. As stated at p. 1065, 'it is therefore necessary to ascertain the sense in which the word 'ethnic' is used in the 1976 Act' and, as in the Court of Appeal, the respondent referred to the Oxford English Dictionary for the exact meaning of the term 'ethnic'. It was observed, at p. 1065, that the 1897 edition gives two meanings:

> The first is 'pertaining to nations not Christian or Jewish; gentile, heathen, pagan'. That clearly cannot be its meaning in the 1976 Act, because it is inconceivable that Parliament would have legislated against racial discrimination intending that the protection should not apply either to Christians or (above all) to Jews. Neither party contended that that was the relevant meaning for the present purpose. The second meaning... was 'pertaining to race; peculiar to a race or nation; ethnological'.

Lord Fraser stated at p.1066 that the term 'racial group' conveys a flavour of race, but cannot have been used in the Race Relations Act, 1976 in a strict racial or biological sense. He said further at p. 1066:

> For one thing [sic] it would be absurd to suppose that Parliament can have intended that membership of a particular racial group should depend on scientific proof that a person possessed the relevant distinctive biological characteristics (assuming that such characteristics exist). The practical difficulties of such proof would be prohibitive, and it is clear that Parliament must have used the word in some more popular sense.

He therefore categorically denied the proposition that the term 'ethnic' has any connection with narrowly conceived biological factors and turned to a wider meaning of 'ethnic', as found in the Supplement to the Oxford English Dictionary of 1972, which was, as cited at p. 1066, 'pertaining to or having common racial, cultural, religious, or linguistic characteristics, esp. designating a racial or other group within a larger system...'. This definition, in the words of Lord Fraser at p. 1066,

...shows that ethnic has come to be commonly used in a sense appreciably wider than the strictly racial or biological. That appears to me to be consistent with the ordinary experience of those who read newspapers at the present day. In my opinion, the word 'ethnic' still retains a racial flavour but it is used nowadays in an extended sense to include other characteristics which may be commonly thought of as being associated with common racial origin.

Lord Fraser then suggested, at p. 1067, the following seven criteria to define a racial group:

> The conditions which appear to me to be essential are these: (1) a long shared history, of which the group is conscious as distinguishing it from other groups, and the memory of which it keeps alive; (2) a cultural tradition of its own, including family and social customs and manners, often but not necessarily associated with religious obser-vance. In addition to those two essential characteristics the following characteristics are, in my opinion, relevant: (3) either a common geographical origin, or descent from a small number of common ancestors; (4) a common language, not necessarily peculiar to the group; (5) a common literature peculiar to the group; (6) a common religion different from that of neighbouring groups or from the general community surrounding it; (7) being a minority or being an oppressed or a dominant group within a larger community.

Taking these criteria into consideration, his Lordship held, at p. 1069, that 'Sikhs are a group defined by reference to ethnic origins for the purpose of the 1976 Act, although they are not biologically distinguishable from the other peoples living in the Punjab'. Lord Fraser's approach is to be seen as a positive and progressive contribution to race relations law. The earlier thesis that the characteristics which are inherited by birth cannot be changed was clearly refuted by the House of Lords. The judgment opens up the possibility of converts or those marrying into a group to become part of that racial group. Thus, as stated by Lord Fraser at p. 1067, for the purpose of the 1976 Act, '...it is possible for a person to fall into a particular racial group either by birth or by adherence, and it makes no difference, so far as the 1976 Act is concerned, by which route he finds his way into the group'.

However, not all members of the House of Lords were prepared to adopt the approach of Lord Fraser. Lord Templeman preferred to state that the group of persons defined by reference to ethnic origins must possess some racial characteristics, namely group descent, a certain geographical origin and a group history. In effect, then, while Lord Templeman made no reference to cultural traditions but emphasised group descent and a common geographical origin, Lord Fraser treated a common geographical origin and descent from a small number of common ancestors as a relevant but non-essential condition and considered that the two major characteristics were alternatives rather than cumulative. The distinction between Lords Fraser and Templeman is that Lord Templeman requires, in effect, three essential characteristics, whereas Lord Fraser identified only two. However, both indicated that 'ethnic' should be interpreted widely, and in a cultural and historical sense. The application of this wide, inclusive definitional paradigm has not been without problems, however, as the following sub-chapters will show.

2.5 Jews

Jewish settlement in the UK has a long history dating back to the Middle Ages (Gartner, 1973; Berghahn, 1984; Lipman, 1954). All Jews were expelled from England in 1290 but managed, more or less secretly, to come back during the following centuries. Sephardi Jews migrated to Britain from Spain and Portugal during the 14th and 15th centuries and. the Sephardim became the largest Jewish group in Britain. Many Jewish migrants came from Germany and Eastern Europe between 1880 and 1905 (Jewish Women in London, 1989: 19). Significant numbers also arrived in Britain during and after the two world wars, mainly Ashkenazi, a national group mainly from the Russian and Austro-Hungarian Empires. Jews from the Sephardi and Mizrachi traditions also came from India, Morocco and Aden. From the 1960s onwards, Jews also migrated from South Africa, driven out by apartheid (Jewish Women in London, 1989: 23). Despite the different geographical origins, they all embrace one religion, Judaism. To what extent would this determine the racial or ethnic identity of the various sub-groups?

Whether or not Jews are a 'racial group' was never much of an issue among historians, politicians or anti-Jewish campaigners. Jews were primarily identified in biological rather than religious terms (Dummett and Nicol, 1990: 98). Anti-semitism regarded Jewishness as something in the blood, irreducible and hereditary, which conversion to Christianity could not alter. Jews were identified with permanent stereotypical characteristics (Dummett and Nicol, 1990: 98-99). Nevertheless, their identity as a separate racial group was said to depend upon whether at least one parent had embraced Judaism. Benjamin Akzin (1970: 261) analysed this rather unusual situation:

> Where Jewish 'nationality' or 'people' is concerned, the minimum objective criterion long prevalent within the Jewish community was that of a minimum objective link with Jewish religion, i.e. either affiliated or as long as the descendant did not convert to another organised faith... Jewish religious law views descent from a Jewish mother as decisive in this connection. So important was that link between nationality and religion in Jewish ranks and quite often and quite sincerely was the Jewish community described by many of its own members as a religious group only, while its character as an ethnic group, as a nationality, was overlooked or even denied.

In the Court of Appeal stage of Mandla v Dowell Lee [1982] 3 All ER 1108, Lord Denning MR made reference to Jews and agreed with the well-known anthropologists, Huxley and Haddon, that Jews are the best-known example of a racial group because of their distinguished racial characteristics. Particular emphasis was placed on Jewish blood, which does not diminish by conversion to Christianity. His Lordship pronounced, at p. 1112:

> Why are 'the Jews' given as the best-known example of 'ethnic grouping'? What is their special characteristic which distinguishes them from non-Jews? To my mind it is a racial characteristic. The Shorter Oxford Dictionary describes a Jew as 'a person of Hebrew race'. Some help too can be found in our law books... If a man desires that his daughter should only marry 'a Jew' and cuts her out of his will if she should marry a man who is not 'a Jew', he will find that the court will hold the condition void for uncertainty. The reason is because 'a Jew' may mean a dozen different things. It may mean a man of the Jewish faith. Even if he was a convert from Christianity, he would be of the Jewish faith. Or it may mean a man of Jewish parentage, even though he may be a convert to Christianity. It may

suffice if his grandfather was a Jew and his grandmother was not. The Jewish blood may have become very thin by intermarriage with Christians, but still many would call him 'a Jew'. All this leads me to think that, when it is said of the Jews that they are an 'ethnic group', it means that the group as a whole share a common characteristic which is a racial characteristic. It is that they are descended, however remotely, from a Jewish ancestor.

However, this approach is simply relying on conventional wisdom and certain prejudices, rather than defining Jewishness in terms of s. 3 of the Race Relations Act, 1976. An alternative approach was evidenced earlier in Re Samuel, Jacobs, Ramsden [1941] 3 All ER 196, Lord Greene MR concluding at p. 203 that whether an individual is a Jew can be established by asking him about his faith. If a person answered 'I am a Jew by faith', that would be a most cogent piece of evidence. The Master of the Rolls did not go beyond 'faith' and did not focus on race or nationality. Similarly in Morgan v Civil Service Commission and the British Library (Case No. 19177/98, EOR Discrimination Case Law Digest, No. 6, Winter 1990, p. 3) the industrial tribunal affirmed the above position and held that Jews 'may be a racial or religious group'. Again in Seide v Gillette Industries Ltd. [1980] IRLR 427, EAT it was conceded that 'Jews' could mean a member of a race or of a particular ethnic origin as well as a member of a religious faith. This view was echoed in King-Ansell v Police [1979] 2 NZLR 531, where it was held that Jews form a group with common ethnic origins. Refusing to adopt the standard dictionary meaning, the court held at p. 534:

> There is no biological means of establishing that Jewish people are a race and that members of the Jewish people have diverse racial origins... Jewishness was much more than a matter of religion only.

These cases stand in contrast to the interpretation offered by Lord Denning in Mandla v Dowell Lee [1982] 3 All ER 1108, CA, where he wished to place emphasis on racial characteristics and casually referred to 'Jewish blood' in defining Jews as an ethnic group. His Lordship's argument is based on the biological requirement, as is evident from his reference to the 'Hebrew race', from which Jews are believed to be descended.

2.6 Gypsies and travellers

Gypsy movements in Britain appeared as early as the beginning of the 16th century. It is often believed that Gypsies came from the East, but their true origin is likely to have been the Northern part of India (Liégeois, 1987: 14). 'Gypsy' may not even be a gypsy word (Liégeois, 1985: 13). It is only one of many words used to identify a person of Romani descent or a person having a nomadic lifestyle. The picture often invoked by 'Gypsy' is of a person travelling with horses or donkeys, collecting scrap metal, rags, rabbit skins or bones, and living by sooth-saying or selling charms. The word is often used interchangeably with 'traveller'. Indeed Gypsies often refer to themselves as travellers, believing this to be a less derogatory expression.

The Chambers 20th Century Dictionary of 1983 describes 'travellers' as 'travelling folk: the name by which itinerant people often call themselves, in preference to the derogatory names gypsies or tinkers'. The Supplement to the Oxford English Dictionary of 1986 identifies a traveller also as a Gypsy. However, Nicholls LJ in Commission for Racial Equality v Dutton [1989] 2 WLR 17, CA at pp. 22-23, stated that the two words 'gypsy' and 'traveller' are not synonymous. His Lordship cited the Oxford English Dictionary of 1933 and the Longman Dictionary of Contemporary English of 1987. According to the former, the word 'gypsy' describes 'a member of a wandering race (by themselves called Romany), of Hindu origin, which first appeared in England about the beginning of the 16th c. and was then believed to have come from Egypt'. One of the meanings given by the Longman definition is that of 'a person who habitually wanders or who has the habits of someone who does not stay for long in one place, in short, a nomad'. Gypsy, it seems, may be defined in terms of both ethnic and cultural characteristics.

The difficulty categorising Gypsies arose because, as one of the leading authorities in Europe on Gypsies, Jean-Pierre Liégeois (1985: 23) comments, 'Gypsies are a rich mosaic of ethnic fragments, very different groups going under different names'. This diversity is reflected in the range of terms used to describe various kinds of Gypsies, prominently 'tinkers',[1] 'diddikois' or 'diddicoy',[2] 'Romani', 'Rom', or 'Romans',[3] 'kalderas', 'kale',[4] 'mumper' and 'posh-cat'.

Gypsies themselves, legislators and the judiciary have attempted to isolate the 'real' Gypsies from this mosaic and to differentiate them from so-called pretenders, such as 'show-men', 'travellers' or simply 'dropouts from house dwelling society' (Adams et al. 1975: 27). The issue of identification has become a dilemma for Gypsies because of the criminalisation of travelling people by English law.

In addition to the Race Relations Act of 1976, three other statutes come into play in respect of Gypsies:

(a) the Highways Act, 1959;

(b) the Caravan Sites Act, 1968;

(c) the Criminal Justice and Public Order Act, 1994.

In Mills v Cooper [1967] 2 WLR 1343, the court was required for the first time to define the term 'Gypsy' in the context of the modern statutory provisions. The court considered s. 127 of the Highways Act of 1959,[5] where the term 'gypsy' is used along with 'itinerant trader' and 'hawker'. Section 127(c) of the Highways Act, 1959 states in essence that, 'if without lawful authority or excuse... (c) a hawker or other itinerant trader or a gypsy pitches a booth, stall or stand, or encamps on a highway, he shall be guilty of an offence'. In Mills v Cooper [1967] 2 WLR 1343, at p. 1348, Lord Parker was not prepared to accept the suggestion that the word 'Gypsy' should be given the dictionary meaning, 'as being a member of the Romany race'. His Lordship stated with confidence, at p. 1348: 'I am...quite satisfied that 'gypsy' in this context cannot bear that meaning'. The court held that the Romany race is too vague a concept to be defined; it would be impossible to prove the race's existence. For Lord Parker, as stated at p. 1349, 'Gypsy means no more than a person leading a nomadic life with no fixed employment and with no fixed abode'. Diplock LJ, in the same case, similarly defined 'gypsy' at p. 1349 as 'a person without fixed abode who leads a nomadic life, dwelling in tents or other shelters, or in caravans or other vehicles'. The interpretations of Lord Parker and Lord Diplock therefore reject racial or ethnic and cultural factors and the popular assumption that a Gypsy is a person of the Romany race.

This interpretation had serious implications when it came to be applied in the Caravan Sites Act, 1968. The Act's main purpose was to control unauthorised Gypsy encampments on public property and to protect the rest of the community from visitation by Gypsies trespassing on land and camping on unregulated sites, causing damage to those areas in which they trespass.[6] Section 16 of this Act defines Gypsies as 'persons of nomadic habit of life, whatever their race or origin, but does not include members of an organised group of travelling showmen, or of persons engaged in travelling circuses, travelling together as such'.[7]

The definition did not focus on the concerns of the Gypsy community, their historical background, their racial and ethnic origin or characteristics. Their cultural, religious or linguistic factors seem to have been given scant attention by the drafters. Above all the Caravan Sites Act failed to lay down an unambiguous meaning of the term. The Department for the Environment was forced to provide clarification in its circular 28/77 (see further Barnet, 1995: 142), to the effect that:

> The definition in Section 16... makes no distinction between different groups of travellers or their trades. It includes romanies, didicoys, mumpers, tinkers-hawkers etc. In law, therefore, the term 'gypsy' refers to a class of persons and is not confined to an ethnic group. Nevertheless, it is clear that gypsies do constitute a cohesive and separate group within our society, with strong internal social ties.

Yet this clarification has itself again neglected the important defining criteria, i.e. the racial and ethnic characteristics. The definition in the Caravan Sites Act, 1968 seems to rely heavily on the decision in Mills v Cooper. The Act and Mills v Cooper both emphasise the nomadic way of life in defining Gypsies. It appears that racial and ethnic characteristics have been purposely neglected, even though Gypsies themselves give prominence to such factors in differentiating themselves from outsiders.

In anchoring the definition of Gypsies in the nomadic lifestyle, the judiciary have been forced to conclude that individuals may move in and out of the category of Gypsy according to their current circumstances. According to Diplock LJ in Mills v Cooper [1967] 2 WLR 1343, at pp. 1349-1350:

> Being a gipsy is not an unalterable status. It cannot be said, 'once a gipsy always a gipsy'. By changing his way of life a modern Borrow may be a gipsy at one time and not a gipsy at another.

Accordingly to claim the status of Gypsy, a person has to move continually from place to place and live in a caravan or similar shelter. This means that true-blooded Gypsies are assumed to lose their Gypsy identity if they settle permanently. In so defining Gypsies, the law forces them to choose between retaining their ethnic identity by continually moving, or losing it if they choose to settle for some time, for instance to allow their children to be educated.

In Horsham District Council v Secretary of State for the Environment, an unreported case cited in R v Shropshire County Council, ex parte Bungay [1991] QBD 23 HLR 195, the appellant's father had been a council tenant for 20 years. The appellant himself had lived in a timber building for 20 years and had not been travelling in that period except to trade shows. It was held that a Gypsy who had lost the nomadic habit of life did not remain a Gypsy for the purposes of the Caravan Sites Act, 1968, even though he remained a Gypsy by descent, culture, tradition or inclination. Delivering the judgment, McCullough J stated as follows, as cited at p. 204 of Bungay:

> The criterion 'nomadic habit of life', as was noted in Circular 28/77 paragraph 5, leads to a certain ambiguity, especially in relation to gypsies who settle for lengthy periods on authorised sites. It is a fact, well recognised both before and since the passing of the Act, that many gypsies – and I use the term ethnically – do settle sometimes for several years, indeed many years, in the same place. Where this happens, as in this case, it may not be easy to determine whether they have lost their status as gypsies for the purpose of the relevant legislation. Clearly there can, and indeed must, come a time when as a matter of fact the nomadic habit of life has been lost. When it is lost the gypsy is no longer a gypsy for the purpose of the Act. He remains, of course, a gypsy by descent, by culture, and by tradition, but that is not the issue. The question is whether he is a gypsy for the purposes of the relevant Act.

A variant of this 'all or nothing approach' was evident in Bungay itself, at p. 204, where the court appears to have accepted that rather than move out of the status of Gypsy, the applicant may merely be holding that status in abeyance. In this case, a Gypsy family, the Bennetts, had lived a nomadic life for several decades. Eventually the family settled and although still living in a caravan, stayed at the same site for some 28 years. Otton J, distinguishing the facts from Horsham, held that the family had not abandoned the nomadic life style, but 'held it in abeyance'. His Lordship stated in Bungay, at p. 206, that 'the family were undoubtedly of gypsy descent' and found that their way of life reflected many elements of the gypsy lifestyle. For example, they were speaking Romany.

Similarly in Greenwich London Borough Council v Powell and another [1989] AC 995, Lord Bridge held at p. 1010:

> I am inclined to conclude from these indications alone that a person may be within the definition if he leads a nomadic life only seasonally and notwithstanding that he regularly returns for part of the year to the same place where he may be said to have a fixed abode or permanent residence.

As a result bona fide Gypsies may not lose their identity by returning to the same residence, whether permanent or not, for part of the year, or for a period of years.

A more radical approach was taken in 1989 in Commission for Racial Equality v Dutton [1989] 1 All ER 306, CA and [1989] 2 WLR 17, at p.18, where the court showed a willingness to import the concept of ethnic origin into the definition of 'Gypsy' within the framework of s. 3 (i) of the Race Relations Act, 1976 and did not confine itself to s. 16 of the Caravan Sites Act, 1968. For the first time in English legal history, Gypsies were identified in Dutton as an 'ethnic group' in the context of the race relations laws. Nicholls LJ stated, at p. 27:

> On the evidence it is clear that such gypsies are a minority, with a long shared history and a common geographical origin. They are a people who originated in northern India. They migrated thence to Europe through Persia in medieval times. They have certain, albeit limited, customs of their own, regarding cooking and the manner of washing.... They also furnish their caravans in a distinctive manner. They have a language or dialect, known as 'pogadi chib', spoken by English gypsies (Romany chals) and Welsh gypsies (Kale) which consists of up to one-fifth of Romany words in place of English words. They do not have a common religion, nor a peculiar, common literature of their own, but they have a repertoire of folk tales and music passed on from one generation to the next. No doubt, after all the centuries which have passed since the first gypsies left the Punjab, gypsies are no longer derived from what, in biological terms, is a common racial stock, but that of itself does not prevent them from being a racial group as widely defined in the Act.

Nicholls LJ also used the criteria introduced by the New Zealand court in King-Ansell [1979] 2 NZLR 531 at p. 543, such as 'self-awareness', 'maintenance of separateness', and historically determined social identity in the group's own eyes and in the eyes of the public. His Lordship held that 'Gypsy' should be defined in conjunction with Lord Fraser's criteria in the House of Lord's Mandla judgment, discussed above. In consequence he found Gypsies to be a 'racial group' defined by ethnic characteristics, taking into consideration their long shared history, common geographical origin, specific culture and social habits.

More recently, however, it appears that the courts have reverted to the approach favoured in Mills. In R v South Hampshire District Council, ex parte Gibb, R v Gloucestershire County Council, ex parte Davies, and R v Dorset County Council, ex parte Rolls and another [1994] 3 WLR 1151, at p. 1161, the Court of Appeal, in giving a definition to the term 'nomadic' in the Caravan Sites Act of 1968, held that this presupposes a person who moves purposefully from place to place. Accordingly, the status of Gypsy would cease if the nomadic life style is relinquished. Referring to the definition in the Caravan Sites Act, the court held that it was capable of embracing persons other than traditional Gypsies, so long as they could be said to have a nomadic mode of life. Purpose is a necessary and characteristic part of the life of a nomad in the sense of the original derivation of that word. Neill LJ on appeal, stated at p. 1161:

> As Lord Donaldson of Lymington MR remarked in Mole Valley District Council v. Smith [1992] 90 LGR 557, 560, the definition in section 16 of the 1968 Act is not a particularly happy definition. In my judgment, however, in the context of Part II of the Act the definition of 'gypsies' in section 16 imports the requirement that there should be some recognizable connection between the wandering or travelling and the means whereby the persons concerned make or seek their livelihood. Persons, or individuals, who move from place to place merely as the fancy may take them and without any connection between the movement and their means of livelihood fall outside these statutory definitions.

This is clearly a retreat to the Mills v Cooper era. The nomadic way of life and the related economic activities therefore appear to decide the group identity of Gypsies. These attitudes have a remarkable similarity with Spanish approaches to, and mythologies about Gypsies. As Liégeois (1987: 134) states, 'as early as the eighteenth century in Spain, the Gypsy ceased to be considered (in legislation) as soon as he settled'. Existing jurisprudence clearly excludes non-nomadic Gypsies, who are committed to following their traditions and preserving their cultural heritage. They would like to be identified as such, but have been excluded from legal protection. In such circumstances, particularly non-white, non-nomadic Gypsies may find enormous problems when they are requested to prove their racial identity in cases where they seek protection under the race relations law. Because they would now again appear to fall automatically into an area where they are neither Gypsies nor members of any other racial group within the meaning of the Race Relations Act, 1976, Gypsies are at a clear disadvantage as far as protection against discrimination is concerned.

2.7 Rastafarians

The Rastafarian movement began in the 1930s in Jamaica (Cashmore, 1979 and 1984b). The founding father of this essentially social movement, partly a reaction to discriminatory practices against blacks in Europe and North America, was Marcus Garvey, a black Jamaican. This distinct culture includes a refusal to cut one's hair or to shave (an obvious parallel to the Sikhs), a commitment to observe certain dietary laws, and prohibitions on homosexuality and contraception. Rastafarians have a common language, a combination of English and Jamaican Patois, and are descended from a common geographical origin.

In Dawkins v Crown Suppliers (Property Services Agency) (a judgment delivered by the South Industrial Tribunal, 28 March 1989) the complainant, Mr. Trevor Dawkins, a Rastafarian, complained to the industrial tribunal that he had been denied a job as a van driver simply because he was not prepared to cut his 'dreadlocks'. He attended the interview wearing a hat over his dreadlocks. He was told that the PSA, the government agency to which he had applied for a job, expected their drivers to have short hair, as they might be required to drive the government's ministers and similar high-ranking civil servants. Since he refused to cut his hair, he was not recruited for the job. His complaint to the industrial tribunal succeeded. By a majority, the tribunal held that Rastafarians are a racial group defined by s. 3 (i) of the Race Relations Act, 1976 (Cashmore, 1989).

The industrial tribunal was divided on whether a shared tradition of under 60 years was long enough to qualify as a racial group, but the majority were of the opinion that the Rastas have a long shared history, and so had fulfilled the necessary criteria identified by Lord Fraser in Mandla (for details see Crown Suppliers (Property Services Agency) v Dawkins [1991] ICR 583 EAT, at p. 592). The test had to be examined in relation to not only the age of the tradition, but also its continuity and persistence. The third member disagreed on the basis that a far longer period of time was required before it could be said that a group possessed a 'long shared history'.

The Employment Appeal Tribunal, by a majority decision, recorded at p. 594, adopted the view of the minority and reversed the industrial tribunal decision, holding that Rastas are not a racial group as defined by the Race Relations Act. Sixty years could not be considered long enough to become a 'racial group'. Moreover, the Tribunal was reluctant to admit that the Rastas have distinctive cultural traditions of their own or a long shared history, as required by the criteria introduced by Lord Fraser in Mandla. Delivering the judgment, Tucker J said at p. 594:

> Applying those tests to Rastafarians, we ask whether they possess any of the characteristics of a race? We very much doubt whether the majority of Rastafarians can claim that they are of group descent, though some of them may be. Their geographical origin is Jamaica. We doubt whether they can be said to have a group history. Lord Templeman held that the Sikhs qualified as a group defined by ethnic origins because they constitute a separate and distinct community derived from racial characteristics. But in our judgment, Rastafarians cannot be so described. There is in our view insufficient to distinguish them from the rest of the Afro-Caribbean community so as to render them a separate group defined by reference to ethnic origins. They are a religious sect and no more. In any event returning to Lord Fraser's test we are unable to agree with the majority of the industrial tribunal that Rastafarians have a long shared history. It cannot reasonably be said that a movement which goes back for only 60 years, i.e. within the living memory of many people, can claim to be long in existence. Its history, in the judgment of the majority, is insufficiently sustained. The fact that the movement has maintained itself and still exists is insufficient. We have no hesitation in disagreeing with the conclusion of the majority of the industrial tribunal on this point, because first we do not regard it as a finding of fact and secondly, even if it were we

would regard it as a finding which no reasonable tribunal could make, and therefore perverse... So far as Lord Fraser's second essential test is concerned, that of a cultural tradition of its own, our view is that Rastafarians are a group with very little structure with no apparent organisation and having customs and practices which have evolved in a somewhat haphazard way.

The Court of Appeal, agreeing with the Employment Appeal Tribunal, held that the Rastafarians do not fall within the meaning of s. 3(1) of the Race Relations Act, 1976. The Court was reluctant to accept arguments based upon statements made by the Home Secretary on the meaning of 'ethnic' during parliamentary debates on the Race Relations Bill (see Crown Suppliers (Property Service Agency) v Dawkins [1993] ICR 517, CA at p. 525).

Mr. Riza, counsel for the appellant, had submitted that the obscurity and ambiguity of the words 'ethnic origin' had not been removed by the House of Lords judgment in Mandla and had been made worse by the difference of approach in the speeches of Lord Fraser and Lord Templeman. Neill LJ disagreed, saying at p. 527 that even though there was some difference between the speeches in their Lordships' judgments, 'the guidance given by the speeches read together was clear and unambiguous for the purpose of deciding the present appeal'. He then sought to rely on King-Ansell v Police [1979] 2 NZLR 531, where Richardson J had declared, at p. 543:

> ...a group is identifiable in terms of its ethnic origins if it is a segment of the population distinguished from others by a sufficient combination of shared customs, beliefs, traditions, and characteristics derived from a common or presumed common past, even if not drawn from what in biological terms is a common racial stock. It is that combination which gives them a historically determined social identity in their own eyes and in the eyes of those outside the group. They have a distinct social identity based not simply on group cohesion and solidarity but also on their beliefs as to their historical antecedents.

Relying on this much-publicised judgment, Neill LJ considered whether Rastafarians could satisfy the criteria of Lord Fraser. He admitted that there were some identifiable characteristics peculiar to Rastafarians, for example, their distinctive form of music, known as 'reggae' and they had adopted a distinctive form of hair-style. However the Court of Appeal ultimately refused to recognise Rastafarians as a racial or ethnic group as defined by s. 3 of the Race Relations Act, 1976 and it was held that Rastafarians had failed to establish their separate identity by reference to their 'ethnic origins'. As the respondent's counsel had argued, there was nothing to distinguish Rastafarians from the rest of the African-Caribbean community – they are a separate group, but not a separate ethnic or racial group (see Crown Suppliers (Property Service Agency) v Dawkins [1993] ICR 517, at pp. 525-528) . The Court of Appeal, therefore, chose to link ethnic origin to its racial aspects again and the wide-ranging, inclusive approach of Mandla was not followed. Why this was done remains to be analysed. It might be erroneous to argue that the Rastafarians have been singled out for non-recognition, since their position as an unrecognised group is shared by Africans, African-Caribbeans generally and by large Asian groups, to which we now turn.

2.8 Muslims and Hindus

Most Muslims and Hindus migrated to Britain directly from the Indian sub-continent, although significant numbers came from East Africa, and many Muslims originate in the Middle East and elsewhere. Among South Asian Muslims, the largest group are the Pakistanis (Shaw, 1988; Pearl, 1986; Saifullah-Khan, 1976; Jeffery, 1972), many originating from Mirpur, a district of Azad Kashmir in today's Pakistan. Others come from various parts of Panjab and the North-West Frontier Province in Pakistan, and from Gujarat in India. Some 90% of Britain's Bangladeshi Muslims originate from the northern district of Sylhet. A large number of East African Asians came from Uganda, Kenya, and Tanzania during the latter part of the 1960s and 1970s. While most of them are Hindus or Sikhs, there are also significant numbers of East African Asian Muslims.

Muslims are identified, and identify themselves, predominantly as a religious group, part of the world-wide Muslim community (ummah). In research based on Manchester in particular, and on Muslims living in Britain in general, it was found that Muslims prefer to be known first and foremost as Muslims (Scantlebury, 1995: 433). This religious identification has probably been a stumbling block to recognition as a 'racial group' under the 1976 Act, in addition to their internal diversity. In Tariq v Young and others (Case No. 24773/88, EOR Discrimination Case Law,

Digest 2 Winter 1989, p. 4) it was held that Muslims are not a racial or ethnic group for the purposes of the Race Relations Act, 1976. The tribunal found that, unlike Sikhs and Jews, Muslims are not bound by a common culture and that it is predominantly the Muslim religion which marks Muslim identity.

It has also been argued that there is no unified 'Muslim' culture. The cultural and social habits of Nigerian Muslims are quite different from those of Pakistanis and Bangladeshis. As such, Lord Fraser's second criterion of a common cultural tradition is not satisfied. Having failed to satisfy either of the first two of Lord Fraser's criteria, the fact that Muslims have similar religious practices is by itself insufficient to establish Muslims as a separate racial or ethnic group, since religion is not one of the criteria given in the relevant sections of the 1976 Act.

This position was affirmed in Morgan v Civil Service Commission and the British Library (Case no. 19177/89, EOR Discrimination Case Law Digest, No. 6, Winter, 1990, p. 3). In both Racial Equality v Precision Manufacturing Services (cited in P. Lewis 1994: 173) and Nyazi v Rymans Limited, EAT/6/88 (cited in UK Action Committee on Islamic Affairs 1993), Muslims failed to achieve legal recognition as a racial group within the meaning of the Race Relations Act, 1976. According to the latter source, Dr. Mashuq Ibn Ally, Director of the Islamic Studies Centre, University of Wales in Lampeter, presented an expert report arguing that there should be no legal hindrance to UK Muslims qualifying as a 'racial group' in terms of the criteria established in Mandla and the Race Relations Act, 1976. Dr. Ally submitted that Muslims as a group were bound together by several common factors, such as shared historical origins, links to the Arabic language as a lingua franca, to the extent that Arabic had become incorporated into many other languages which Muslims used, as well as a nurtured geographical link. Just as Jews were encouraged to visit Israel, Muslims were required to make the pilgrimage to Mekka, which established a geographic origin in the mind. He had also emphasised that Muslims should be recognised as an ethnic group since they were not part of the wider community. In other words, distinctiveness from the rest of society was said to make up an element of Muslim ethnicity, too.

Could Muslims and Hindus, as Pakistanis, Bangladeshis and Indians, argue that discrimination on religious grounds amounts to racial discrimination? Recent unreported cases suggest that Muslims have not been able to convince the judiciary that religious discrimination amounts to unlawful indirect discrimination against a particular religious group. Examples that have come to our notice include Farhath Malik v British Home Stores [1980]; Yasin v Northwest Home [1993]; Azam, Bhayat and others v J H Walker [1994], all cited in the CRE Bulletin for 1997, in which the CRE has argued that discrimination against Muslims or Hindus, in certain cases, may constitute indirect racial discrimination.

At present, the picture is unclear. A number of important cases have been settled out of court, thus avoiding that the law become clarified. There seems to be some method behind keeping Muslim claims for recognition in limbo. Only detailed investigation would allow anyone to make more specific comments. It is evident, however, that the current situation is perceived by Muslims (comparing themselves with the Sikhs, who are recognised as a 'racial group') as blatantly discriminatory, thus leading to more vigorous calls for reform and the removal of unfair discrimination against them by the institutions of the English legal system. Perusal of the Muslim press certainly creates an impression of victim mentality.

The picture is no better for Hindus. It is often said that there is still no legal authority on the position of Hindus as a 'racial group'. While it is unlikely that no cases have ever been brought to the lower tribunals, only detailed research would give us a clearer picture. It would seem that Hindus, too, encounter legal opposition at all levels to recognition as a separate ethnic group. Apart from the many internal diversities and sectarian differences among the British Hindu population, they, too, are perceived as a religious group, and thus not entitled to recognition under the race relations law.

2.9 The position of smaller sub-groups

Smaller sub-groups of South Asians, like the Pushtuns, Sylhetis and Comillians, originate from the North-West Frontier Province of Pakistan or from certain parts of Bangladesh. Most of them are followers of the Muslim faith, but there are a few Christians and Hindus. Would it be a viable strategy for such smaller groups (of which there are many in Britain) to seek recognition as 'racial groups' under English law?

In Abdul Khayum (Case No. 40306/93, EOR Discrimination Case Law Digest, No. 21 Autumn 1994, p. 2), an application by a descendant of the

'Pushtun' tribe in the North-West Frontier Province of Pakistan for the post of project manager at the Pakistan Muslim Centre in Sheffield was rejected, allegedly on racial grounds. The tribunal held that as Pushtuns were not recognised as a distinct community by themselves and by others, they did not constitute an ethnic group within the meaning of s. 3 of the Race Relations Act, 1976. This was despite the fact that during the proceedings it was found that Pushtuns have a long shared history, their own cultural traditions, use the Pushto language and specific literature with poetry, song and dance, live in a separate geographical area and have a separate legal system supervised by elders. Further the strict seclusion of women and the giving of asylum to outsiders were said to distinguish Pushtuns from other communities in Pakistan. These criteria do appear to fit within Lord Fraser's test and so give credence to a claim for recognition as a separate ethnic group. The tribunal, however, preferred to base its decision on the fact that Pushtuns follow the Muslim religion, as do other neighbouring groups such as Panjabis. It was held therefore that they should be considered as only a religious group.

In Kabir v Bangladesh Women's Association (Case No. 10026/92, EOR Discrimination Case Law Digest, No. 18 [Winter 1993], p. 2), the London North Industrial Tribunal ruled that the Sylhetis were not a racial group as defined by the Race Relations Act, 1976. In this case, Mrs. Kabir, who was employed by the Bangladesh Women's Association, complained that she had been dismissed because she was not a member of the Sylheti community like most of the staff. The complainant came from Comilla, another district in Bangladesh, while the defendant officials were from Sylhet, the district of Bangladesh from which most British Bangladeshis originate. Instead of deciding whether Mrs. Kabir was a member of the Comillians, the tribunal held that Sylhetis were not a racial group, which meant that the Comillians, too, could not be such a group.

In both Abdul Khayum and Kabir, reference was made to the need for groups which claim the status of a 'racial group' to be in some form 'oppressed'. This is probably outside Lord Fraser's test as well as beyond s. 3 of the Race Relations Act, 1976. Whichever way one turns, the somewhat open-minded, liberal-sounding and comprehensive framework of recognition for 'racial groups' under English law as laid down by the House of Lords in Mandla v Dowell Lee [1983] 1 All ER 1062, has proved not to be as inclusive and as welcoming as it at first appeared.

Notes to chapter 2

1 The term 'tinker' is particularly used to identify travellers from an Irish background. See details in Adams et al., 1975.

2 More properly, the term 'diddikois' is used to describe 'gorgios' or Gypsies of the half-blood. See Adams et al., 1975: 41.

3 A 'Romani' is generally identified as a true Gypsy or true-blooded Gypsy. Hair and skin are supposed to be black, and they speak the 'Romani' language.

4 Those from the North of Wales call themselves 'Kale', an old Romani word for 'Black'. For details see Liégeois, 1987.

5 S. 127(c) of the Highways Act, 1959 states that, 'if without lawful authority or excuse...(c) a hawker or other itinerant trader or a gypsy pitches a booth, stall or stand, or encamps on a highway he shall be guilty of an offence'.

6 See West Glamorgan County Council v Rafferty and others [1987] 1 WLR 457, R v Secretary of State for Sales and another, ex parte Gilhaney CA, and sections 10 and 12 of the Caravan Sites Act, 1968.

7 It is now repeated by s. 80 (i) of the Criminal Justice and Public Order Act, 1994 and re-enacted in s.80 (2)(b) which states that '...gypsies means persons of nomadic habit of life, whatever their race or origin, but does not include members of an organised group of travelling showmen, or persons engaged in travelling circuses, travelling together as such'.

Chapter 3

Judicial attitudes towards ethnic minorities and their customs

The indifference to the challenges of immigration and rights of migrants was replaced after the 1950s by legislation controlling immigration and prohibiting social discrimination. The judiciary holds the key role in the implementation and interpretation of this legislation, so should be seen as independent arbiters in disputes. However, judges cannot and do not remain isolated from the social and political debate. In this chapter, we examine the extent to which the judiciary was able to remain impartial in the fevered social and political debates about immigration and the rights of migrants.

Some have found the English judiciary wanting. Its membership continues to be limited and restricted; it is seen as aloof and cocooned from reality; it shares a common set of values; and it is by its nature conservative and concerned to preserve the status quo. J. A. G. Griffith (1985: 134) summed it up:

> Judges are concerned to preserve and to protect the existing order. This does not mean that no judges are capable of moving with the times, or adjusting to changing circumstances. But their function in our society is to do so belatedly. The law and order, the established distribution of power both public and private, the conventional and agreed view amongst those who exercise political and economic power, the fears and prejudices of the middle and upper classes, these are the forces which the judges are expected to uphold... in the societies of our world today they do not stand out as protectors of liberty, of the rights of man, of the underprivileged....Their view of the public interest when it has gone beyond the interest of govern-

ment, has not been wide enough to embrace the interests of political, ethnic, social or other minorities.

Few members of the judiciary are black or Asian. The essentially male, white middle-class judiciary is not always impartial towards the new ethnic minorities and some judicial comments are insensitive. Understandably, many ethnic minority people believe the courts to be instrumental in encouraging negative and harmful attitudes which have accentuated the divisions between the various social groups.

3. 1 Deportation and repatriation

Some members of the judiciary were simply opposed to the immigration of blacks and Asians and the consequent requirement to adapt to a pluralist society. The claims for judicial recognition of multicultural aspects in British society were criticised by Lord Radcliffe (1969: 39):

> It is true, of course, that its union embraced several different nations and, more relevantly, that in the course of the history it has absorbed by immigration a number of diverse racist strains: out of all this, as we believe, there has emerged a homogeneous people with no seriously conflicting differences of culture or purpose.

African-Caribbeans and Asians were blamed for all social ills, the development of a ghetto culture, as well as unemployment, housing problems and dishonesty. They were accused by a judge in 1986 of jumping the queue on council housing lists and job vacancies (The Times, 24 October 1986, cited in Pannick, 1987: 80). As Master of the Rolls, Sir John Donaldson commented thus on a Mr. Taj Mohd. Swati's attempt to visit places of interest in the UK: '[t]he venture has not been a success, because he was refused permission to enter and the only places of interest which he has been able to visit were the airport and the Ashford Remand Centre' (R v Secretary of State for the Home Office, ex parte Swati [1986] 1 All ER 717, at p. 719).

Other judges have been quick to ascribe blame for violence in the inner cities to Asians and African-Caribbeans. Paul Gordon has highlighted several such instances. In one, Judge Gwyn Morris in 1975, sentencing five young black defendants, told them:

> These attacks became a monotonous feature in the suburbs of Brixton and Clapham, areas which within memory were peaceful,

safe and agreeable to live in. But the immigrant settlement which has occurred over the past 25 years has radically transformed that environment. Those concerned with maintenance of law and order are confronted with immense difficulties. (The Times, 16 May 1975, cited in Gordon, 1983: 96)

A Magistrate at Marlborough Street said in open court that most of the migrants 'come to this country just to thieve' (The Daily Telegraph, 10 April 1973, cited in Gordon, 1983: 96). Judge Wild at Cambridge Crown Court warned two ethnic minority defendants, '[t]his all came about because you got drunk and it is a pity that you did not have the decency to stand up and admit it. But then, as people about the courts know, people of your origin never admit anything, well, hardly anything'. (The Guardian, 25 January 1978, cited in Gordon 1983: 96). A Magistrate at South London Magistrates Court warned a black defendant (cited in Cain and Sadigh, 1982: 92):

Whatever you do in your country I don't know, but you don't tell lies in this country, get that into your thick head.... If you're going to live in England you're going to behave like an Englishman and tell the truth or you can leave... we are sick of you and your like.

The repatriation of New Commonwealth migrants was seen as a possible solution. Colonel R. L. G. Thorpe, the senior magistrate and alderman of the city of London, confessed in open court that he was an active member of an organisation which advocated the repatriation of migrants. Addressing two black defendants, brought before his court for failure to pay a fine, he asked them whether they had ever thought of going back to Barbados, and said that he was a member of an organisation which would gladly pay their fare (The Guardian, 2 February 1978, cited in Gordon, 1983: 83).

Deportation as a punishment is normally only used in extremely serious cases. It effectively destroys the individual's social environment and family connections. Deportation 'will often inflict more hardship than a term of imprisonment....In addition, deportation often carries a moral stigma, and will normally disqualify the individual from re-entering the United Kingdom while the order is in force' (Evans 1983: 259). Deportation is available only in the case of aliens, yet some judges have attempted to mould the common law to allow them to deport, or as Gordon (1983: 115) noted, to use 'quasi-deportation'.

In R v Ayu [1958] 1 WLR 1264, the appellant James Ayu, a Nigerian, had lived and worked in Britain between 1939 and 1958 – when individuals from the Commonwealth could live in the UK as they pleased. Mr. Ayu was prosecuted for dwelling in a house for an unlawful purpose and committed for sentence as an 'irrecorrigible rogue'. He was sentenced to 12 months imprisonment by the Magistrates' Court at Brighton and the court attached a condition that the defendant should return to Nigeria and stay there for five years. This binding over order was in fact a deportation order, for which there was no power under the Justices of the Peace Act, 1361 and the Aliens Order, 1953. Even though the expulsion order was reversed by the Appeal Court on technical grounds, Lord Parker, whilst not commenting on the legality of the order, said in R v Ayu [1958] 1 WLR 1264 at p. 1266: 'I should add that this case shows very clearly the need which has already been canvassed, I understood, in other quarters for there being a power to deport a man such as this'.

The judgment probably had a significant impact on immigration legislation. Changes were introduced in the Commonwealth Immigrants Act, 1962 and the Immigration Appeals Act of 1969 by the Immigration Act, 1971. Section 7 of that Act made it lawful to deport an individual who was required to get an entry clearance certificate before entering the country, effectively removing the privilege of immunity from deportation enjoyed by Commonwealth citizens (Evans, 1983: 258). This Act also contains a provision which allows a judge to recommend deportation upon conviction, provided the defendant has attained the age of 17 years. If a defendant can prove immunity from deportation on the grounds of being a 'patrial',[1] the court cannot impose such a punishment unless there is an extradition request made by another country.

Some judges have pushed the issue further. In 1982, an expulsion order was made against a British-born black teenager who was a 'patrial' under the British Nationality Act, 1981. Carl William, aged 18 years, had been charged with theft. The court, not being able to deport a British citizen, made an order binding him over with a requirement that he was to stay away from Britain for five years. The National Council for Civil Liberties identified this as 'repatriation by the back door' (Gordon, 1983: 115).

3.2 Negative attitudes

The judiciary has expressed general concerns about the presence of migrants in various contexts. Lord Radcliffe extra-judicially spoke about the numbers of African-Caribbean and Asian migrants in cities and the possible effects on the socio-legal infrastructure. He saw a problem in 'inserting into a fairly complex urban and industrial civilisation a large alien wedge, which is in many ways as ready to isolate itself within that community as some members of the community are to keep it isolated' (Radcliffe, 1969: 39). He described migrants as a 'menacing problem' (Radcliffe, 1969: 36) and suggested that 'the English cities might be surrounded by colonies of migrants workers' (Radcliffe, 1969: 38). All his concerns were only over what he called the 'coloured migrants' who carried with their colour 'a fling of strangeness and all that strangeness implies' (Radcliffe, 1969: 47).

Over 20 years later, Roger Davies, the 'angry magistrate' at Horseferry Street in Central London, spoke thus for taxpayers throughout Britain: 'We are mad in this country. Other countries are not as generous as we are. It is high time that something was done about dishing out money in this way. It offends many of us' (Daily Mail, 20 November 1993). He reprimanded the British government for becoming a 'soft touch for foreign scroungers', allowing them to live off the state. More recently, Judge Ingeborg Bernstein at Liverpool County Court referred to Valentine Reid, a mixed-race defendant, as a 'Nigger in a woodpile' (The Times, 7 February 1996). The defendant appealed against the conviction, one of the grounds being that this remark had unduly influenced the jurors. It was revealed in the appeal court proceedings that the trial judge had immediately apologised for her 'inadvertent remark' but, as Peter Herbert, the defence counsel, pointed out, the judge had displayed racial bias, however unintentional, and had thereby prejudiced the minds of jurors. Waite LJ with concurrence of Morrit LJ, rejected this argument, saying that 'it was fanciful to suggest that any jury would have been influenced by the remark' (The Times, 7 February 1996).

In 1977, John Kingsley Read, chair of the British National Party, commenting on the death of an Asian youth, is alleged to have said, '[o]ne down, a million to go' (Gordon, 1983: 95). He was prosecuted for incitement to racial hatred. The original common law offence was codified by s. 70 of the Race Relations Act, 1976 which inserted a new subsection A after s. 5 of the Public Order Act, 1936. Section 5(A) of this Act stated that a person commits an offence if:

(a) he publishes or distributes written matter which is threatening, abusive or insulting; or

(b) he uses in any public place or at any public meeting words which are threatening, abusive or insulting;

in a case where, having regard to all the circumstances, hatred is likely to be stirred up against any racial group in Great Britain by the matter or words in question.

The offence is punishable with six months imprisonment or a fine of £1,000 or both, on summary conviction, or with two years imprisonment or an unlimited fine, or both, on indictment. These provisions were amended and re-enacted in s. 17 of the Public Order Act, 1986.

To prove the guilt of the defendant, the words used must amount to a direct incitement to violence or public disorder. Originally, the prosecution was not required to prove the intention (mens rea) of the defendant but this position is now changed. The words or behaviour used must be threatening, abusive or insulting and the prosecution must now prove that the actions of the defendant 'must either have been intended to stir up racial hatred or be likely to do so' (for details see Stone, 1994: 253).

Directing the jury in the case against Read, McKinnon J advised them that the law against incitement to racial hatred did not cover reasoned argument in favour of immigration control or even repatriation. He continued (as cited in Gordon, 1983: 95):

Goodness knows, we have a million and a half or more unemployed already and that all the immigrants are going to do is to occupy the jobs that are needed by our local population. These are matters upon which people are entitled to hold and to declare strong views expressed in moderate terms... It is difficult to say what it is that this defendant is alleged to have done that amounts to a criminal offence.

The defendant was praised as a man who had the guts to come forward in the past and stand up in public for what he believes in. The judge (Gordon, 1983: 95) warned Mr. Read to be cautious in future when makings statements on similar matters:

You have been rightly acquitted but in these days and in these times it would be well if you were careful to use moderate language. By all means propagate the views you may have but try to avoid involving the sort of action which has been taken against you. I wish you well.

These comments by a judge were addressed to the chairman of an organisation which openly advocated violence against 'coloured' migrants and their repatriation, if necessary by force. Mr. Read's original comment, it is submitted, is neither a reasoned argument nor would it be tolerated under public order offences, so the comments of McKinnon J seem neither impartial nor objective. Later, McKinnon J was able to obtain the permission of the Lord Chancellor not to preside over cases involving racial questions.

In a similar case, R v Malik [1968] 1 All ER 582, the leader of the Racial Adjustment Society, a black activist, Mr. Michael Abdul Malik, was convicted to twelve months imprisonment in November 1967 for using insulting words to stir up racial hatred against white people at one of the rallies organised by his organisation. In the same month, another four black activists were fined for making speeches at Speaker's Corner. Civil libertarians complained rightly that the law designed to protect blacks and ethnic minorities was being used against blacks more vigorously than against racist activists (Cox, 1975: 249).

Another distinguished judge, Lord Denning, extra-judicially remarked that: 'Even though in this society there were Saxon, Dane, and Norman, they all became 'English' which were one race... they shared the same religious beliefs... above all they adhered uniformly to the rule of law' (Denning, 1982: 75). Freedom of speech guarantees make it respectable still to voice negative attitudes about 'immigrants' and to make openly racist comments. The law does not appear to concern itself with the effects that this freedom has on those against whom such comments are directed.

3.3 Juries

Compared to civil rights campaigns in the United States, the United Kingdom has poor mechanisms for providing a fairer racial mix in juries. The fear is that jurors would be manipulated through the 'race card', the OJ Simpson trial of 1995 being held up as an example.

Doubts have been expressed over the suitability of black and Asian jurors. Lord Denning is alleged to have written about black jurors: 'They are white and black, coloured and brown...some of them came from countries where bribery and graft are accepted....and where stealing is virtue so long as you are not found out ...black, coloured and brown people do not have the same standards of conduct as whites'.[2]

Similarly Lord Chief Justice Taylor, in a speech given to the Leeds Race Issues Advisory Council, stated that the idea of multiracial juries represents the 'thin edge of a particularly insidious wedge...we must on no account introduce measures which allow the state to start nibbling away at the principle of random selection of juries' (The Times, 1 July 1995).[3] This rejected recommendations by the Royal Commission on Criminal Justice that in exceptional circumstances it should be possible, before beginning a trial, for either prosecution or defence counsel to make an application for a trial judge to select a multiracial jury with at least three ethnic minority members (see Ingman, 1994: 197). The determination to protect the status quo in relation to jury selection can be seen in R v Ford [1989] 3 All ER 445, where Lord Lane CJ held that parties must be prepared to accept random jurors as they come, and that the trial judge has no discretion to interfere with the composition of the jury in order to secure a jury of a particular ethnic group.[4] Criticising this judgment, Peter Herbert, Chair of the Society of Black Lawyers and a member of the Judicial Studies Board, noted that the Ford judgment finally abolished the existing rights of the defendant's counsel to exercise three peremptory challenges (see details in Herbert, 1995: 1138).

In England and Wales, ethnic minorities are not adequately represented in juries. Recent research discloses that in Birmingham, with its high ethnic minority settlement, only 0.7 per cent of jurors were African-Caribbeans, Indians and Pakistanis. Defendants from an ethnic minority background are prevented from being tried by juries representative of their community and so better able to understand their behavioural patterns. In consequence, many Blacks and Asians are sceptical about the criminal justice process. An opinion poll conducted by Harris Research for BBC 2 in November 1995 found that 78 per cent of Blacks and Asians (and 38% of white respondents) were of the view that they could not trust white juries and that non-white defendants were more likely to be wrongly convicted than whites on the same charge (The Times, 28 November 1995).

3.4 Responses to ethnic minority customs: Romance, sex and discipline

The wish of ethnic minority people to continue to apply their own customs and personal laws has provided some of the most difficult challenges for legislators and the judiciary. It is traditional to interpret the problem in terms of assimilation and cultural pluralism. Assimilation involves the incorporation of minorities into the dominant majority, while cultural pluralism encourages respect for the distinctive cultures of ethnic minorities. The terms themselves are unhelpful: 'assimilation' and 'pluralism' are merely the ends of a spectrum of approaches. Some judges have lacked sophistication in cases where the customs of migrants were seen to clash with the customs of the majority community. Judges frequently misunderstand ethnic minority cultures, behavioural patterns and personal laws, and have shown scant sympathy for different perspectives.

In Vinod Bhatia v IAT [1985] Imm AR 50 CA, Vijay Kumari, a British resident and widow in the UK, wanted to marry an Indian citizen, Mr. Bhatia. Mr. Bhatia's application for entry to this country as a fiancé was refused. So began a complicated court procedure which lasted for nearly six years. Arguments presented by the applicant seemed not to be understood by the judge. The court was told, wrongly, that a Hindu widow could not marry again. The marriage had been arranged by the woman's parents, who were also living in Britain and had been unable to find a suitable husband for their daughter in Britain, so placed a matrimonial advert in the Hindustan Times in India. If a second marriage were unacceptable, why would Vijay Kumari's parents have done this? The court stubbornly insisted that 'it is rare for a Hindu woman who is divorced to find another husband' (Vinod Bhatia v IAT [1985] Imm AR 50, at p. 51). There was no happy ending – after the long litigation struggle, Mr. Bhatia was so disgusted that he refused to marry the sponsor.

Similarly, in R v Immigration Appeal Tribunal, ex parte Naushad Kandiya and ex parte Aurangzeb Khan [1990] Imm AR 377 CA, Taylor LJ, agreeing with the adjudicator, questioned the appellant as to why the husband, who sought entry clearance to enter Britain, was departing from the traditions in Pakistan according to which the wife goes to the husband's home, not the other way round.[5] Yet in contemporary Indian, Bangladeshi and Pakistani societies, whose industrialisation has led to an unprecedented migration to urban areas, it is not uncommon to see men leaving villages to marry women settled in the booming industrial cities (Shah, 1979: 132). The increasing practice of 'trans-continental marriages' between the sub-continent and people of the same origin living in different countries all over the world means that it is not uncommon for bridegrooms from the subcontinent to come to the bride's home in the UK. The couple may establish their own home at once, or live for a time with the bride's family. Traditions are not static but respond to social need, in this case, to find suitable bridegrooms for Asian women living in the UK, exacerbated by the trend among British Asian men to look to India, Pakistan or Bangladesh for brides.

Senior members of the judiciary have misunderstood the nature of South Asian arranged marriages and the possibility of 'romance' between the parties before the marriage (see Sachdeva, 1993: 159-165 on the dangers of pleading love). These recurring legal problems do not appear to be tackled adequately by judicial training. In R v Immigration Appeal Tribunal, ex parte Manjula Jethva [1990] Imm AR 450, the wife was a British citizen who, on a visit to India, met her future husband at a circus in May 1985. They fell in love and married within weeks. The husband's application for entry clearance was refused because their story of a 'love marriage' was unlikely; it was assumed that such marriages are rare in the sub-continent. Each was interviewed separately as to how they fell in love, discrepancies in their 'story' were alleged (a common strategy to justify a refusal in such cases), and the husband's application was refused. Popplewell J upheld the decision of the Immigration Appeal Tribunal, which had agreed with the original decision to refuse entry clearance, making reference to an earlier Tribunal decision in Pindi Dass v Secretary of State for the Home Department [5388], where the adjudicator had expressed his doubts about the occurrence of 'love marriages' in the sub-continent. Details are found in the case report at p. 454 (see also Sachdeva, 1993: 159-160). Popplewell J therefore concluded at p. 454:

> I find nothing in the decision of Pindi to suggest that their view is mistaken. The Immigration Appeal Tribunal is probably the most experienced tribunal in relation to marriages that exist in the world. Even those of us who sit doing Crown Court Office work have some familiarity with arranged marriages.

Yet romance in the Indian sub-continent is neither unusual nor surprising. Neither is it surprising that a girl brought up in Britain should fall in love at first sight with a man from a relatively poor economic and social background. The determining factor in a marriage is not always wealth or background. Recent Western trends in pre-marital cohabitation need not be mirrored in all ethnic groups. The Immigration Appeal Tribunal and the Divisional Court failed to appreciate the nature of individual behaviour within the context of demographic and cultural changes in the sub-continent and took recourse to cultural stereotypes.

Stereotypical views were also evident when Francis Middleton, while sentencing a white man for having unlawful sexual intercourse with a 13 year old Asian girl, asserted that 'girls mature much earlier in the East.... until recently marriages were arranged at a very early age. In the form of marriage that takes place there, intercourse occurs before marriage. This may have predisposed her to this action' (cited in Gordon, 1983: 97). The case was about an alleged rape, and need not have concerned itself with Asian arranged marriages nor child marriages, nor the rates at which girls mature in the sub-continent grow biologically faster than their Western counterparts. And his remarks about pre-marital sex are false. Although a marriage is arranged when the parties are still children, married life does not begin until adulthood. Nor would sexual intercourse be permitted before the marriage.

In Mohamed v Knott [1968] 2 All ER 563, Lord Parker similarly assumed that young girls in African countries develop earlier than their European counterparts. He stated, at p. 568, that 'it is certainly natural for a girl to marry at that stage. They develop sooner, and there is nothing abhorrent in their way of life for a girl of thirteen to marry a man of twenty-five'.

Different customs are illustrated in the case of R v Derriviere [1969] 53 Cr App R 637, concerning the use of excessive force by the defendant in disciplining his child. Derriviere, a West Indian father, was prosecuted for assault and battery. English law permits parents to apply 'reasonable' force to their children for the purpose of punishing them. Derriviere argued that his own customs allowed for more severe disciplining of children. He was found guilty and sentenced to six months imprisonment. On appeal, Lord Widgery CJ, when pronouncing the judgment, admitted at p. 638 that cases of this kind raised difficult issues.

The unfamiliarity of ethnic minority individuals with local practices and standards may be considered a mitigating factor at the sentencing stage. Thus in R v Adesanya (The Times, 16 July 1974, cited in Poulter, 1989: 123) the punishment imposed on the accused was considerably less than could have been expected, had not the injury been inflicted within the context of the family's Nigerian customs. Mrs. Adesanya was charged with assault and battery following the incision of tribal marks on the face of her two boys. The injuries were inflicted in a festival atmosphere in the presence of friends and relatives – some of whom also bore tribal scars. The infliction of tribal marks was not criminal or sinister – it was to affirm the children's ethnic identity and to enable them to become full members of their tribe. The court was informed about the custom by a member of the Nigerian Embassy in London. The decision to find the mother guilty was reached with some reluctance and is reflected in the leniency of the sentence.

3.5 Judicial responses to statutes concerning new migrants and their rights
3.5.1 Immigration and exclusion
In the context of immigration and race relations legislation, judicial inter-pretation has often been less than generous to members of ethnic minority communities. The motives of those claiming rights of entry have often been a focal point. Should it, for instance, be automatically assumed that marriages of convenience are used to bypass immigration controls? (Shah, 1979: 132). Lord Denning illustrated this all too common judicial presumption in R v Chief Immigration Officer, ex parte Salamat Bibi [1976] 1 WLR 979 CA. Mrs. Bibi had come from Pakistan with her two children to join her husband, a British citizen and a businessman who was perfectly able to support his wife and children. There was no question of their becoming a burden on the state. The validity of the marriage entered into in Pakistan in 1952 was not disputed. The wife was following tradi-tion by coming to Britain to live with her husband and there was then no restriction on wives coming to join their husbands.

The case centres on a series of alleged lies Mrs. Bibi told the immigra-tion officer – she stated that she was coming to meet her husband and that her stay in England would be a short one. When her husband was ques-tioned, he stated that his wife was coming to start their marital life in this country, should the Home Office grant permission. Mrs. Bibi and her two children were refused entry clearance because of such alleged discrepancies and were sent back. She appealed against this order. Her counsel, Mr. Louis Blom-Cooper QC argued that Article 8(1) of the European Convention on Human Rights, 1950 guarantees that everyone has the right to respect for his private and family life. Lord Denning was swift to deal with this point and held, at p. 985:

> The Convention is drafted in a style very different from the way which we are used to in legislation. It contains wide general statements of principle. They are apt to lead to much difficulty in application... At last we came to a decision. We put aside the Convention altogether as being of no use.

His Lordship was then able to conclude, at p. 985:

> Coming back to this case, it seems to me that the immigration officer was right to go by the rules: and by the rules, beyond all question, the immigration officer was entirely right to refuse entry to this lady and her two children. She has no visa. She had no current entry clearance.

Lord Denning's statements (further details are found at Denning, 1982: 281-282) aimed to mislead. The husband in this case was a settled Commonwealth citizen and had been an ordinary resident in the UK since 1967 and had indefinite leave to remain. The term 'ordinary resident' was interpreted in Levene v Commissioners of the Inland Revenue [1928] AC 217, at p. 225, by Viscount Cave LC to the effect that 'the term connotes residence in a place with some degree of continuity and apart from accidental or temporary absence'. The husband therefore came under s. 1(2) of the Immigration Act, 1971, which provides that:

> ...indefinite leave to enter or remain in the United Kingdom shall, by virtue of this provision, be treated as having been given under this Act to those in the United Kingdom at its coming into force, if they are then settled there (and not exempt under this Act from the provisions relating to leave to enter or remain).

Here the phrase 'those in the United Kingdom' refers to aliens as well as Commonwealth citizens. Having been a Commonwealth citizen, the husband as an ordinary resident had a right to remain indefinitely. Therefore he was entitled to bring his wife and children to the UK, provided the children were under 16 years of age, under s. 1(5) of the Immigration Act of 1971 and there should have been no need for litigation. Section 1(5) clearly provides:

> The rules shall be so framed that Commonwealth citizens settled in the United Kingdom at the coming into force of this Act and their wives and children are not, by virtue of anything in the rules, any less free to come into and go from the United Kingdom than if this Act has not been passed.

The clear purpose of this provision was to preserve the statutory rights of entry conferred to wives and children under s. 2(b) of the Commonwealth Immigrants Act, 1962. To justify the immigration officer's refusal to issue an entry clearance certificate to Mrs. Bibi, Lord Denning argued that the husband could not be considered a Commonwealth citizen when the Immigration Act, 1971 came into force. His wife, in consequence, was not entitled to seek protection under the above provisions. Lord Denning's view seems to be based on the fact that Pakistan left the Commonwealth in 1973, but this was only on 1 September 1973, according to the Pakistan Act, 1973 and the Immigration Act, 1971 came into force on 1 January 1973. By that time, the husband's position as a Commonwealth citizen living as an 'ordinary resident' in the UK was secured. Mrs. Bibi should have been recognised not primarily as a citizen of Pakistan but as the lawful wife of a husband settled in the UK, whose wife and children under 16 years of age had an entitlement to come into the UK 'as of right' (see further Macdonald, 1969: 67).

Lord Denning's argument that s.1(2) of the Immigration Act, 1971 does not confer rights for 'those in the United Kingdom' is also incorrect. Lord Denning said, at p. 983: 'I do not think that section gives any right to the wives and children to come in without entry clearance'. However, rather than interpreting and expressing a firm judicial opinion on this section, His Lordship seemed to be speculating. The main purpose of the section was to create and confer rights on individuals from Commonwealth countries who had been living in the UK before the passage of the Immigration Act, 1971, so there was a right to family reunion.

However, Lord Denning held that Mrs. Bibi should not be allowed to enter the UK and went on to describe her as a person who could speak no English and who told lies to the immigration officer. The judgment effectively ruined her marriage. Humanitarian considerations, ethics or the UK's long-standing principles or commitment to Commonwealth citizens had no place in this judgment. The downgrading of the obligations imposed by the European Convention on Human Rights, 1950 to a general statement of principles is questionable, but it is indicative of the negative tone of the entire judgment.

Like Lord Radcliffe, Lord Denning was unhappy to see large numbers of new migrants coming to the UK as spouses and dependants claiming British citizenship. His negative views on the migration of Asians can also be discerned in R v Secretary of State for the Home Department, ex parte Phansopkar and ex parte Begum [1976] QB 606 at pp. 615-616, discussed in chapter 1. These cases exemplify how prominent members of the judiciary intervened in the political debate about the desirability of Britain's immigration policies.

3.5.2 Race relations law and the denial of protection

As we saw in chapter 2, racial discrimination in both public and private employment and housing was first prohibited under the Race Relations Act, 1965. Criminal sanctions were introduced for incitement to racial hatred. The Race Relations Board was established to secure compliance and to investigate breaches. However, the 1965 Act was subject to amendments in the Race Relations Act, 1968 because the limited powers of the Race Relations Board had been criticised and many discriminatory activities were not covered by it. The 1968 Act stipulated a more proactive role for the Race Relations Board but was in turn replaced by the Race Relations Act, 1976 which extended its protective framework to include indirect discrimination and sought to define discrimination based on racial grounds.

From the very beginning, some members of the judiciary remained unconvinced of the need for legislation to control discrimination. Race relations law and anti-discriminatory measures were seen as a perversion of pure English law. Right-wing anti-migrant politicians were worried that such measures would be used by 'strangers' as legal weapons to overcome and dominate the rest (Powell, 1969, cited in Fitzpatrick, 1987: 129). Judicial attitudes were based on English law's traditional support for the concepts of freedom of choice and contract, which meant that for judges it remained not self-evident that it should now be wrong to discriminate. Commenting on the Race Relations Act of 1968, Lord Radcliffe said that part one of this Act, which outlawed discrimination in areas such as the provision of goods, facilities and services, employment, trade unions, housing, accommodation, and business and other premises, advertisements and notices, was a mistake (Radcliffe, 1969: 45). He argued that 'freedom of choice' and 'freedom of preference' should be preserved at whatever cost, since these rights had for centuries been the hallmark of Western democracy. Why cannot a restaurant owner decide who should be allowed in? He should not be punished for his reluctance to serve a black or coloured person, since he was entitled to choose his customers according to common law principles (Radcliffe, 1969: 45-47). Judge Harold Brown corroborated, saying in the Brighton Corporation case (unreported, cited from The Guardian, 2 August 1969 in Lester and Bindman, 1972: 96):

> It seems curious that if a landlord closes the door on a coloured applicant merely because of his colour he might well get into serious trouble. But if he closes his door on white people with children merely because they have children, he is under no penalty at all.

There is a significant body of case law showing a lack of sympathy for the basic aims of the legislation, a trend which began with Dockers Labour Club v Race Relations Board [1974] 3 WLR 533 HL. In this case, a Mr. Sherrington went with a Mr. Moulding, a member of the Dockers' Labour Club, to visit that club. Sherrington sought and obtained admission as an associate. A little while later, he was asked by the club secretary to leave, since it was against the rules of the club to admit coloured people. The issue was whether the Labour Club had failed to provide services as a 'section of the public' to Mr. Sherrington within the meaning of s. 2 of the Race Relations Act, 1968. If the club fell within the category of 'public sector' then it could not deny the admission of Mr. Sherrington on the grounds of colour, because the public sector was bound by the 1968 Act to provide services without taking into consideration a person's colour or race. Affirming the position taken in Charter and others v Race Relations Board [1973] 1 All ER 512 HL, the House of Lords unanimously held that the words 'section of the public' did not apply to members or associate members of social clubs. The law would not interfere even though discrimination was being practised on the basis of colour or race.

Lord Diplock was not particularly convinced of the wisdom of the race relations legislation and its attempt to regulate the social behaviour of individuals and said, at p. 540:

In the field of domestic or social intercourse differentiation in treatment of individuals is unavoidable. No one has room to invite everyone to dinner. The law cannot dictate one's choice of friends.

His Lordship saw no reason why discrimination against ethnic minorities could not be practised if that was the wish of the individual. He continued, at p. 540, that '[t]he arrival in this country within recent years, of many migrants from disparate and distant lands has brought a new dimension to the problem of the legal right to discriminate against the strangers'. He considered the new legislation an intrusion into the private lives of individuals and wished to see it as no more than 'a 'code of conduct' to be followed in day to day transactions between ordinary citizens' (p. 541). His Lordship's opposition to the Commission for Racial Equality is well illustrated in London Borough of Hillingdon v Commission for Racial Equality [1982] IRLR 424, at p. 430. He was critical of the CRE's investigation into employment practices at public expense. This judgment was instrumental in destroying the backbone of the race relations legislation and has affected subsequent attempts by the CRE to use its investigative powers against the discriminatory practices of employers. In R v Commission for Racial Equality ex parte Prestige Group plc [1984] 1 WLR 335 and Commission for Racial Equality v Amari Plastics Ltd. [1982] 2 All ER 499 CA, the CRE was subjected to severe criticism for investigating discriminatory practices by institutes, employers and service providers. The judiciary was gradually curtailing the investigative powers of the CRE (for details see Gregory, 1987: ch. 6).

Further erosion occurred in Home Office v Commission for Racial Equality [1981] 1 All ER 1042, which confirmed that the immigration control mechanism enshrined in the Immigration Act, 1971 was excluded from the supervision of the Race Relations Act, 1976. The case arose because the CRE wished to investigate allegations of discriminatory practices against migrants by the immigration authorities, particularly by officers in the Home Office. The CRE's decision to investigate was alleged to have been 'precipitated by the allegation that an Indian woman arriving at Heathrow Airport in order to marry her fiancé had been subjected to a virginity test' (Gregory, 1987: 118). The CRE tried to launch an inquiry under s. 43(1) and s. 48(1) of the Race Relations Act, 1976. Under s. 43(1), the Commission has the following duties:

(a) to work towards the elimination of discrimination;

(b) to promote equality of opportunity, and good relations, between persons of different racial groups generally; and

(c) to keep under review the working of this Act and, when they are so required by the Secretary of State or otherwise think it necessary, draw up and submit to the Secretary of State proposals for amending it.

Based on these statutory powers, the CRE is legally entitled to make investigations under s. 48 (1), which provides:

Without prejudice to their general power to do anything requisite for the performance of their duties under section 43(1), the Commission may if they think fit, and shall if required by the Secretary of State, conduct a formal investigation for any purpose connected with the carrying out of those duties.

The Home Secretary, objecting to the request of the Commission for investigation into immigration procedures and practices, stated that immigration control did not come under the supervision of the Race Relations Act, 1976. The CRE relied on s. 20(1) of the 1976 Act, which provides:

It is unlawful for any person concerned with the provision (for payment or not) of goods, facilities or services to the public or a section of the public to discriminate against a person who seeks to obtain or use those goods, facilities or services –

(a) by refusing or deliberately omitting to provide him with any of them; or

(b) by refusing or deliberately omitting to provide him with goods, facilities or services of the like quality, in the like manner and on the like terms as are normal in the first-mentioned person's case in relation to other members of the public or (where the person so seeking belongs to a section of the public) to other members of that section.

In Kassam v Immigration Appeal Tribunal [1980] 2 All ER 330 CA, it had been held that s. 20(1) covers essentially 'market place activities' or activities akin to the provisions of 'goods and services' and is not intended to cover immigration services. Ackner LJ gave a restrictive meaning to the word 'facilities', effectively excluding immigration services from the control of race relations laws when he stated, at p. 335:

> The word 'facilities' in that section is flanked on one side by the word 'goods' and on the other by the word 'services'. This suggests to my mind that the word 'facilities' is not to be given a wholly unrestricted meaning but must be limited or confined to facilities that are akin to goods or services.

In concurring with this view, Stephenson LJ held that the Secretary of State is merely exercising statutory powers to control immigration and any facilities he may provide in the course of his exercise do not come under s. 20(1) of the Race Relations Act, 1976. Referring particularly to the provisions of s. 20 (1) he stated, at p. 334 that,

> ...read in their natural and ordinary meaning they are not aimed at and do not hit the Secretary of State concerned with giving leave to enter or remain in the exercise of his powers under the 1971 Act.

In following Kassam and in particular referring to the words 'goods, facilities or services', Wolf J concluded in Home Office v Commission for Racial Equality [1981] 1 All ER 1042 that the Secretary of State or his immigration officers or entry clearance officers could not be held responsible for any violation of discrimination within the provisions of the Race Relations Act, 1976, as they are not legally bound to provide services for 'immigrants' because:

(a) immigrants do not fall into the category of 'public or section of the public';

(b) immigration services, control or regulations do not fall into the category of services intended by s. 20(1) of the Race Relations Act, 1976.

Wolf J further held that immigration officers, including Ministers, are there to regulate and control immigration into the UK, so they are not providing any facilities or services. Approving the ratio decidendi of Kassam, Wolf J stated that the words 'facilities' and 'services' contained in s. 20 (1) did not cover the giving of leave to enter or remain by the Secretary of State under the Immigration Act, 1971 and asserted that 'the existence of immigration control and the enforcement of that immigration control was not discrimination within the Race Relations Act' (p.

1048). Neither was any discrimination by those officers unlawful within the meaning of the above Act. In Amin v Entry Clearance Officer, Bombay [1983] 2 All ER 864, at pp. 873-879, Lord Scarman had delivered, with Lord Brandon, a powerful dissenting judgment in which he had refused to accept the reasoning in Kassam, considering the decision both 'limited' and 'irrational'. His Lordship considered that immigration officers were engaged in providing services to the public and that immigrants should be treated as a section of the public. Entry into the UK for study, visit or settlement is certainly a facility and one which the Secretary of State has within his power under s. 3(2) of the Immigration Act of 1971 to provide. Therefore these officers should be considered as providing services and facilities within the meaning of s. 20 of the Race Relations Act, 1976.

Consequently, immigration officers, while using the Immigration Rules, can discriminate against would-be migrants on any grounds whatsoever. In fact, the current set of Immigration Rules, which came into operation on 1 October 1994, says so quite clearly in para 2 of HC 395:

> 2. Immigration Officers, Entry Clearance Officers and all staff of the Home Office Immigration and Nationality Department will carry out their duties without regard to race, colour or religion of persons seeking to enter or remain in the United Kingdom.

As the CRE has argued, it is mostly migrants from the Indian subcontinent who have become victims at the hands of immigration officers (Home Office v Commission for Racial Equality [1981] 1 All ER 1042 at p. 1045). But judges have been reluctant to intervene and thus to strengthen the position of the race relations laws in the suppression of discriminatory practices. Judges have been unsympathetic to the efforts of the CRE to take actions when discriminatory practices are being applied against people on racial or ethnic grounds. It is no surprise that, in the process, the CRE has become a spectator in the face of widespread discriminatory practices in the UK.

The negative response to the primary aim of the legislation is further evident in a large number of cases involving black and Asian workers and individuals living in the UK. Relevant cases are R v Immigration Appeal Tribunal, ex parte Kotecha [1983] 1 WLR 487; Suthendran v IAT [1976] 3 WLR 725; R v Secretary of State for the Home Department, ex parte

Choudhary [1978] 1 WLR 1177; Zamir v Secretary of State for the Home Department [1980] 2 All ER 708.

The Court of Appeal decision in Mandla v Dowell Lee [1982] 3 All ER 1108 (see chapter 2.4 above) provides a telling example of the judiciary's restrictive approach to legislation designed to protect ethnic minority communities. The case involved analysis of the term 'racial group' in the Race Relations Act, 1976. Mr. Seva Singh Mandla, an orthodox Sikh, took his son to see the headmaster of Park Grove School in Birmingham with a view to obtaining a place for his son at the school. Both Mandla and his son wore turbans. The headmaster, Mr. Lee, asked Mandla whether he would consent to his son removing his turban and cutting his hair, and Mandla replied that this was completely out of the question. The headmaster then wrote a letter to Mandla, saying (Mandla v Dowell Lee [1982] 3 All ER 1108 CA, at p. 1110):

> Thank you for bringing your son to see me. As I promised, I have given much thought to the problem and I have reluctantly come to the conclusion that on balance it would be unwise to relax the school rules with regard to uniform at the moment. I do not see any way in which it would be possible to reconcile the two conflicting require-ments. May I wish you well in your efforts to promote harmony and peace, and I hope you find a suitable school for Gurinder without difficulty.

Mandla was determined to contest the case. Only if Sikhs were held to be members of a racial group as defined by s. 3(1) of the Race Relations Act, 1976 could he seek legal protection against racial discrimination on the grounds of race, colour or ethnicity. He was given legal assistance from the CRE, which was severely criticised by Lord Denning at p. 1111:

> The Commission, however, did not let the matter rest. They pursued the headmaster relentlessly. They interviewed him. They demanded information from him. Eventually they decided to assist Mr. Mandla in legal proceedings against him.

Lord Denning does not acknowledge the legal duty of the CRE to take up such cases. As we saw in chapter 2.4, despite the assistance of the CRE the applicant lost his case in the county court and in the Court of Appeal, where Lord Denning, Oliver and Kerr LJ unanimously refused to accept that Sikhs are a 'racial group' as defined by the 1976 Act. Lord Denning, while dismissing Mandla's appeal, expressed sympathy for the head-master who had been subjected to 'relentless' pressure and continued, at p. 1111:

> The headmaster appeared before us in person. He has not the means to instruct counsel and solicitors. He put his case moderately and with restraint. He has himself done much research in the India Office Library and elsewhere. It must have taken him many hours and many days.

His Lordship indirectly criticised the wisdom of the new race relations statutes and admitted that they are difficult to understand and apply. On the issue of discrimination itself, he stated at p. 1114 (as already cited in ch. 2, p. 38 above), that it remained perfectly lawful to discriminate against groups of people to whom one objects, as long as they are not a 'racial' group under the terms of the 1976 Act.

The critique of the CRE continued in the judgment of Oliver LJ. He disliked the way the CRE had hounded the headmaster and held, at pp. 1117-1118:

> Throughout Mr Dowell Lee appears to have behaved with the greatest courtesy and restraint. After an entirely courteous corres-pondence with the first plaintiff, he found himself the subject of a visitation from a representative of the Commission for Racial Equality and the papers before us contain the notes of an interview with him at which he appears to have been deliberately interrogated with a view to extracting admissions of racial bias and at which barely concealed threats of 'investigation' were made unless he modified the stance which he had adopted. Thereafter he, whose proper business was running his school in a way which to him seemed most suited to the needs of his students, found himself involved in an action, fostered and supported by the Commission...

> As it is Mr Dowell Lee has been compelled to waste a great deal of his time and the resources of the school in defending himself against charges which could hardly have been levelled at any target less deserving of them. He has been dragged through two courts at enor-mous expense in order, apparently, to establish a point which no doubt is a difficult and important one, but is now entirely academic for both plaintiffs. It seems to me a great pity that it should have been

thought necessary to test it at the expense of an entirely blameless individual who has done no more than to seek in the best way that he knows how to run his own business in his own way.

Kerr LJ also announced in his speech at p. 1118, that this was 'a difficult and troubling case' and his criticism, too, was aimed at the CRE for creating unnecessary trouble for the headmaster. Dismissing the appeal, he said, at p. 1123:

Meanwhile the boy has gone to another school wearing his turban... I would add my disquiet to what Lord Denning MR and Oliver LJ have already said about the events which have led up to these proceedings. The Commission for Racial Equality is clearly highly motivated and does useful work in cases where there is clear evidence, or real ground for suspicion, that racial discrimination exists and is practised. But this is not such a case. This school was demonstrably conducted harmoniously on a multiracial basis. I have read in the evidence the notes of the interview of the headmaster by an official of the commission. In parts this reads more like an inquisition than an interview, and I can see no basis whatsoever for what I can only describe as harassment of this headmaster. All that the commission has achieved in this case, as it seems to me, is to create racial discord where there was none before.

As we saw, this decision of the Court of Appeal was reversed by the House of Lords which was particularly scathing of some comments made by the Court of Appeal. Criticising Lord Denning's judgment, Lord Fraser stated that he considered the strictures on the Commission and its officials entirely unjustified but recognised, in Mandla v Dowell Lee [1983] 1 All ER 1062 HL, at pp. 1070-71, that the inquiries of the Commission 'will be resented by some' for no justifiable reasons.

The lack of enthusiasm for race relations law has continued. In Commission for Racial Equality v Amari Plastics [1982] 2 All ER 499, the Race Relations Act of 1976 was considered by both Griffiths LJ and Lord Denning MR to be unworkable, intimidating and extremely cumbersome. Lord Denning remarked at p. 503 that 'the CRE has been caught up in a spider's web spun by Parliament, from which there is little hope of escaping'. The CRE was asked by Griffiths LJ in this case, at p. 506, to take all necessary representations which they considered useful to the

Secretary of State before embarking upon further embarrassing investigations against employers. Similarly, in Commission for Racial Equality v Prestige Group plc [1984] 1 WLR 335 at p. 347, Lord Diplock warned that before engaging on futile investigative adventures the CRE should think about whether it was appropriate to incur the substantial expenses, 'all of which come out of the pocket of the taxpayers'. The judicial position taken in this case has 'thwarted the intention of Parliament' (Munro, 1985: 201).

In consequence the CRE has never been allowed to evolve into an institution which could effectively investigate discriminatory practices of employers. It seems that the superior courts have done everything to weaken the CRE, particularly its investigative powers. Echoing this view, the first Chairman of the Commission, David Lane (1987: 15-16) wrote:

> Some decisions by the courts, up to and including the House of Lords, seemed unduly restrictive and did not reflect the intentions of Parliament regarding the Commission for Racial Equality's use of its strategic powers. Our cutting edge in law enforcement was badly blunted.

Yet not all the blame should be laid at the hands of the courts, since the legislation, with its unclear definition of 'race', contributed to the restrictive and damaging interpretations which hampered building a truly multiracial society.

3.6 Positive developments: Attempting to understand 'the other'

The cases considered so far show a less than sympathetic judicial approach, but they do not provide the complete picture. Some cases deal more sympathetically with ethnic minority groups and with individuals from them and run counter to the general criminalisation of ethnic minorities, evidenced for example by an extended debate in Vol. 16 No. 1 [October 1989] of New Community.

A somewhat bizarre example of judicial leniency was highlighted by Pannick (1987: 133-134) through the 'farcical' case of Sardar Tejendrasingh, who had filed a case in the Cambridge County Court in 1983 to recover some debts. He did not retain a lawyer and conducted his own case. In court Mr. Tejendrasingh refused to stand while addressing the judge, explaining that he had 'no respect for this country or its civilization or its courts' (Pannick, 1987: 133). Following unsuccessful attempts to persuade Mr. Tejendrasingh to comply with court etiquette, Judge Garfitt told him that until he gave an undertaking that he would obey the orders of the court and stand, his case would not be tried. Mr. Tejendrasingh appealed against this order. In the Court of Appeal, in November 1985, Sir John Donaldson MR and two other senior judges struck a compromise with this litigant, allowing him to address them while sitting down, but they still held that he would have to stand up before the County Court judge. The Court of Appeal emphasised, as noted by Pannick (1987: 134), that 'it is customary to stand in court while presenting evidence or argument and that there are practical reasons for this: to preserve order in court and to assist audibility'. The obstinacy of this Sikh gentleman went unpunished. It would have been very easy to make an example of him.

The position was much the same in the case of McKenzie v McKenzie [1970] 3 WLR 472, and it made legal history. Mr. McKenzie, a Jamaican, was a defendant in a divorce case. Like Mr. Tejendrasingh, he was not an admirer of the British legal system, nor of the legal profession. He failed to retain a solicitor or to obtain legal advice. During the proceedings, the presiding judge noticed that McKenzie was consulting a young man who was sitting by him, taking notes and assisting and ordered McKenzie's friend from the court. Later it was revealed that the so-called amicus curiae of McKenzie was in fact a barrister. Mr. McKenzie appealed against the order of the court, arguing that litigants should be allowed to have a friend instead of a solicitor taking notes and advising them. The Appeal Court allowed his application and 'McKenzie friends' became part of the legal culture. This has not prevented a judge from referring to them as 'ubiquitous animals' (Holgate, 1991: 617-618).

Other judges have shown considerable tolerance to the attitude of certain members of ethnic minority communities but one cannot be sure whether or not this is on account of race. Lee Ryan, a young black man who won £6.5 million from the National Lottery, purchased three dogs, six luxury cars, a helicopter, and a mansion worth £1 million. He was tried for car theft, an offence he had allegedly committed before the lottery win. Before going to court, he held a small press conference and stated that he could not expect a fair trial because of his colour. He was given only an extra seven days imprisonment for contempt of court after shouting 'bullshit' at the Crown Court judge in front of the jury and a large gathering of tabloid journalists (The Daily Mirror, 20 April 1996). Journalists expressed their surprise about this lenient punishment. Similarly the woman judge presiding in the case of a black girl, Debra 'Styler' Read, so named because of her clothes, took no action when 'Styler' referred to her as 'a bitch' as she left the court (Gilroy, 1987: 72).

Judge Michael Argyll went out of his way to help Everton Samuel, a Rastafarian of Jamaican origin, accused of possessing cannabis. Samuel had been on the dole for two years and informed the court that he was awaiting the result of a job application. The judge adjourned to allow him to contact the employer, spent his lunch-break pleading with the firm's director and eventually obtained a promise that the company would do everything possible to find Mr. Samuel a position as a trainee electronic worker. However, when he was asked whether he was willing to take the employment, he refused. The case was then postponed and the defendant asked to give his decision when the case was recalled. Meanwhile, the tabloid press had launched an attack, with headlines including 'Lazy Rasta', 'Cheeky little Rasta angers judge', 'Pot smoking Rastafarian on the dole for two years' (for details see Gilroy, 1987: 72-73). Judge Argyll received hate mail for his leniency towards 'this lazy little pot smoking Rasta'. When the case was recalled, Mr. Samuel was not prepared to change his mind and was alleged to have said, 'If the judge likes to buy me a car, I'll take the job' (Gilroy, 1987: 72). At this point, Judge Argyll lost his patience and imposed a two year suspended sentence. He warned the accused, as cited in Gilroy (1987: 73):

> I have to tell you that your attitude has done your own people no good. The court has received a number of letters from fascists and anarchists, all anonymous, which have ended up in the waste bin. Your manner merely feeds the prejudice of those people who think that anybody who is coloured is automatically unfit to be a member of society.

Sympathy is not always sufficient. Most migrants, perhaps without realising the possible consequences – particularly in family and matrimonial matters – have continued to apply their personal laws and customs in Britain and elsewhere (see now in detail Pearl and Menski 1998: ch. 3) to protect their separate ethnic, racial and religious identity. But Muslims, for example, have found that certain traditions and practices which are legal in their native countries, are illegal in the United Kingdom (Rath,

Groenendijk and Penninx, 1995: 106). Research reveals that in the Muslim community in Norwich, for example, traditional family relationships continue to exist without reference to civil requirements for marriage registration (Nielsen, 1987: 389). It is common for Muslims (and other ethnic minorities) to continue their traditions in the organisation of family relationships, social intercourse, religious matters and petty disputes. An example is found in R v Imam of Bury Park Jame Masjid, Luton and others, ex parte Sulaiman Ali and 304 others, QB, 30 August 1991, reported in The Times, 13 September 1991.

Language difficulties and unfamiliar processes of litigation discourage many members of ethnic minorities from seeking legal redress. The strange atmosphere replete with centuries-old rituals surrounded by police, prison and lawyers with black gowns and wigs terrify the new ethnic minorities (King, 1978; Wilkinson, 1985-86: 481). The court language can sound harsh and strange, even for those who are fluent in English. Speaking particularly of African-Caribbeans, a black magistrate, C. G. Duncan (cited in Wilkinson, 1985-86: 482) wrote:

> They learn standard English in school, but their domestic and social language is generally a patois. This means that they are quite seriously disadvantaged in a court setting where the language used is precise, formal and sometimes impenetrably legalistic.

Some judges have accepted aspects of a different culture with which they are familiar. Gordon (1983: 96) wrote that '[o]ther judges have claimed for themselves some sort of understanding of the background and cultures of immigrants who come before them'. Thus, Judge Solomon at Middlesex Crown Court, imposing a sentence on a Jamaican youth who was sentenced for allowing himself to be driven in a stolen car, claimed that the tragedy of the West Indies is the lack of family life, as we understand it here in Britain (cited in Gordon, 1983: 96). In 1981, in the 'Newton Rose Trial', a black man was charged with the murder of a white man. The trial judge advised the potential jurors that if they held strong views against black people they should inform the court that they did not wish to serve (Gordon, 1983: 96). In R v Gregory (cited in Herbert, 1995: 1139-1140), a trial judge at Manchester Crown Court showed considerable sympathy and understanding in a case where David Gregory, a black man, was prosecuted for robbery. When the jury retired to consider the verdict, a member of the jury gave a note to the judge indicating that some jury members were racially prejudiced. The trial judge re-convened the jury, reminded them of their oath and warned them that any thoughts of prejudice of one form or another, for or against anybody, must be put out of their mind. On appeal, Ward J identified such instances as 'novel' and 'delicate' (see details in Herbert, 1995: 1139). In R v Saiman Thomas, the trial judge advised the jurors before the trial that they should be free from any prejudice when ethnic minority defendants are involved (see Herbert, 1995: 1139).

There are, however, limits to sympathy. The cases of Derriviere and Adesanya, discussed above, still resulted in convictions of the accused, albeit with more lenient sentences. Judges have often found it difficult to grasp the underlying principles of personal laws and customs of new migrants. Adapting to the multicultural population has been difficult for the judiciary. Lord Parker CJ humbly admitted the difficulty in studying this 'difficult realm of law' in Mohamed v Knott [1968] 2 All ER 563 at p. 565, while Lord Widgery LJ observed that some cases raise difficult issues in R v Derriviere [1969] 53 Cr App R 637 at p. 638.

Some judges have complained that they have not been given formal training and have been forced to depend on expert evidence (see Gerils, 1995: 260). His Honour Judge Lind-Smith expressed a similar view in Kaur v Singh [1972] 1 All ER 292 at p. 293. Referring to marriage practices among the Sikhs, he stated that some areas of ethnic minority customs presented some difficulty for him and considered the possibility of transfer of the case to a judge of the Probate, Divorce and Admiralty Division. As is evident from many cases, judges have been exposed to new cultural phenomena in a totally haphazard, piecemeal way.

The judiciary's unfamiliarity with matters of ethnic minority practices and concepts has precipitated a number of training initiatives. Magistrates demanded a special training programme as far back as 1983 to learn about the experiences and behavioural patterns of various ethnic groups, so as to avoid misconceptions and myths about their particular situation (Wilkinson, 1985-86). Special training programmes were run by voluntary organisations in Manchester, Sheffield and at the University of Birmingham in the 1980s. In 1991 the Justices Clerks' Society established a group to consider the possibility of establishing a training programme (Gibson, 1994: 282). As Lord Chancellor, Lord Mackay appreciated the importance of training for judges about racial groups and awareness of cultures, traditions, and personal value systems and officially established a programme costing £1 million lest minority groups lose faith in the legal process (Pannick, 1987: 5).

Academics who are experts on the customs and personal laws of ethnic minorities are sometimes invited to deliver lectures and take part in seminars. District Judge Stephen Gerils (1995: 260) gives some insight into how such seminars are being conducted :

> Four years ago, the Judicial Studies Board announced the formation of the Ethnic Minorities Advisory Committee (EMAC) chaired by Mr. Justice Brooke, with Trevor Hall, Community Relations Consultant to the Home Office, as its vice-chairman. It embarked on a modest training programme. At first, this consisted of a handbook and a lecture of about one to one and a half hours which was slotted in the middle of the periodical residential refresher courses which all judges must attend... EMAC has now recognised the shortcomings of the previous course and has introduced a '24-hour' seminar on racial awareness which is streets ahead of its predecessors. The new course, with its emphasis on discussion rather than lecture, represents a considerable leap forward in increasing the awareness of judges to ethnic minority issues and their relationship to the matters that they have to deal with.

In these seminars the focus is on basic demographic information, problems in the use of languages, names and systems of address, oaths and oath taking, significant cultural differences, issues of communication, including body language, and the need to avoid generalisations. The Ethnic Minorities Advisory Committee (EMAC) held special sessions on civil and family matters and issues relating to children. Training was given to High Court judges, circuit judges, recorders, assistant recorders, stipendiary magistrates and lay magistrates. EMAC has now evolved into ETAC, the Equal Treatment Advisory Committee, chaired by Mr. Justice Dyson. It operates under the supervision of the Judicial Studies Board and comprises South Asian, Caribbean, African and white members. The Lord Chancellor's Department is now more actively recruiting magistrates from ethnic minority communities. During 1992-95, several hundred magistrates from ethnic minority backgrounds were appointed.

Problems still remain. Some judges are opposed to any kind of seminars which concentrate on ethnic factors (Daily Mail, 7 February 1996). Rising awareness may force judges to seek opinions from experts, whose opinions may be wrong or misleading. But without expert guidance, judges may be misled by the parties before them, especially if one side is not represented. In Kaur v Singh [1972] 1 All ER 292 CA, the judge allowed a petition for nullity based upon wilful refusal by the husband to consummate marriage, having been told – by a dishonest wife in the absence of the husband – that it was the husband's duty in Sikh custom to make the arrangements for the marriage, when in fact this is the obligation of the wife's side. Such mistakes are avoidable, but expert guidance may need to be sought.

Despite 'ethnic' training, some judges rightly or wrongly believe that there is still the option of enforcing conformity to the predominant culture. In some older cases, judges openly took the view that it was necessary to educate migrants and their descendants about how they should live in this country 'according to our way of life' (Mohamed v Knott [1968] 2 All ER 563, at p. 568) or how they should conduct themselves 'without violating the ethos of Christendom' (see Baindail (otherwise Lawson) v Baindail [1946] 1 All ER 342 CA, at p. 344-5). Today, such assimilationist comments would not be voiced openly. However, the widespread belief that education of the young members of ethnic minorities will lead to a weakening of traditional customs still carries much weight among the legal profession.

One should not forget that not only judges make an input into legal proceedings, solicitors and barristers would appear to require specialist training, too, to be able to bring out any relevant cultural dimensions of a case. Generally speaking, the tendency to think and argue in assimilationist terms remains strong, and it is not clear just how efforts by the law to recognise multicultural aspects can lead to a better justice system. We address this issue further in the next chapter, in the wider policy context of legal pluralism.

Notes on chapter 3

1 'Patrials' comprise citizens of the United Kingdom and Colonies who (a) were born, adopted, registered or naturalised in the United Kingdom or Ireland; (b) were born to or legally adopted by a parent who at the time of the birth or adoption was a citizen of the United Kingdom and Colonies by one of the ways specified in (a); or (c) had a grandparent who satisfied the same criteria; or (d) had at any time been settled in the United Kingdom and Islands and had at that time been ordinarily resident there for the last five years. For details see Evans, 1983: 259.

2 This passage does not appear in Denning, 1982 but is cited by Gordon, 1983: 110. Gordon states (id.) that after threats of legal action by two black Bristol jurors the book was hastily withdrawn and the above passage was removed.

3 The Lord Chief Justice's Practice Direction of 1973 requires that the jurors should be chosen 'at random' from the appropriate panel. This position has been consistently applied by the English legal system. See further the Practice Note at [1973] 1 All ER 240, per Lord Widgery CJ. This was reaffirmed by Lord Lane CJ in 1988, see Practice Note [1988] 3 All ER 177. In the same year, the Attorney-General approved this position, see Practice Note [1988] 3 All ER 1086, at 1087. For the Attorney-General's guidelines on this see Note at [1980] 2 All ER 457. Relevant material is also found in the Juries Act 1978 together with the Juries (Disqualification) Act, 1984.

4 See further the opinion of Lord Denning MR in R v Crown Court at Sheffield, ex parte Brownlow [1980] 2 All ER 444, at p. 452 and Lord Campbell CJ in Mansell v R (1857) 8 E&B 54, at pp. 80-81.

5 A similar argument was put forward by the British legal delegation in Abdul Aziz, Cabales and Balkandali v UK [1985] 7 EHRR 471.

Chapter 4

Legal pluralism in the British context

In this chapter we consider to what extent legal pluralism, a concept virtually unknown in European legal systems yet common in Afro-Asian jurisdictions, could enable English law to accommodate the customs and personal laws of ethnic minorities. Legal pluralism 'refers to the situation where two or more laws interact' (Hooker, 1975: 6). The basic difficulty with such a definition, however, is that much depends on the meaning given to 'law'. Migrants inevitably brought awareness of their personal laws and customs with them to the UK but soon experienced clashes with English concepts and legal rules. Many have realised that their laws have to a large extent been deprived of official legal recognition. The way in which these clashes or interactions were managed, but not resolved, is a major subject of this chapter.

We showed in chapter 1 that political debates in the post-1945 period about ethnic minorities and their incomplete assimilation had a significant impact on the attitudes of judicial personnel and jurists. Customs were ridiculed or looked upon with disdain and suspicion, branded by some leading politicians as 'insanitary or uproarious' or described as coming 'straight from the field' (Elton, 1965: 66). Particular disdain was reserved for the customs of Indian migrants who, unlike Caribbean migrants, were unable or unwilling to adhere to English norms. Lord Elton (1965: 70) illustrated the prevailing view:

> The West Indians at least wish for integration. Unlike the Asians, they besiege social workers for advice. Moreover, they speak our language, they share many of our traditions and most of them are

Christians; indeed in some respect life in Jamaica distinctly resembles that in mid-Victorian England. But few Asians even desire integration. They have their own cultures, and not unnaturally they display not the slightest desire to adopt ours.

Many migrants had no wish to discard their traditions and value systems. Aware of conflicts between the desire to continue customs and concern not to antagonise the indigenous population, migrants more or less consciously developed adaptive measures which varied from generation to generation, from group to group, and from individual to individual. In the 1950s and 1960s, customs and personal laws were practised more or less in seclusion and were not a matter of common knowledge. Open demands for recognition of specific customs were rarely voiced. Rastafarians were more active than other African-Caribbeans in asserting their ethnicity. Hindus adopted a lower profile approach than Muslims and Sikhs, who resorted to vigorous lobbying for recognition of their socio-legal concerns. Demands for recognition were often interpreted as a claim for preferential treatment at the expense of the indigenous community and were vigorously questioned: Why should particular customs be given a special place in English law? The fight by Sikh activists for the right to wear turbans and beards generated defensive arguments. One Labour MP said in a parliamentary debate (see Berkeley, 1977: 136):

> The Sikh communities' campaign to maintain customs inappropriate in Britain is much to be regretted. Working in Britain, particularly in the public services, they should be prepared to accept the terms and conditions of their employers. To claim special communal rights, or should they say rights, leads to a dangerous fragmentation within society. This communalism is a canker; whether practised by one colour or another it is to be strongly condemned.

Similarly the Muslim campaign for the legal recognition of Islamic laws, at least those dealing with the family, was described as an implied call for the legalisation of polygamy (Akhtar, 1989: 127). The main issue did not go away: to what extent should the personal laws of ethnic minorities be accommodated in the domestic legal system?

4.1 Pluralism as a legal theory

The concept of legal pluralism is borrowed from sociologists and has only recently been introduced to legal studies (van den Berg, 1992: 451; McLennan, 1995). Scholars have attempted to interpret obligation patterns of sub-groups in industrialised societies in terms of pluralism (Merry, 1988: 872; van den Bergh, 1992: 451). The idea itself is not new, but has never been encouraged by lawyers, especially in Western Europe, where the predominant view is that different legal systems cannot exist within the one-nation-state structure. In the ideal model, administration of justice and government is structured within a monistic framework. Pluralist structures and ideas were considered cumbersome, difficult to administer and dangerous. Yet opposition to pluralist theory did not prevent European jurists and policy makers from encouraging former African and Asian colonies to practise legal pluralism (Hooker, 1975). Another view is that legal plurality as an ancient feature in such systems was left intact by the colonisers for their own interests, because they did not want to be governed by the laws of the people whose territories they now ruled. Some migrants in Britain are quick to point out that the current British scenario is a kind of reversal and use this as an argument for recognition of their own personal law in Britain today.

Legal pluralism contradicts the notion that law is a monolithic, unified set of rules. Its proponents argue that centralist theories suffer from a number of inadequacies. Firstly centralist theories have to rely on the existence of one set of rules and values. Griffiths (1986: 4) unambiguously rejects the notion of monolithic legal norms and sees legal uniformity as 'a myth, an ideal, a claim, an illusion' (see also Galanter, 1981: 4 and 18; Merry, 1988: 871). Any centralist attempt, argues Galanter (1981: 5), would be similar to making all spoken languages into a common written language. He continues:

> No one would deny the utility or importance of written language, but it does not invariably afford the best guidance about how to speak. We should be cautioned by the way that it is our tendency to visualise the 'law in action' as a deviant or debased version of the higher law, 'the law of the book'.

Centralist ideology also holds that all justice should be dispensed through one system of courts, the state's courts and its arbitration system. This is clearly impossible in practice, since most disputes between people never go to any form of court, anyway. The development of various alternative dispute resolution techniques and informal justice give the lie to the exclusive competence of one set of courts (Merry, 1988: 874; generally McLennan, 1995). Galanter (1981: 17) points out that we have to,

> examine the courts in the context of their rivals and companions...we must put aside our historical perspective of legal centralism, a picture in which state agencies (and their learning) occupy the centre of legal life and stand in a relation of hierarchic control to other, lesser normative orderings such as the family, the corporation, the business network.

Finally, centralist systems pay insufficient respect to customs or customary laws. Diamond (1992) shows how customs were viewed as a modality of primitive society. Many Western jurists believe that the dominant state laws will eventually extinguish customs, personal laws and the normative orderings of sub-groups. They argue for the adaptation of the dominant culture and legal system by sub-groups and the prohibition of non-state laws on the grounds of repugnance or public policy, which would lead to a monistic legal system (Diamond, 1992). In consequence, the only source of legitimacy in modern societies is the state's law, and its only recipients are individuals (McLennan, 1995: 46). In such a society there tends to be a lack of tolerance; minorities are repressed and are discouraged from continuing their religious and cultural activities (Raz, 1974: 68). Referring to Western European countries that refuse pluralism, Raz (1974: 70) argues that 'there is the view of the superiority of the secular, democratic, European culture, and a reluctance to admit equal rights to inferior oppressive religious cultures, or ones whose cultural values are seen as limited and less developed'. Raz sees tolerance of minority customs as an extension of the classical liberal concept of constitutional, civil and political rights.

Progress towards acceptance of pluralism has been hampered by the difficulty of finding a sufficiently robust definition of legal pluralism. Griffiths (1986: 1) discussed legal pluralism in line with Sally Falk Moore's standard definition as the 'presence in a social field of more than one legal order' (see further Merry, 1988: 877; Pospisil, 1971; Van den Bergh, 1992: 451). In this model, the state laws still have a role in regulating individual behaviour whilst allowing personal laws and customs to be used in matters specific to particular communities and situations. Van den

Bergh (1992: 451-454) suggests that pluralism should be viewed not as a situation but as a process that develops over time, a complex pattern of continuous interactions. Many sub-orderings operate independently, most evidently in contemporary multi-ethnic and multi-religious systems. Galanter (1981: 20) asserts that 'law in modern society is plural rather than monolithic, that it is private as well as public in character and that the national (public, official) legal system is often secondary rather than a focus of regulation' (see further Merry, 1988; Pospisil, 1971). It seems agreed that in a pluralistic legal regime several sets of laws may be administered in several sets of institutions (Griffiths, 1986: 5; also Griffiths, 1985).

Even in Westernised systems, then, legal pluralism operates in all but name; personal laws and customs of sub-groups are applied sometimes with the blessing of the state and in most instances without any official sanction. In Chiba's terminology (see below) they would be 'unofficial laws'. However, do we call that 'legal pluralism', or is it merely social diversity? Though the gaps between the laws of sub-groups and of states are visible, and distinctions between the two can be made, both Griffiths (1986) and Merry (1988) argue that such divisions are constructed, man-made phenomena. Whatever we call them, in reality these two systems are interacting constantly, creating tensions as well as contributing to each other. Such a system is operating as a pluralistic entity. For Pospisil (1971) sub-groups are not constrained by sets of rules or laws of political society. They may have their own laws and rules which mould their behaviour and are responsive to conflict scenarios. Allott (1980: 7-8) agreed, subject to the proviso that such rules must not empower illegal groups and organisations like the IRA and the Mafia.

The prominent Japanese jurist Masaji Chiba critically analysed modern Western jurisprudence, based on Hellenistic and Christian views of men and women, as Western 'model jurisprudence' (Chiba, 1986: 2). His 'three-level structure of law' (Chiba, 1986: 5) emphasised that the jurisprudence of any contemporary society cannot be identified as a unified, uniform system. The state cannot control the whole of the law, as socio-cultural aspects of legal principles are not totally subject to outside control. Since cultural practices continue to evolve and develop separately from the state, the totality of the law is always plural, consisting of different systems of laws interacting harmoniously as well as creating conflict. Chiba (1986: 5-6) distinguishes 'official laws', 'unofficial laws' and 'legal postulates'. A legal postulate 'is a value principle or value system specifically connected with a particular official or unofficial law, which acts to found, justify and orient the latter' (Chiba, 1986: 6).

The first category, official laws, are sanctioned by the legitimate authority of the country, i.e. Parliament, State Assemblies or a monarch and may have little relevance to the lives and customs of individuals. Ethical, cultural and religious practices are reflected in the second category, the unofficial laws, rules which are not explicitly sanctioned and recognised by the state but exist in social reality. Unofficial laws operate on their own, without the blessing of the authorities, sanctioned by the general consensus of the people who practise them. Chiba argues, in essence, that this consensus more or less indirectly influences the formation of official state laws. The 'legal postulates', seen as complementary, consist of established legal principles such as natural justice, morality and equity. They may relate particularly to litigation, encouraging individuals to settle their disputes in a cultural context outside official courts. Chiba's main point is that these 'legal postulates' influence the way in which official and unofficial law develop in practice, thus illustrating the point that the actual, living law is culture-specific and diverse, rather than value-free and uniform.

It is not the function of this chapter to attempt to resolve the above conflicts and to arbitrate on opposing theories. We merely advocate that pluralism offers a better approach to dealing with conflicts caused when ethnic minority groups wish to maintain their own culture and values. Indeed, it could be questioned whether this is the right way to put it, since legal problems can be caused by the intransigence of the official law rather than by the mere presence of minorities.

It is our observation that English jurists and courts, dominated by legal centralist perspectives, have dealt inadequately with claims by ethnic minorities for the acceptance of customs and different value systems. We now illustrate our argument that a wider acceptance of alternative perspectives offered by legal pluralism would result in more just and equitable decisions in our so-called modern multicultural society.

4.2 Legal pluralism in the British context

Increased ethnic minority presence in Britain during the last four decades has not led to a doctrinal debate on legal pluralism that could inform the thinking of the judiciary. English lawyers have shown slight enthusiasm for legal pluralism. The literature is sparse, focused on theory (particularly Griffiths, 1986), and rarely linked to ethnic minority studies (see critically Menski, 1993: 242). Most of the debate has been conducted from a Western perspective of the role of law, with a tendency to reduce the significance of customary laws by arguing the universal applicability of Western law, and to misrepresent ethnic minority customs as somehow deficient and, more lately, violative of basic human rights norms (Poulter, 1987). This led almost inevitably to the adoption of an inappropriate methodology in analysing the validity of customs and their interactions with the dominant law. We consider each of these issues in turn.

The jurisprudential debate shifted in the mid-1980s when writers like Chiba (1986) began to argue that Western laws have unduly claimed universal applicability. Misconceptions about the superiority of Western notion of state laws were earlier challenged by Galanter (1981: 1):

> The view that the justice to which we seek access is a product that is produced or at least distributed exclusively by the state, a view which I shall for convenience label 'legal centralism' is not an uncommon one among legal professionals.

Legal pluralism opposes claims of the superiority or dominance of one legal system at the expense of other normative orderings or personal laws of sub-groups. As Griffiths (1986: 48) says, 'the state has no more empirical claim to being the centre of the universe of the legal phenomenon than any other element of the system does'.

Attempts to bolster the superiority of Western values and laws are aided by constant attacks on the culture and values of others. Western jurists claim that customs in some cultures are underdeveloped, rigid and inappropriate in developed societies. This strategy was pursued by Poulter (1986) and is evident in his final work (Poulter, 1998). Customs are often referred to derogatorily as 'ancient' (Allott, 1980: 60) and the impression is created that they belong to a less advanced stage of development. In his discussion of the limits of law arising from the nature of society, Allott (1980: 51) cited Alf Ross, who had written in an earlier study:

The transition from customary law to legislation is immensely important in the evolution of any society. Customary law is conservative; it relies on traditional and static patterns of behaviour. Those bound by it act as their fathers did. This does not mean that customs are unchangeable, for they may be adapted to changing conditions; this adaptation is slow and unplanned, lacking calculation and rational understanding of the requirements of a change in conditions.

Of those more sympathetic to the claims of legal pluralism in Britain, Bainham (1995: 238) has argued that although there are good reasons to justify the accommodation of cultural and religious practices, particularly in the field of family law within certain limits, the idea of 'multi-culturalism' in family law should be supported to encourage diversity in lifestyles. This support is, however, qualified because 'those family practices regarded as oppressive, especially perhaps oppressive of women or children, cannot... be supported' (Bainham, 1995: 239, see also Hamilton, 1995). This cautious approach can be traced back to Pearl (1972: 120-121), who emphasised that in view of the migrants' desire to maintain their customs and Britain's multicultural history, 'the recognition of alien customs, so long as they do not fall below minimum standards of public policy would appear to be a valuable contribution to the enhancement of racial harmony'.

Poulter (1987: 593) argued that ethnic minorities should not be allowed to 'endanger the integrity of the social and cultural core of English values' and adopted a monistic view of the role of law in a nation-state, testing customs against the concept of international human rights, which are largely a product of the West and its values (see now Poulter, 1998). The three tests against which customs are to be judged are based on so-called European and international human rights standards, on reasonableness, repugnance or abhorrence to English core values, and on public policy.

These terms present difficulties. They are open-ended and are by their very nature defined by the value system of those applying them – so are hardly universal. Can one justify one value system assessing the reasonableness of the cultures of other communities in Britain? It seems inappropriate to adopt a purely Western perspective of the abstract ideas of 'reasonable', 'repugnant' and 'abhorrent to justice and morality' to judge the cultural values of ethnic minorities. Customary behaviour of migrant groups should also not be judged against the background of a potential threat to Western morality. As Diamond (1992: 195) pointed out,

> ...morality continues to be reduced to or confused with legality. In civil society we are encouraged to assume that legal behavior is the measure of moral behavior... efforts to legislate conscience by an external political power are the antithesis of custom: customary behavior comprises precisely those aspects of social behavior which are traditional, moral, and religious, which are, in short, conventional and non-legal. Put another way, custom is social morality. The relation between custom and law is, basically, one of contradiction, not continuity.

The repugnance test has received some prominence in the literature because of its colonial antecedents in Africa (see Allott, 1980: 115). The test was first used in the former colonies of the British and French empires (Fawcett, 1990). Its basis is that the non-white colonial subjects were considered barbaric, their traditions, values and personal laws arbitrary, discriminatory and harmful to Western civilisation. Indigenous laws, therefore, were only allowed 'as long as they were not repugnant to natural justice, equity, and good conscience or inconsistent with any written law' (Merry, 1988: 870). Poulter's insistence upon a virtual repugnancy test and a morality filter advocated not pluralism but temporary toleration of 'the other', based on human rights standards as enshrined in the European Convention on Human Rights and the International Covenant on Civil and Political Rights and also the Convention of Consent to Marriage, and the Convention on the Elimination of All Forms of Discrimination Against Women. Poulter selected a number of human right principles as guidelines in legal toleration:

- right to life and liberty;
- freedom from torture;
- absence of slavery or forced labour;
- fair trial;
- respect for private and family life;
- freedom of thought, conscience, religion and expression.

We argue that these principles were carefully chosen to support the argument for non-recognition of ethnic minority customs, allowing Poulter (1987: 597) to claim that 'these rights and freedoms collectively represent a significant portion of the hard core of English public policy'.

Poulter (1987) developed the proposition that a custom can only be valid if it can be tolerated within the official dominant system. The term 'legal toleration' is more paternalistic than 'legal pluralism' (Poulter, 1987: 593). Law makers and the judiciary should tolerate only 'civilised customs' which are not repugnant to English values. Poulter (1987: 591) favoured defined guidelines 'as to what official recognition to such customs can be expected from legal institutions, government departments and administrative agencies'. The same approach is evident in his study of Asian traditions in English law (Poulter, 1990a), which seeks to educate Asians about English legal concepts. Poulter's methodology led him to conclude that most aspects of ethnic minority culture and tradition are repugnant and oppressive in comparison with standard norms of English civilisation and should not be tolerated. Cultural tolerance cannot become, argued Poulter (1987: 593), a cloak of oppression and injustice within migrant communities.

This approach ignores one of the universal truths, namely that 'something which is lawful one side of the mountain may be unlawful on the other side' (van den Bergh, 1992: 451). Allott (1980: 45) had concluded earlier that 'no one can be forced to do anything merely by a law. No law can compel any particular course of action, even if the law is accompanied by a sanction'. Allott saw law not as a draconian set of rules but rather as a living element within a society, responding to the socio-cultural and religious needs of particular individuals, groups and society at large. Following migration, what has happened to the axiom that law is culture-specific? Are we saying that once people migrate to a new place, they have to accept the legal system of their new home and abandon their own legal traditions?

Poulter (1987) developed a list of unacceptable customs in relation to English law:

- female circumcision, described as 'cruel, inhuman or degrading' (p. 601);

- polygamy, which should be prohibited because it involves violation of the fundamental right to sexual equality in the formation and dissolution of marriage (p. 609);

- religious ways of slaughtering animals. Abolition of s. 36(3) of the Slaughterhouses Act, 1974 might be justified according to current notions of public policy (pp. 611-612);

- religious processions on public highways. These cannot be justified because they are often noisy and boisterous and interfere with the free flow of traffic and pedestrians (p. 611);

- talaq should not be allowed since no judicial hearing takes place (p. 601);

- child and forced marriages should be prohibited, because they violate children's rights; and

- the toleration of turbans is also an ambiguous issue (p. 612).

Poulter (1986: 124-125) wrote in some detail about the difficult issue of how to handle the unilateral talaq:

> ...divorce by repudiation, in the Islamic world at any rate, is clearly discriminatory against wives. Talaqs are, however, countenanced by the Muslim faith and in so far as any improvement in the status of married women in this regard is concerned one must clearly look principally to the countries concerned for significant reforms. A start has been made in some of them, such as Tunisia, Pakistan and Bangladesh, but it would be presumptuous to imagine that English law can make a real contribution in this direction simply by denying validity to the small numbers of talaq divorces which might occur in this country. Even so, to authorise the pronouncement of talaqs here would seem to run counter to prevailing attitudes towards sexual equality in marriage and could well involve a violation of the UK's international obligations to respect human rights... On the other hand, refusal to authorise talaqs in England would not, it is thought, violate the religious freedom of Muslims since there is obviously nothing in Islamic doctrine which actually requires a man to put away his wife in this manner.

Poulter wrote elsewhere (1987: 601):

> Parliament should not recognise talaq even though it ran counter to an ancient religious tradition applicable to millions of followers of Islam, because the practice of talaq violates a number of important human rights provisions.

The assertion that a talaq is arbitrary and denies a fair trial in terms of modern human rights norms is popular but misleading. Although the Muslim husband has been given the right of unilateral repudiation, divorce is not looked upon with favour among Muslims and carries a stigma. Divorce was permitted by the Qur'an but portrayed as highly undesirable. Further, informal arbitration procedures involving the immediate family, the community and religious leaders – though these are not, in the eyes of many Western jurists – legal proceedings, may put pressure on husbands not to divorce. Legal systems should be interpreted to cover non-legal forms of normative orderings as well as the state's court system (Merry, 1988: 870). Even in traditional Muslim countries like Pakistan, both parties may be given an opportunity to present their case in arbitration. This may enable a wife can stop a husband from divorcing her, a right not given under the Family Law Act, 1996 to a wife under English law. In Britain, in unofficial talaq proceedings, both parties may represent their case before an arbitration panel consisting of religious and community leaders, in a procedure derived from classical Islamic law which implements checks and balances to try and ensure that justice is done in cases of both talaq and khula (khula allows a Muslim wife to divorce her husband). The Islamic scholar Maulana Abdul 'Ala Maududi, referring to talaq, states that 'the man is given the right to divorce his wife but at the same time several checks have been placed on him' (see Maududi, 1993: 34-5). In fact, talaq and khula, in the view of Islamic jurists, should be exercised only as a last resort. More recently, Poulter (1995: 85) insisted on several 'points of absolutely irreducible conflict' in family law, including the talaq. Such examples show that the dominant culture's approach to ethnic minority customs remains flawed. It is impossible to judge the customs of ethnic minorities against a completely different set of values.

The institution of marriage illustrates this point further. The Western perspective on marriage is of a contract entered into freely by two equal parties primarily for the fulfilment of individual objectives. If contrasted with Asian and African marriages, this renders them instruments of oppression foisted on unwilling and immature parties. In neither African-Caribbean nor Asian culture does the relationship between husband and wife depend on the Western notion of equality between the sexes. Marriage is based on many obligations, of which the respect for each other's roles in the domestic and public sphere is recognised as paramount. Husbands and wives have separate marital duties to perform, and the marriage is not based on lust or the personal ambitions of either party. Family life amongst ethnic minorities, in particular Asians, is viewed on a grander scale that just the individualistic. 'Getting married is more than a matter of contract between two individuals; it has, in the context of the Hindu notion of dharma, implications for the world at large' (Menski, 1987: 196). Muslim marriages are based on spiritual ideals of the need to promote morality, chastity and preserve human civilisation (Maududi, 1993). As Maududi summarises at p. 29, 'Allah does not like men and women whose only aim is the satisfaction of their sexual lust'. Some Western writers now recognise that the Western concept of equality between sexes should not necessarily be the common yardstick of marital life (see Hamilton, 1995: 2). Tolerance should not be limited to the concepts and rights recognised by Western civilisations or their legal systems.

Poulter (1990b: 165) suggested that 'cultural pluralism must be recognised by the English legal system as an integral part of modern English society and as one of the key elements of our liberal democracy' but seems to stop short of legal pluralism, asserting that ethnic minorities should conform to English law and its value systems. Poulter (1990b: 164) wrote about British Muslims:

> In the first place, they should bear in mind just how flexible and accommodating many of the provisions of English law are and ensure that they use the existing system to the full to suit their own purposes. This applies particularly to such issues as arranging marriages, performing weddings in mosques, organising a child's religious education at school (or elsewhere), paying mahr on divorce and executing a will.

That customs should only be used and recognised when they are not in conflict with the state's law is an ideal of monism, which van den Bergh (1992: 453) regards as an obsolete concept that ignores the capacity of law to develop through customary mechanisms more coherently than from legislative interventions. Law-making procedures in a traditional social setting can be truly democratic, in that many members of the group take part in forming and reforming personal laws and customs. The assertion that customs lack consensus and coherence, or that they are morally wrong, is incorrect and unjust.

Ethnic minorities have understandably responded to the lack of appreciation of their customs by closing in on themselves and operating outside the traditional legal system. Assisted by the gradual development of organised networks of community and communications structures, focused around religious and community centres, ethnic minority groups have evolved self-regulatory obligation systems which are applicable and understandable to themselves. Senior members of the community or religious leaders are sometimes brought in to manage these obligations and regulatory procedures but there is also much informality and a search for 'righteousness' on a case-by-case basis. Over time, this process has resulted in the organic development of customs and specific personal laws of ethnic minorities in Britain, which may avoid official channels and the official legal processes This can be seen in areas such as marriage, divorce, dowry, gift-giving, parental discipline, transfer of property and child care. Though customary arbitration procedures may not fit in with the Western legal system, their decisions are generally honoured and implemented through a mixture of sanctions and ostracism.

Menski (1987; 1988; 1993) has observed how British Asians adapt to English law whilst practising their personal laws and has traced their process of constructing a new kind of law, a blend of personal laws and English law. Though Menski's early focus has been on the application of Hindu personal laws in Britain, in particular Hindu marriage, his more recent writing is mainly on Muslims, showing how Shari'a law operates through community and religious networks in reshaping the lives of Muslims in a British context. Pearl and Menski (1998, ch. 3) introduce the concept of English shariat, 'Angrezi shariat', as a pluralistic end product of this complex process. Menski's observations confirm that most migrants prefer their own customs to English law in resolving disputes and implementing their obligation systems. Strong evidence is now emerging that many migrants do not necessarily follow legal requirements as expected by English law (see Hamilton, 1995: 50). Considering why a low rate of marriage registration was reflected in the national census, Hamilton (1995: 50) concluded:

> Another possible reason for the low rate of Muslim marriages is that Muslims are deliberately circumventing marriage laws and marrying according to Muslim customs with no registration of marriage.

This concurs with the view of Menski that Hindus and Muslims have, for some time, been engaged in law-making processes of their own, while admitting the importance of formal obedience to English law. Thus Menski (1993: 244-245):

Continued observation in this field now leads me to write about the emergence of new forms of Hindu, Muslims and even Sikh laws in Britain that are different from their subcontinental prototypes, for the very reason that their development took place in Britain and in a complex interplay with the demands made by English law. In many cases, thus, I would say that, from the perspective of the persons concerned, a modified version of their traditional laws has been developed and is being followed in the new land rather than the official 'law of the land'. The latter is not being ignored, of course, but the actual legal development takes place in the modification of the traditional laws, not in the sphere of English law. In addition, we are now beginning to see some areas of English law that are significantly influenced by the presence of large numbers of Asians.

Thus, what we can witness in Britain today, the moment we allow ourselves to abandon preconceived notions of the superiority of everything European, is the gradual emergence of what may be called 'Asian laws' in Britain, or 'British Asian laws', as Asians here negotiate a co-existence between the requirements of English law and of traditional forms of South Asian laws.

Similar views, especially on the role of unofficial arbitration procedures, can be found in the earlier literature. Galanter (1981: 3) suggested it is wrong to expect all disputes to be arbitrated in official courts and argued that the majority of disputes, in particular ethnic minority disputes, do not end up in the state's courts (see also Chiba, 1986). It is naive to believe that the state's courts would deliver justice – quite the reverse – or understand the nature of disputes in their proper cultural context, or respond to disputes which may be complicated and shrouded in mystery. Noonan (1976) pointed out that even the most superior and esteemed courts have not been able to dispense justice or respond to the needs of litigants. The notion that all disputes will be fully adjudicated by official courts is a 'monstrous proposition' (Galanter, 1981: 4).

Menski has been critical of English lawyers' refusal or inability to recognise the emerging laws and processes among British Asians. English lawyers, in his observation, tend to stick to the notion that the unified legal system is best for dealing with disputes and crimes. They continue to consider Western cultures and legal systems superior to those of non-Western laws and believe that English law alone should be followed as the law of the land (Menski, 1993: 242). Yet the customs of both African-Caribbeans and Asians have continuously been developing and adapting to the needs of new legal and social environments. Menski's pioneering contribution to the debate on legal pluralism in the British context is helpful in challenging traditional myths about the personal laws of ethnic minorities, particularly of Asian background, and in identifying the areas in which the development of personal laws among ethnic minority groups has taken place.

4.3 Legal pluralism in English courts

Ethnic minority people may find difficulty in complying with the values of English law, which may seem contrary to their own or a challenge to their obligation systems, regarding family, religious and cultural matters, and the institutions dealing with them. Therefore our focus on legal pluralism in English law is limited to these areas of contention.

Ethnic minorities may wish to steer clear of any involvement with English law. This is a difficult issue, since a citizen is, for example, guilty of an offence if he fails to respond to a constable's call for assistance in keeping the peace (Smith and Hogan, 1996: 47). Further, under s. 17(1)(a) of the Theft Act, 1968 it is an offence to fail to complete documents for accounting purposes (see R v. Shama [1990] 2 AllER 602) – problem for immigrants from Bangladesh in the early 1950s and 1960s, even when formal documents were generally not required.

Ethnic minority individuals who wish to understand the dominant cultural values face difficulties when these are in flux, as often happens in family law. Recently, the House of Lords restated the law relating to rape within marriage in R v R [1991] 4 All ER 481, holding that the rule that a husband cannot be criminally liable for raping his wife if he insists on sexual intercourse without her consent no longer forms part of the law of England. Husband and wife are now regarded as equal partners in marriage in English law, but this may not correspond to the views of ethnic minority communities.

The same might apply to English views on the rights of children, as in the case of Gillick v West Norfolk Area Health Authority [1986] AC 112 and its interpretation of the Child Abduction Act, 1984, as amended by the Children Act, 1989 (see also Sherry v El Yamani [1993] Cri LR 536). The changing responses to domestic violence, particularly in R v Ahluwalia

[1992] 4 All ER 889 CA, which allowed evidence of 'battered women syndrome', based on the defence of provocation as a valid defence to homicide (see also R. v Thornton [1992] 1 All ER 306 CA), may be seen by ethnic minorities as an attack on the integrity of family life.

Ethnic minority individuals whose values conflict with the dominant law have suffered for non-compliance. In child care cases, ethnic minority parents may find themselves challenged by allegations of falling below the level of acceptable parenting, a criterion used to justify the intervention of state agencies in the family, or of the criminal law (see s. 31 of the Children Act, 1989).

Other cases have arisen in the realm of employment law. In Ahmad v Inner London Education Authority [1978] 1 All ER 574, not accepting a particular value system cost a man his livelihood. The applicant, Mr. Ahmad, was an orthodox Muslim, employed as a teacher by the defendants. To attend a local mosque for prayers every Friday, he was absent from school for some 45 minutes. He refused to accept a part-time contract for 4.5 days a week and resigned instead. His claim for unfair dismissal was rejected. His right under Art. 9 of the European Convention on Human Rights, 1950 to manifest his religion in practice and obser-vance was held to be subject to the education authority's rights under the contract of employment. By absenting himself he was in breach of contract. Many early migrants experienced similar hostilities at the hands of the judiciary (see R v Sarwan Singh and R v Sagoo below).

The judicial response to customs perceived to be in conflict with Christian and/or English values has varied from indifference to outright hostility. The courts have not operated the presumption that all legal systems are equal (Fentiman, 1992: 143) but require migrants to conform to English law. Such traditional thinking on foreign customs was ex-pressed by Judge King-Hamilton QC in R v Adesanya, a case only reported in The Times of 16 and 17 July 1974 (see Poulter, 1986: 151):

> You and others who come to this country must realise that our laws must be obeyed... [I]t cannot be stressed too strongly that any further offences of this kind in pursuance of tribal traditions in Nigeria or other parts of Africa... can only result in prosecution. Because this is a test case... I am prepared to deal with you with the utmost leniency. But let no one else assume that they will be treated with mercy. Others have now been warned.

In Mohamed v Knott [1968] 2 All ER 563 QB, the lower court had chosen to vilify a migrants' custom, in this case a child marriage validly entered into in Nigeria. The case was referred to Southwark North Juvenile Court under what was then s. 62 of the Children and Young Persons Act, 1933 for a 'Fit Person Order'. The magistrates commenting on the marriage said, as cited at p. 567 of the case report:

> Here is a girl, aged 13, or possibly less, unable to speak English, living in London with a man twice her age to whom she has been married by Muslim law. He admits having had sexual intercourse with her at a time when according to the medical evidence the development of puberty had almost certainly not begun. He intends to resume intercourse as soon as he is satisfied that she is adequately protected by contraceptives from the risk of pregnancy. He admits that before the marriage he had intercourse with a woman by whom he has three illegitimate children. He further admits that since the marriage, which took place as recently as January of this year, he has had sexual relations with a prostitute in Nigeria from whom he contracted venereal disease. In our opinion a continuance of such an association notwithstanding the marriage, would be repugnant to any decent-minded English man or woman. Our decision reflects that repugnance.

On appeal the ruling was reversed by the Divisional Court. Lord Parker CJ conceded that since this marriage was valid in Nigeria, it was recognised and valid by English law. The Fit Person Order was revoked. The higher court would perhaps not have been so tolerant if the couple had had links with England. In such a case the courts would have expected the couple to comply with English standards, according to which marriages of persons under 16 are void.

The lack of a pluralistic perspective from the judiciary is surprising, considering that legal pluralism was encouraged in British colonies. Hamilton has written (1995: 94):

> For many religious minority groups, particularly non-western immigrant groups, maintaining their religious way of life means adhering to traditional customs, moral values and legal principles. Complying with civil legal requirements in relation to the regulation of the family may upset these traditional beliefs, and weaken the religious bonds

within the community. Many minority religious groups have a rather stricter attitude towards morality and the family than that exhibited by the civil system of family law, and fear that their standards of morality will decline if their members are subject only to the requirements and values of the civil system....

Further, immigrant communities from countries with a plural legal system find it difficult to see why western nations cannot accommodate such legal pluralism. They point to the fact that Britain in its colonial period accepted such a system, and see no reason why, now that there are substantial religious minorities in England, such a system could not be introduced. For many this is seen as an issue of religious freedom and religious toleration, and a matter of free exercise of religion.

Requests for the recognition of personal laws by some early migrants were flatly rejected. Esop [1836] 7C & P 456 held that it was not a defence for a native of Baghdad to argue that sodomy was not a criminal offence in his own country (see Smith and Hogan, 1996: 83; Amin, 1985: 26). In R v Barronet and Allain (1852) Dears CC 51, it was held that it was not a valid defence to murder for a Frenchman to state that duelling was legal in France (Smith and Hogan, 1996: 83). Not content merely to reject claims for recognition of customs, some judges have gone on to condemn and vilify the customs of ethnic minorities.

4.4 Family law cases

Ethnic minority claims for the retention and recognition of customary practices arise particularly in family law cases, causing conflict with a judiciary determined to impose the values of Christian society. We discuss here evidence from cases relating to polygamy, divorce and marriage solemnisation.

4.4.1 Polygamy

According to classical Islamic law, a man may marry up to four wives. While Turkey, Tunisia, Pakistan, and some other countries have restricted the practice – which does not mean that polygamy does not occur there – polygamy is openly practised in many African and Asian countries, among Muslims, some Jews, orthodox Hindus, some sections of Buddhists, and in many African tribal groups. Prior to the promulgation of the Hindu

Marriage Act of 1955 in India, Hindus and Sikhs could marry as many wives as they chose (see R v Sarwan Singh [1962] 3 All ER 612, at p. 613). In some countries, men are also allowed to keep 'secondary wives', such as 'concubines' (tsipsis) in classical Chinese law, though marriage in customary Chinese law is based on the concept of monogamous marriage (see Lee v Lau [1964] 2 All ER 248 at p. 252). Muslims and many Africans practise polygamy, which is valid by their personal laws and in compliance with traditional cultural values.

When early Muslim immigrants married or wanted to marry English Christian women, this was neither welcomed by the civil authorities nor appreciated by the judiciary. Many had come alone, leaving their wives and children at home and married local white women whilst their first marriages were still valid. Some immigrants found themselves subject to the criminal law if they attempted to remarry in this country. They may have been surprised to learn that English law does not consider the bona fides of the individual in prosecutions for bigamy. English law requires merely an intention to go through the second marriage ceremony without obtaining a divorce as a basis for criminal conviction. In The King v Naguib [1917] 1 KB 359, it transpired that Mr. Naguib, an Egyptian Muslim, came to England in 1901 and married Miss Annie Wheeler in 1903. In 1914 he married again while his first marriage was subsisting. It was revealed in the trial for bigamy that he was also party to an earlier marriage, solemnised according to Islamic law in Egypt in 1898. As a Muslim, he genuinely believed that he could marry four wives but he was found guilty and sentenced to imprisonment with hard labour for eight months.

Another polygamist, Mr. Sarwan Singh, by birth an Indian Sikh, was charged at West Bromwich Quarter Session before the Assistant Recorder and a jury with committing bigamy under s. 57 of the Offences Against the Person Act, 1861. This defined the crime of bigamy by saying, in essence, that any married person marrying any other person during the life of the first husband or wife, whether the second marriage shall have taken place in England or Ireland or elsewhere, shall be guilty of felony. R v Sarwan Singh [1962] 3 All ER 612 shows that before migrating to Britain, this man married a Sikh woman in 1944 in Jullundur, then part of British India. Being an orthodox Sikh, he could have as many wives as he chose. He entered into a further marriage in Britain without obtaining a divorce. He was acquitted on the basis that his first potentially poly-gamous marriage could not be used as a basis for bigamy because poly-gamous marriages did not create any legal rights or obligations under English law.

While this was the standard response of English family law to such cases for a long time (see further below), this judgment was overruled in R v Sagoo [1975] 1 QB 885 CA. In this case a Kenyan Sikh, Mr. Mohinder Singh Sagoo, had migrated to England with his wife in 1966 and then acquired a British domicile of choice. On 19 March 1973, he married Miss Ushaben Patel while the marriage with his first wife sub-sisted. His change of domicile had had the effect of turning his first potentially polygamous marriage into a monogamous marriage. Thus he was found guilty of bigamy.

The frequent requests by Muslims for application of their personal laws in the area of family law have been refused. The Law Commission Report No. 53 of 1973 concluded that there is no justification for amend-ing the current law (Hamilton, 1995: 50-51). However, many Muslims and others have valid polygamous marriages, entered into abroad, so questions of legal recognition frequently arise. A major issue in English civil law has therefore been whether to recognise and give effect to poly-gamous marriages.

English law demands conformity with English standards and will only recognise a marriage entered into in England as legally valid if it satisfies the formality and capacity requirements of English law. As a consequence of s.11(b) Matrimonial Causes Act, 1973 a polygamous marriage entered into in England is void. A polygamous marriage entered into outside England and Wales will also be void if either party was at the time of the marriage domiciled in England (s.11(d) Matrimonial Causes Act, 1973). This has now been amended by the Private International Law (Mis-cellaneous Provisions) Act, 1995 which abolishes the concept of the potentially polygamous marriage. The amended section now reads that '...a marriage is not polygamous if at its inception neither party has any spouse additional to the other'.

English courts were initially totally hostile to polygamous marriages entered into outside England and Wales by those domiciled abroad. The foreign marriage was made to satisfy the much-cited definition of mar-riage given by Lord Penzance in Hyde v Hyde and Woodmansee (1886) LR 1 P & M 130 at p. 133:

...Marriage has been well said to be something more than a contract, either religious or civil – to be an institution. It creates mutual rights and obligations, as all contracts do, but beyond that it confers a status. The position or status of 'husband' and 'wife' is a recognised one throughout Christendom: the laws of all Christian nations throw about that status a variety of legal incidents during the lives of the parties, and induce definite rights upon their offspring. What, then, is the nature of this institution as understood in Christendom? Its incidents vary in different countries, but what are its essential elements and invariable features? If it be of common acceptance and existence, it must needs (however varied in different countries in its minor incidents) have some pervading identity and universal basis. I conceive that marriage, as understood in Christendom, may for this purpose be defined as the voluntary union for life of one man and one woman, to the exclusion of others. There are no doubt countries peopled by a large section of the human race in which men and women do not live or cohabit together upon these terms – countries in which this institution and status are not known. In such parts the men take to themselves several women, whom they jealously guard from the rest of the world, and whose number is limited only by considerations of material means. But the status of these women in no way resembles that of the Christian 'wife'. In some parts they are slaves, in others perhaps not; in none do they stand, as in Christendom, upon the same level with the man under whose protection they live. There are, no doubt, in these countries laws adapted to this state of things – laws which regulate the duties and define the obligations of men and women standing to each other in these relations. It may be, and probably is, the case that the women there pass by some word or name which corresponds to our word 'wife'. But there is no magic in a name; and, if the relations there existing between men and women is not the relations which in Christendom we recognise and intend by the words 'husband' or 'wife', but another and altogether different relations, the use of a common term to express these two separate relations will not make them one and the same, though it may tend to confuse them to a superficial observer. (emphasis added)

This was taken as providing a comprehensive test against which the validity of all marriages could be judged (see further Brinkley v Attorney

General [1890] 15 PD 76, at p. 80) and for some time English law would not recognise as valid any marriage that fell foul of any of Lord Penzance's four conditions. A polygamous marriage, not being of 'one man and one woman' was considered void. Hyde v Hyde concluded in this regard at p. 133:

> We have in England no law framed on the scale of polygamy, or adjusted to its requirements. And it may well be doubted whether it would become the tribunals of this country to enforce the duties (even if we knew them) which belong to a system so utterly at variance with the Christian conception of marriage, and so revolting to the idea we entertain of the social position to be accorded to the weaker sex.

In refusing to recognise polygamous marriages, Lush LJ in Harvey v Farnie, 6 PD 35, at p. 53, stated:

> Marriage in the contemplation of every Christian community is the union of one man and one woman to the exclusion of all others. No such provision is made, no such relation is created, in a country where polygamy is allowed, and if one of the numerous wives of a Mohammedan was to come to this country, and marry in this country, she could not be indicted for bigamy, because our laws do not recognise a marriage solemnised in that country, a union falsely called marriage, as a marriage to be recognised in our Christian country.

In Warrender v Warrender, 2 Cl and F 488, at p. 532, Lord Brougham wrote:

> Marriage is one and the same thing substantially all the Christian world over. Our whole law of marriage assumes this; and it is important to observe, that we regard it as a wholly different thing, a different status from Turkish or other marriages among infidel nations, because we clearly never should recognise the plurality of wives, and consequent validity of second marriages...

The influence of the above cases was evident in Rex v Hammersmith Superintendent Registrar of Marriage, ex parte Mir-Anwaruddin [1917] 1 KB 634, where Darling J commented at p. 649:

> ...yet it is plain that not one of such unions could give the women espoused the status of wife according to English law, for if it did

those certificates would permit of polygamy, which our law forbids; they would indeed amount to licences to commit three separate felonies.

Swinfen Eady LJ, in the same case, asserted at p. 657 that non-Christian countries basically did not know what a 'wife' was. The practical effect of these early decisions was to prevent parties to polygamous marriages from claiming any form of matrimonial relief. In Sowa v Sowa [1961] 1 All ER 687, at p. 690, Holroyd LJ affirmed that parties to a potentially poly-gamous marriage were simply not considered husband and wife, and that the matrimonial jurisdiction of the courts did not extend to giving relief in relation to potentially polygamous marriages (see also Risk v Risk [1950] 2 All ER 973 and De Reneville v De Reneville [1948] 1 All ER 56 CA). In Ohochuku v Ohochuku [1960] 1 All ER 253, the court refused to assume jurisdiction to dissolve a polygamous marriage or to adjudicate on rights arising from such unions, although the parties were Christians and there-fore their marriage was actually monogamous. The court held that Nigerian marriages were potentially polygamous (see further Lee v Lau [1964] 2 All ER 248; Muhammad v Suna [1956] SC 366).

The outright rejection of polygamous marriages entered into outside England and Wales, which as a result of migration now had connections to England, brought with it many obvious practical difficulties. In Baindail (otherwise Lawson) v Baindail [1946] 1 All ER 342 CA, Lord Greene MR faced the question whether a husband in a potentially poly-gamous marriage, which had taken place in India according to Hindu rites, should be recognised as a 'husband' in nullity proceeding initiated by the petitioner wife, who was the second wife of the respondent and an English Christian. On the one hand, the precedent of Hyde v Hyde pre-vented the Court from even considering the legality of a polygamous marriage. On the other, Lord Greene wanted to help the English woman by declaring her marriage void which meant admitting that the res-pondent's previous marriage was valid. Lord Greene held, at p. 346:

What was his status on 5 May 1939? Unquestionably it was that of a married man. Will this status be recognised in this country? English law certainly does not refuse all recognition of that status. For many purposes, quite obviously, the status would have to be recognised.

Lord Greene finally offered support at p. 347, stating that common sense and reasonable policy required that the courts are bound to recognise

Indian marriages as valid for some limited purposes. It was relevant that polygamous Hindu marriages were legal in British India. However, such a marriage would be an effective bar to any subsequent marriage in this country, a position accepted in Coleman v Shang (alias Quartney) [1961] 2 All ER 406.

Hence, courts in England and Wales were no longer precluded from granting matrimonial relief or making a declaration concerning the validity of a marriage by reason only that the marriage in question was entered into under a law which permits polygamy (see now Matrimonial and Family Proceedings Act, 1994; Family Law Act, 1996).

Baindail was developing an approach first evident in the Sinha Peerage Case (1939) 171 Lords Journals, 350 (details in Baindail v Baindail [1946] 1 All ER 342, at pp. 348-349), where the judiciary showed its willingness to consider polygamous marriages for limited purposes, for example in such issues as legitimacy of the children and property right. In Srini Vasan (otherwise Clayton) v Srini Vasan [1945] 2 All ER 21, on facts virtually identical to Baindail, referring to a Hindu marriage which was potentially polygamous and contracted in India, it was stated that the denial of legality would be contrary to common sense and justice. It was held by Barnard J at p. 22:

> The question which I have to decide is whether this Hindu marriage, notwithstanding its polygamous character, is recognised by this court when exercising its matrimonial jurisdiction invoked in this case. It would be strange if English law were to afford no recognition of polygamous marriages when one realises that England is the centre of a great Empire whose Mohammedan and Hindu subjects number many millions...

It was further held at p. 23:

> To deny recognition of a Hindu marriage for the purpose in hand, would, in my opinion, be to fly in the face of common sense, good manners and the ordered system of tolerance on which the Empire is based; and, as I decide, to deny such recognition would be bad law.

Similarly in Shahnaz v Rizwan [1964] 3 WLR 759, a constructive approach was taken by the judiciary at p. 759:

> ...a polygamous or potentially polygamous marriage which was lawful by the personal law of the parties and by the lex loci celebrationis was not regarded as an unlawful marriage under English law, although the English courts would not enforce such a marriage or any right arising specifically by virtue of the marriage relationship between the parties.

Therefore a migrant, domiciled in a country that allows polygamy, may enter into a polygamous marriage that will be recognised by the English courts, provided that the marriage is entered into outside England and Wales by persons not domiciled in England and Wales, both parties have the capacity to enter into the marriage by the law of their lex domicilii and the marriage complies with the formalities of the lex loci celebrationis. In Khoo Hooi Leong v Khoo Chong Yeok [1930] AC 346 and Bamgbose v Daniel [1954] 3 All ER 263, the courts were prepared to take account of polygamous marriages for the purpose of ascertaining such important rights as succession.

The tolerance first shown in the above cases is most evident in Cheni (otherwise Rodriguez) v Cheni [1962] 3 All ER 873, where the main issues centred on incest and polygamy between a Jewish uncle and niece. According to expert evidence such relationships, unlike aunt-nephew relationships, were permissible. The marriage in question was potentially polygamous at the date of the ceremony but monogamous at the date of the proceedings. The court showed a progressive approach to personal laws, admitting that it was no longer advisable to assess cultural arrangements in terms of Christianity alone and emphasised that there was no justification for condemning such cultural practices. It was stated at p. 879 that '[i]t is now clear that English courts will recognise for most purposes the validity of polygamous marriages, notwithstanding that they are prohibited by Christianity'. Sir Jocelyn Simon P said that even though the marriage appeared to be offensive to the conscience of English norms, the court would seek to exercise common sense, good manners and a reasonable tolerance and held, at p. 883:

> Whatever test is adopted, the marriage in the present case is, in my judgment, valid. I do not consider that a marriage which may be the subject of papal dispensation and will then be acknowledged as valid by all Roman Catholics, which without any such qualification is acceptable to all Lutherans, can reasonably be said to be contrary to

the general consent of Christendom. The passage which I have quoted from Story himself and from those who have commented on him bear this out. If the general consent of civilised nations were to be the test, I do not think that the matter can be resolved by, so to speak, taking a card vote of the United Nations and disregarding the views of the many civilised countries by whose laws these marriages are permissible. As counsel for the husband observed, Egypt, where these people lived and where the marriage took place, is itself a civilised country. If public policy were the test, it seems to me that the arguments of the husband, founded on such inferences as one can draw from the scope of the English criminal law, prevail. Moreover, they weigh with me when I come to apply what I believe to be the true test, namely, whether the marriage is so offensive to the conscience of the English court that it should refuse to recognise and give effect to the proper foreign law. In deciding that question the court will seek to exercise common sense, good manners and a reasonable tolerance. In my view, it would be altogether too queasy a judicial conscience which would recoil from a marriage acceptable to many peoples of deep religious convictions, lofty ethical standards and high civilisation. Nor do I think that I am bound to consider such marriages merely as a generality. On the contrary, I must have regard to this particular marriage, which has stood, valid by the religious law of the parties' common faith and the municipal law of their common domicile, unquestioned for thirty five years... In my judgment, injustice would be perpetrated and conscience would be affronted if the English courts were not to recognise and give effect to the law of the domicile in the present case. I therefore reject the prayer of the petition asking that this marriage be declared null and void.

Apart from these few cases, most reported decisions illustrate how members of the judiciary would use the pretext of connection to England as a justification to reject the acceptance of polygamous marriages in other cultures. Judges searched for the common ground to respond to the issues raised by ethnic minorities in the post-war era without violating their Christian values.

The case law also reflects that when there was a possible economic impact on the state, the courts did not hesitate to arbitrate the matter, irrespective of the validity of marriages in the eyes of English law. In Din v National Assistance Board [1967] 1 All ER 750, the appellant Imam Din married Rasul Bibi in Pakistan in 1948 according to Islamic rituals while already married to another wife in Pakistan. The marriage was therefore polygamous. He brought Rasul Bibi and four children to England and later deserted them. This led the National Assistance Board to make weekly payment of £7.16s to Rasul Bibi and her children, all under 16 years. The National Assistance Board later brought proceedings against Din to recover the money they had paid in pursuance of s. 43(2) of the National Assistance Board Act, 1948. Din's counsel took advantage of the faulty earlier reasoning by the English courts to argue that his client's marriage to Rasul Bibi was a polygamous marriage which did not create any legal rights or obligation between parties in the eyes of English law. Using a test of common sense and justice (p. 753), Salmon LJ was quite prepared to accept the rights and obligation arising out of a poly-gamous marriage in relation to the Act of 1948. His words, at p. 753, reveal the economic reasons behind his generosity:

> It would perhaps be as remarkable as it would be unfortunate, if a man, coming from a country where he is lawfully married to a woman and is lawfully the father of her children, may bring them here and leave them destitute, with impunity, so that when the National Assistance Board is obliged to come to their assistance, he can avoid all responsibility and thereby throw the whole burden of maintaining his wife and children on the public.

In Bibi v Chief Adjudication Officer [1998] 1 FIR 375 the Court of Appeal in following Din refused to award widowed mother's allowance to the first wife in an actual polygamous marriage.

This decision confirms that recognition of polygamous marriages will vary. When it suits the state, judges will be prepared to give or not, as the case may be, full legal recognition to overseas polygamous marriages, even though the cultural norms of the migrants' new home appear to be offended.

4.4.2 Divorce

The substance of English divorce law has changed considerably since the introduction of civil divorce in 1857. The present divorce law under the Matrimonial Causes Act of 1973 retains the vestiges of a judicial hearing, with parties referred to as petitioner and respondent. In practice, since the introduction of the 'special procedure' to facilitate quicker disposal of cases, English divorce is more akin to an administrative process. The Family Law Act, 1996 (originally scheduled to be implemented by 1999) will create a conciliatory framework in which divorcing couples are encouraged to work out their own arrangements for the future, the role of the court being merely supervisory. Such reforms are also designed to save the state money. It is still unclear what effects these new procedures will have on ethnic minority couples wishing to divorce.

To what extent has English law taken official notice of the fact that members of ethnic minorities continue to divorce according to their own laws and customs? In many cases, the divorce took place abroad. In England, a marriage can only be dissolved by judicial proceedings under the Matrimonial Causes Act, 1973 (or, where trialed, under the Family Law Act, 1986). Some ethnic minority laws allow divorce by agreement of the parties or even by the unilateral act of one party. Such processes, while not that far removed from present (and future) English law, have caused considerable difficulty for the courts. Two forms of divorce causing difficulties are the talaq and the get.

In classical Islamic law, a talaq can be given by the husband in the absence of the wife and without a reason. It involves merely writing or stating three times, 'I divorce you'. If this talaq is pronounced in triple form and is assumed to take instant effect, it is referred to as a 'bare talaq', which is seen as particularly bad because it is not a process but an instant action, and it allows the divorced woman no defence mechanisms. A get is a letter of divorce issued according to Jewish rabbinical law, a bill of divorce obtained by a Jewish couple.

English law will recognise foreign divorces that are valid by the law of the couple's common domicile or by the religious law of the parties. In Lee v Lau [1964] 2 All ER 248, a divorce obtained in Hong Kong with the agreement of the wife was accepted as valid. In Pemberton v Hughes [1899] 1 Ch 781, even though Lindley MR was not prepared to accommodate legal recognition for foreign judgments carte blanche, it was held that a judgment by a foreign court of competent jurisdiction will be treated as conclusive, provided that the proceedings do not offend English notions of substantial justice. In Russ (otherwise Geffers) v Russ (otherwise De Waele) [1962] 3 All ER 193, a divorce obtained in Egypt in an appropriate Muslim court was recognised. In Varanand v Varanand

(1964) 108 Sol Jo 693 (also reported in The Times, 25 July 1964, cited in Radwan v Radwan [1972] 3 All ER 967, at p. 971) Lord Scarman stated that there was no legal barrier to recognising the validity of a divorce proclaimed in a foreign embassy, nor could there be any legal issues preventing the recognition of a marriage celebrated there.

In Qureshi v Qureshi [1971] 1 All ER 325, this legal recognition was even extended to a talaq pronounced in England where both parties were domiciled in Pakistan. While in Joseph v Joseph [1953] WLR 1182 recognition was refused, in Har-Shefi v Har-Shefi [1953] 1 All ER 783, a get issued in Israel was recognised as valid. Pronouncing the judgment, Denning LJ (as he then was) stated at p. 789:

> ...the petitioner is an English woman resident in this country, intending to make her life here, and she wants to know how she stands in this country. All she asks the English courts to do is to tell her whether she is to be regarded in this country as a single or as a married woman. It is a matter of the utmost importance to her and to others, and I see no reason why she should be forced to go to Israel to have the matter determined.

His Lordship stated, at p. 789, that he saw 'no reason today why the court of this country should not decide on the validity of a Jewish divorce according to the law of Israel...'. The effect was to recognise the dissolution of a marriage without the involvement of the state or courts. This position has since been affected by statute, when the Domicile and Matrimonial Proceedings Act, 1973 laid down that no extra-judicial divorce obtained anywhere in the British Isles should be recognised in England. This has now been re-enacted in the Family Law Act, 1986.

The get will be recognised as 'proceedings' where it is pronounced in another country that recognises its validity and the parties are domiciled there. A get pronounced in Egypt was recognised in Sasson v Sasson [1924] AC 1007. In Salvesen (or van Lorang) v Austrian Property Administrator [1927] AC 641 a similar approach was taken. Although a get pronounced in England will not be deemed capable of dissolving a marriage, the get may have some other relevance.

In Joseph v Joseph [1953] 1 WLR 1182 CA, both parties were Jewish and had married in 1926. After a very unhappy family life, the husband deserted his wife in 1936. Mrs. Joseph later tried to divorce her husband on the ground of his desertion for 10 years. In 1948, after considerable correspondence between the parties, the husband finally agreed to give her a get at the Beth Din in London. In 1951 she petitioned for divorce from an English court but her application was refused. In the Appeal Court, Somervell LJ in agreement with Jenkins and Hodson LJJ refused her application and confirmed the first instance decision. Both the Commissioner and the learned judges failed to appreciate the many years of desertion by the husband. Somervell LJ said at p. 1183:

> The conclusion to which I am driven is that the wife, by obtaining this get and insisting upon it in the way in which she did, had consented to her husband living apart from her and that, from that moment, there was no desertion of the wife by the husband. That remains the position, unless it can be said that there has been any conduct of the wife or the husband to take the matter out of the category of a consensual living apart.

It was further held at p. 1183:

> I think that that conclusion is inescapable. She did ask for this document and for a divorce valid according to Jewish law. There is no suggestion that both parties did not realise that it had no legal effect in English law and, indeed, the wife's evidence emphasises that, in that she wanted it because, in her opinion at any rate, it would be effective in Shanghai;... I do not see how one can avoid the conclusion that she was terminating her husband's desertion by bringing about the state of affairs as between them, that they were to live apart. He was not therefore in a position to come back to her, and if he had sought to do so she was entitled to say that she must abide by the decision of the get.

Mrs. Joseph (who was not English) had asked the court to declare her civil status as a single person so that she could re-marry. She pleaded that her marriage should be dissolved or the divorce obtained by get should be recognised. The plea was very similar to that in Har-Shefi, which was refused (Har-Shefi was decided on 6 March 1953, Joseph was decided on 15 July 1953).

Where the marriage has some connection to England, the courts are less generous also in recognising talaq divorces, for two main reasons. Firstly, the talaq as a unilateral repudiation by the husband seems to lack natural justice much like English divorce law of the 19th century.

Secondly, the common law rule of the wife's dependant domicile meant that a wife would automatically obtain her husband's domicile, so that a wife living in England might have a domicile in Pakistan. If domicile was the true test of divorce jurisdiction, an English wife living in England could be subject to a valid talaq, as illustrated in R v Hammersmith Superintendent Registrar of Marriages ex p. Mir-Anwaruddin [1917] 1 KB 634.

Dr. Mir-Anwaruddin, an Indian Muslim, came to London to qualify as a barrister. He married an English woman, Miss Ruby Hudd, on 18 March 1913. She deserted him and Dr Mir-Anwaruddin repudiated their marriage by talaq and decided to marry another English woman. He asked the Registrar of Marriage in the District of Hammersmith to issue a certificate and licence to marry his new bride. According to Mir-Anwaruddin, the registrar wilfully and without cause refused to issue the certificate and licence. He challenged the decision of the Registrar in person. His arguments were in essence:

* as a Muslim he could marry up to four wives;
* as a Muslim he could repudiate his marriage by way of talaq without going through the English legal process, and it applies to a Christian just as to a Muslim wife;
* as a Muslim he could practise his personal laws, Islamic law, wherever he happened to live.

Regarding the assertion that his marriage to Ruby Hudd was dissolved validly in this country by the operation of the law of his religion, Mir-Anwaruddin was reminded that talaq was not tolerated by English courts because it was considered barbaric and inhuman. Mir-Anwaruddin argued that Ruby Hudd had acquired his domicile automatically upon marriage to him. He contended that he had always remained an Indian Muslim and had never acquired an English domicile. He argued that his personal law should apply to both him and Ruby Hudd. In his view, his talaq was valid in Islamic law so its legality could not be questioned by English law. The court rejected Mir-Anwaruddin's claims and severely criticised the way in which Ruby Hudd was divorced by talaq. In essence, Dr. Mir-Anwaruddin could neither validly enter a Muslim marriage in Britain, nor divorce his wife (see Darling J, at p. 650). Swinfen Eady LJ noted at p. 660:

That is the proposition which the appellant has sought to make good here, by power in pais, by writing under his hand, and without even the concurrence of the wife, without accord between them, at the mere will of the husband, to put her away, and then say that this English marriage is thereby dissolved. In my opinion it is quite impossible to maintain that argument.

Finally, Mir-Anwaruddin was warned that if he tried again to treat English law in a recalcitrant way he could be 'in grave peril' (p. 650). The comments of the courts are illustrative of a negative approach to other religions. The Court of Appeal chose to deal with the applicant's claim through the imposition of Christian beliefs rather than based on policy objections to a unilateral divorce process. The applicant was bluntly reminded, at p. 645, that he was living in a Christian country where a talaq was illegal because it was against the ethos of Christianity.

A similar approach was still taken some thirty years later in Maher v Maher [1951] 2 All ER 37, where the court refused to recognise the validity of a talaq pronounced by a Muslim husband over his English wife. Mr. Maher, domiciled in Egypt, married an English woman, Miss Kathleen Mary Collet, in a civil ceremony in Cambridge while he was studying there. After graduation he disappeared and later Mrs. Maher was divorced in Cairo at the Court of Personal Status. Judge Barnard, while admitting the right of divorce by way of talaq according to Egyptian customary law, refused to recognise the divorce because the wife had not been given prior notice. Since Mrs. Maher had acquired her husband's domicile on marriage, the court should have had no difficulty in recognising the validity of the divorce effected in Egypt in terms of private international law. Indeed, Judge Barnard admitted at p. 38:

> It must be borne in mind, however, that the declaration of divorce by the husband in accordance with the law of his religion is regarded as a valid divorce by the law of the domicile.

He also acknowledged at p. 38:

> It is the established rule of English law that domicile is the true test of divorce jurisdiction, and the courts of England will recognise as valid any divorce which is granted by the courts of the country where the parties are domiciled, even on a ground which is not a ground for a divorce in England.

Barnard J adopted the argument, submitted on behalf of Mrs. Maher, that recognition of such unilateral repudiation by an English court would be contrary to natural justice. He also stated that once a marriage was registered before a Registrar in compliance with English matrimonial law, that marriage could not be dissolved by operation of talaq, an approach approved in many subsequent cases. Judge Barnard seemed to be annoyed about the behaviour of foreigners, who came to the UK on a temporary basis, marrying local white Christian women merely for pleasure, and then divorcing them by way of talaq. He declared at p. 39:

> The marriage between the wife and the husband was a civil marriage pursuant to the Marriage Acts, 1811 to 1939, which laid down certain regulations for the contracting of monogamous marriages. It was a marriage in the Christian sense and cannot be dissolved by a method of divorce which is appropriate to a polygamous union. I, therefore, find that the marriage solemnised between the wife and the husband is a valid and subsisting marriage, the Mohammedan divorce being inappropriate to such a union. To hold otherwise would not only be contrary to the law as I understand it, but would both encourage and sanction the purely temporary unions of English women and foreigners professing the Mohammedan religion during their limited residence in this country.

The courts showed similar disregard for the values of those immigrants who had adopted an English domicile. In Radwan v Radwan [1972] 3 All ER 967, an Egyptian Muslim had married a Christian woman, Mary Isobel, at the Egyptian consulate in Paris in 1951 according to Islamic law. In 1956 he acquired a British domicile and settled permanently in England. In 1970, he obtained a talaq divorce at the Consulate General of the United Arab Republic in London, following a classical talaq procedure, proclamation before two witnesses, and a subsequent grant a divorce. Not satisfied with the Islamic talaq, Mrs. Radwan filed a petition for dissolution of marriage according to English law on the ground of her husband's cruelty. The case concerned the validity of proceedings conducted in the Consulate General of the Arab Republic. An affidavit of the Deputy Consul General of the Consulate General of the United Arab Republic of Egypt in London was produced. It stated inter alia:

- The Egyptian Consulate in London is regarded as being Egyptian territory on Egyptian soil; and

- The divorce obtained by the husband at the Consulate on 1 April 1970, and registered in Cairo on 8 April 1970, is valid and recognised by Egyptian law; and

- The steps taken by the husband in obtaining the divorce were the prescribed legal steps in such cases.

This position was supported by an expert in Egyptian law. Since the divorce occurred in a foreign country, argued Mr. Radwan, it should be recognised within the meaning of s. 2(a) of the Recognition of Divorces and Legal Separations Act, 1971. The judges had to seek legal advice from the Counsel for the Queen's Proctor but, following this opinion, the court refused Mr. Radwan's claim that the talaq obtained in the Consulate amounted to a divorce in a foreign country. Diplomatic premises were part of the territory of the receiving state and not of the sending state and therefore the decree of divorce obtained by the husband from the Consulate General of the United Arab Republic in London could not be recognised under the 1971 Act as it was not obtained by judicial or other proceedings in a country outside the British Isles.

Today it is evident that some ethnic minorities, especially Muslims, have for a long time assumed that they could continue their customary divorce practices in Britain. Muslims of Pakistani origin, while domiciled in England, attempted to divorce by following Islamic traditions or the requirements of the Muslim Family Laws Ordinance, 1961 of Pakistan. These procedures were invoked locally in a mosque, or before a solicitor or at the High Commission by making a proclamation of talaq. English judges were not prepared to accept such a talaq if it was proclaimed in Britain. In the Recognition of Divorces and Legal Separations Act, 1971, extended grounds for recognition of foreign divorces were introduced. This recognition was, however, dependent on the divorce being obtained by 'judicial or other proceedings'. A divorce obtained outside the British Isles by means of judicial or other proceedings would be regarded as valid only if it was obtained in a country where either spouse was habitually resident or domiciled or a national of that country. The term 'proceedings' was not defined. The Law Commission (Report No. 34, Cmnd. 4542, para 18) gave a generous interpretation to the effect that 'our courts recognise any divorce whatever the form, method or ground, provided that the court in the state of origin has jurisdiction in our eyes'. The courts were given an opportunity to decide that even a bare talaq constituted 'proceedings', thereby removing the distinction between those divorces obtained by proceedings and those not so obtained. Regrettably, the courts chose not to adopt such an interpretation, which would have favoured ethnic minorities. The opportunity arose in Quazi v Quazi [1979] 3 All ER 424 CA, where a divorce had been obtained in Pakistan under the Muslim Family Laws Ordinance, 1961. It was assumed that this Ordinance required the husband to send a written notice to the chairman of a local administrative body, the Union Council, who would put in motion arbitration procedures. This was not therefore a case of 'bare talaq'. The Court of Appeal held that the requirements of the Ordinance did not constitute proceedings under the 1971 Act because they did not require any decision or certificate to make the divorce effective. This was reversed by the House of Lords in Quazi v Quazi [1980] AC 744, where Lord Scarman suggested a more constructive approach to the 1971 Act, holding at p. 824:

> For these reasons I construe section 2 as applying to any divorce which has been obtained by means of any proceedings, i.e. any act or acts, officially recognised as leading to divorce in the country where the divorce was obtained and which itself is recognised by the law of the country as an effective divorce. Specifically, 'other proceedings' will include an act or sequence of acts other than a proceeding instituted in a court of law as, indeed, Parliament must have thought when enacting section 16 of the Domicile and Matrimonial Proceedings Act, 1973.

One problem remained, though, the 'bare talaq'. If it did not fall under 'proceedings', did proper proceedings necessarily require an arbiter, a hearing, an appearance by both parties, and notice to the respondent? Was there a minimum content of proceedings? Could a bare talaq be regarded as 'other proceedings' for the purposes of the Recognition of Divorces and Legal Separations Act, 1971? The speeches in the House of Lords showed sufficient diversity for later decisions to adopt different approaches. Sharif v Sharif (1980) 10 Fam Law 216 concluded that the provisions of ss. 2 to 5 of the 1971 Act could not apply to a bare talaq. In Zaal v Zaal and another [1983] 4 FLR 284, the courts used a sense of justice and public policy to refuse the validity of a talaq pronounced in Dubai. Here the wife, who was English, had married a Dubai national in Dubai under Muslim customary law and a child was born in July 1975.

The family lived in Dubai and visited England regularly. During a visit in 1978 the husband told the wife the marriage was over. On 10 June 1978, in Dubai, the husband pronounced a talaq whereby, according to the law of his country, residence and domicile, he effectively divorced the wife. Whilst recognising that the bare talaq was 'proceedings' for the purposes of the Recognition of Divorces and Legal Separations Act, 1971, the Court relied on s. 8 to refuse recognition of the talaq. The relevant part of section 8(2) states:

> Subject to subsection (1) of this section, recognition by virtue of this Act or of any rule preserved by section 6 thereof of the validity of a divorce or legal separation obtained outside the British Isles may be refused if, and only if –
>
> (a) it was obtained by one spouse –
>
> > (i) without such steps having been taken for giving notice of the proceedings to the other spouse as, having regard to the nature of the proceedings and all the circumstances, should reasonably have been taken; or
> >
> > (ii) without the other spouse having been given (for any reason other than lack of notice) such opportunity to take part in the proceedings as, having regard to the matters aforesaid, he should reasonably have been given; or
>
> (b) its recognition would manifestly be contrary to public policy.

Bush J stated in Zaal v Zaal, at p. 289:

> Is it then manifestly against public policy for an English court to give recognition to a bare talaq? It would not be right to lay down a general rule. I have to look at this bare talaq pronounced in the circumstances of this case and I have come to the conclusion that it would manifestly be contrary to public policy to recognise the divorce. I have come to this conclusion on the restricted ground that what was done, though properly done according to the husband's own customary laws, was done in secrecy so far as the wife was concerned. The first this wife knew of it the deed was done and she was divorced in fact and in law and it was irrevocable and binding according to the law of the husband's state. No opportunity was given to enlist the aid of her or the husband's relatives in repairing the breach.

Common justice requires that some notice other than a casual threat ought to be given for so solemn a proceeding. It is this that in this case offends one's sense of justice and jars upon the conscience and brings me to the conclusion... that to recognise this talaq divorce would be manifestly against public policy.

The court refused to recognise the talaq even though Bush J conceded (at p. 289) that the purpose of the 1971 Act was to enable the recognition of other countries' divorces. In Viswalingham v Viswalingham [1980] 1 FLR 15, a divorce obtained in Malaysia was held contrary to the 'ideas of substantial justice'.

The issue was resolved by the Court of Appeal in Chaudhary v Chaudhary [1984] 3 All ER 1017. The husband had travelled to Kashmir to declare a talaq against his wife who was in Britain at all material times. The Court of Appeal held that the marriage could not be ended by a bare talaq. It was held at pp. 1030-1031 that proceedings must 'import a degree of formality and at least the involvement of some agency....of or recognised by the state having a function that is more than simply probative.' In attacking the way a talaq was obtained, it was held at p. 1018:

In according recognition in the United Kingdom to overseas divorces 'obtained by judicial or other proceedings', s.2 (a) of the 1971 Act was not intended to give unlimited recognition to all foreign divorces obtained by any means whatsoever. In order to be recognised on the basis that it was obtained by 'other proceedings' a foreign divorce had to be obtained by means which entailed more than a mere unilateral or consensual act of either or both parties to the marriage, regardless of how formal or solemn the act was or what ritual or ceremony accompanied it.

The Law Commission in its 1984 report No 137 (Cmnd. 9341) at paragraph 6.11 recommended that the phrase 'judicial or other proceedings' should be extended to include any acts by which a divorce may be obtained in the country concerned. The effect would be that a bare talaq would be recognised. The proposal was, however, rejected by the government, Lord Hailsham commenting (House of Lords Debates, 1984 Hansard, Vol. 473, cols 1081-1082):

Such divorces are informal, arbitrary and usually unilateral. More importantly, there is often no available proof that what is alleged to have taken place has taken place at all. In addition, these divorces are almost exclusively obtained by men and therefore discriminate against women. Finally particularly where the wife is resident abroad, such divorces provide little or no financial protection.

As a result the Family Law Act, 1986 draws a distinction between overseas divorces obtained abroad by means of proceedings (s. 46(1)) and those divorces obtained other than by means of proceedings, i.e. bare talaqs (s. 46(2)). The latter are required to meet more stringent criteria.

Recognition of overseas divorces was also not extended to cases, classed as a 'transnational divorce', where only part of the proceedings took place in England and Wales. Thus, attempts by ethnic minority spouses resident in Britain to invoke customary procedures without having to return to Pakistan or other countries failed. Attempts to emulate the procedural provisions of the Muslim Family Laws Ordinance of 1961, which applies to Muslim citizens of Pakistan wherever they live, have not been legally recognised. For some time, the High Commissioner for Pakistan in London was required to perform the role of Chairman of an Arbitration Council, as provided by the 1961 Ordinance, which in effect treated Britain as a part of Pakistan. Not surprisingly, the English courts refused to recognise this process (see Qureshi v Qureshi [1971] 1 All ER 325 and Radwan v Radwan [1972] 3 All ER 967).

In R v Registrar General of Births, Deaths and Marriages and another, ex parte Minhas [1977] QB 1, the facts were that the husband had come to England in 1961 and had acquired British nationality while retaining Pakistani nationality. His wife refused to join him because she did not want to leave Pakistan. In February 1973, he issued a talaq in England against his wife, a copy was sent to her and a copy to the Chairman of the local Council in Pakistan. In so doing, the husband had tried to fulfil the requirements under s. 7 of the Muslim Family Laws Ordinance, 1961. Three months later, Mr. Minhas travelled to Pakistan and was granted a divorce by the Union Council after a hearing. He then returned to England in 1974 and tried to marry another Pakistani woman in Eccles. The Superintendent Registrar of Marriages refused to authorise this marriage, arguing that the husband's earlier divorce was not acceptable. Mr. Minhas moved for an order of mandamus directing the Registrar to issue a licence. It was argued by the Registrar that the alleged divorce did not occur completely in Pakistan, so that it would not fall within the meaning of ss. 2 and 3 of the Recognition of Divorces and Legal Separations Act, 1971. The former wife was at all material times a Pakistani national, so there could not be any barrier to recognising Minhas's divorce, however, it was refused by Park J in agreeing with Lord Widgery, emphasising that part of the proceedings had occurred in the British Isles.

In R v Secretary of State for the Home Department, ex parte Ghulam Fatima and R v Secretary of State for the Home Department, ex parte Shafeena Bi [1985] QB 190, Taylor J came to the conclusion that a Muslim divorce obtained before a solicitor (otherwise following the procedure laid down in the Muslim Family Laws Ordinance, 1961) by way of talaq would not be recognised as an overseas divorce, because the pronouncement of talaq occurred in Britain, while the divorce was ultimately obtained in Pakistan. The House of Lords in Re Fatima [1986] AC 527 HL, held that 'proceedings' meant a single set of proceedings which had to be instituted in the same country as that in which the divorce was ultimately obtained.

The re-enactment of the 1971 Act in the Family Law Act, 1986 resulted in a change of wording. Section 46(3)(a) of the 1986 Act requires one of the parties to be habitually resident or domiciled or a national of the overseas country at the date of the commencement of the proceedings and additionally specifies that the divorce must by s. 46(1)(a) be effective under the law of the country in which it was obtained. As such, where a husband is a national of Pakistan and pronounces a talaq in England which is 'obtained' in Pakistan, the talaq should now be recognised.

However, the option to adopt this interpretation, which would be sympathetic to the needs of ethnic minorities, seems to have been lost as a result of Berkovits v Grinberg [1995] Fam 142. In this case the husband and wife, who were both Israeli citizens, were married in Israel in 1975. Subsequently the husband became habitually resident and domiciled in England. In 1988 the husband, who wished to remarry, had a Jewish get written in England which was delivered to the wife in Israel. The dissolution of the marriage was effective under the law of Israel. The matter came to court after the Registrar General in England advised the husband that the divorce would not be recognised. The petitioner, Rabbi Bernard Berkovits, an ecclesiastical judge for the federation of Synagogues, brought the case as a test case for several other members of the Jewish faith in a similar predicament and petitioned the court for a declaration pursuant to s. 55 of the Family Law Act, 1986 that the get be recognised as a valid divorce obtained in Israel. Wall J rejected the claim of the petitioner and thus left the situation unresolved. This interpretation seems to go against the clear wording of the statute. The defects in Wall J's argument become apparent at p. 157:

> In my view the word 'obtained' connotes a process rather than a single act. To obtain a divorce a party must go through a process, in the same way that a person obtains a university degree or any other qualification. If that process is part of a judicial process (proceedings) and therefore linked to one judicial authority, it seems to me that there is logic and sense in saying that the proceedings must begin and end in the same place. Accordingly, the mere fact that the divorce is 'obtained' in the sense of 'finalised' or 'pronounced' in one country cannot in my judgment dissociate the process of 'obtaining' it from the proceedings in which it was obtained.

More fundamentally, Wall J dismissed the significant policy arguments against such an interpretation. This judgement had the effect of creating a 'limping marriage' and denying the possibility of ethnic minorities following their own divorce systems unless they were prepared to travel to the country of their nationality. Dealing with this point, it was stated at p. 160:

> I have also come to the conclusion that policy considerations such as those discussed here are properly a matter for Parliament and not for the courts. If, for example, there is a distinction to be drawn between a talaq and a get it is a distinction which Parliament must draw after the full public debate on all the questions of policy which arise. Accordingly, the question as to whether or not in an increasingly multiracial and multi-ethnic society the refusal to recognise the transnational divorce can or should continue is a matter for Parliament, and should not influence my interpretation of the statute. That interpretation must mean, as I have found, that the Israeli get in this case cannot be recognised and the petition must be dismissed.

This conclusion seems again at variance with previous comments where the judge accepted that the 'policy' in this area had been laid down in R v Secretary of State, ex parte Ghulam Fatima [1985] QB 190. The decision has little to commend it, it has 'far reaching implications for the Jewish community in the UK, and also for the Muslims and other communities' (Reed, 1996: 102). As noted, the decision creates a limping marriage, it favours the rich who can fly out to Pakistan or Israel and it leaves the wife in this case in an extremely vulnerable position. The opportunity to provide a pluralist perspective in this area of the law appears to have been lost, at least for the moment.

4.4.3 Marriage solemnisation

To be legally valid, a marriage solemnised in England and Wales must comply with the formalities and capacity requirements of the Marriage Acts, 1949-1996, otherwise it will be void under s. 11 Matrimonial Causes Act, 1973. Most members of ethnic minorities, and certainly not only Muslims, have sought to preserve customary patterns of marriage solemnisation, although the observance of customary rituals would not lead to recognition by English law. While ethnic minorities in Britain appear to consider this an area of law central to their cultural traditions, the English courts have been reluctant to recognise the validity of ethnic minority marriages celebrated in England which failed to comply with the requirements of the Marriage Acts.

A number of cases illustrate the legal problems which have arisen. In R v Bham [1965] 3 All ER 124, Mr. Bham had performed a marriage ceremony between a Muslim male, Mr. Seedat, and an English Christian woman in a private house in Gloucester. Mr. Seedat had gone to the local Registrar of Marriage to give notice of their intended marriage, but his application to have the marriage registered was refused. He then decided to marry according to Islamic law. Having obtained the consent of the girl's parents, the couple went to see Mr. Bham, who eventually solemnised their marriage in a private house. Mr. Bham also issued a marriage certificate purporting to confer the status of husband and wife on the couple under Islamic law. He was subsequently prosecuted and it was alleged that he had solemnised a marriage in violation of s. 39 of the Marriage Act, 1836.

The Court of Criminal Appeal quashed the conviction on the ground that the ceremony performed did not prima facie confer on the parties the status of husband and wife in English law; therefore it did not constitute solemnisation of marriage within the meaning of s. 75(2)(a) of the Marriage Act, 1949. Hence, in addition to not being recognised, this marriage was even denied the status of being void. The couple, in effect, were treated in English law as a couple who had merely cohabited and their efforts to go through any form of marriage ceremony were entirely disregarded by the legal system.

In R v Ali Mohammed, decided by Birmingham Assizes in March 1943 and cited in R v Kemp [1964] 1 All ER 649, a marriage was simply registered under Islamic law in violation of s. 39 of the Marriage Act, 1836, which was later replaced by s. 75 of the Marriage Act 1949. Humphrey J noted, as cited in R v Kemp [1964] 1 All ER 649 at pp. 653-54:

> In order to offend against this section... the solemnisation of matrimony must be at least the ceremony which prima facie will confer the status of husband and wife on those two persons – at least prima facie – and I cannot think that there is any evidence on which any jury could say that this religious ceremony, so performed on this occasion, had that effect or was intended to have that effect, or that anybody thought it could have that effect; and I cannot think that it would be right that any jury should convict the defendant of having solemnized a marriage in England when he has said some form of words to people... in my opinion the defendant has not been shown, and there is no evidence on which any jury could find that he has been shown, to have solemnised a marriage within the meaning of the Marriage Act, 1836.

In Rahman [1949] 2 All ER 165, Mohammed Hussain Mia, who was already a married man before he migrated to Britain, had attempted to marry Mary Jane Brown on 12 December 1947 according to Islamic law without a special licence and in a place other than a Church or Chapel. Mr. Rahman was prosecuted for solemnising a marriage without proper legal authority in violation of English marriage law. Neither Mr. Mia's marriage nor his alleged right to solemnise a marriage in Britain were recognised.

A more generous approach to the recognition of ethnic minority marriages has been taken in a recent case involving Coptic Orthodox Christians. In Gereis v Yagoub [1997] 1 FLR 854, a decree of nullity was obtained of a marriage which had been conducted in an unregistered church by a priest who was not authorised to solemnise marriages and where no notice had been given to the Superintendent Registrar and no certificate or licence to marry had been issued. The decision was based on the fact that the marriage bore all the hallmarks of a marriage recognisable to English law and to Christian values. Had the church been registered, there would of course have been no question about the validity of this marriage.

4.4 Accommodation

It would be wrong to conclude the chapter without recognising that both in case law and statute some attempt has been made to accommodate the value systems of ethnic minorities. For example, in Banik v Banik [1973] 3 All ER 45, Davies, Lawton and Stephenson LJJ were willing to consider whether a Hindu wife could claim that her divorce would cause 'grave hardship' within the meaning of s. 4 of the Divorce Reform Act, 1969. She pleaded, at pp. 47-48:

> The dissolution of the marriage will result in grave financial and other hardship to me in that my husband will be unable or unwilling to continue making maintenance payments to me. My husband knows and knew when he married me that I was a devout believer in the Hindu religion. A Hindu woman looks to the spiritual aspect of dying as a married woman rather than for any material benefit. A Hindu woman will be destitute as a divorcee. If I am divorced, I will, by virtue of the society in which we live and the social attitudes and conventions existing in it, become a social outcast. The dissolution of this marriage would result in grave financial and other hardship to me. I and other members of the community in which we live regard the divorce as anathema on religious and moral as well as social grounds. My husband knows the humiliation and degradation I will suffer spiritually and socially if the court grants a decree.

The respondent wife's request for consideration of her hardship in terms of her cultural values was sympathetically listened to by the court, even though in the ordinary hearing her pleas were, in the words of their Lordships, 'pooh-poohed' by Ormrod J. The case was remitted for rehearing by another judge to inquire into the alleged hardship raised by Mrs. Banik in her petition. Pending the hearing, an order for alimony of £12 a month was made.

In R v Bibi [1980] 1 WLR 1193, Mrs. Bibi, a Muslim widow aged 49, had been sentenced to three years in prison for taking part in drug smuggling. She had been sentenced despite her plea that she had had to act under the pressure of her brother-in-law. In the Appeal Court proceedings, the social inquiry report concerning Mrs. Bibi's cultural and family patterns was considered by way of judicial notice and it was revealed that her brother-in-law, with whom she lived after the death of her husband, had asked her to hide cannabis. Her cultural background was considered relevant in viewing the obligations she felt to her immediate relatives and household and her prison sentence was reduced to six months, the time she had already spent in prison. Lord Lane CJ commented, at pp. 1195-1196:

> It is apparent that she is well socialised into the Muslim traditions and as such has a role subservient to any male figures around her. Contact with society around is not encouraged and it is her role to remain within the house... Should the Begum Bibi be found guilty of these alleged offences she must undoubtedly find herself in a most serious position. Because she has assumed the traditional role of her culture any involvement in these offences is likely to be the result of being told what to do and the learned need to comply. Traditionally her role revolves completely around her home and as such she is probably unaware of a great deal of what is happening in society around her.

Lord Lane said further, at p. 1196:

> In the light of that history, it would not be safe to credit her with the same independence of mind and action as most women today enjoy. The effect of any term of imprisonment upon her, however short, would inevitably be traumatic, though she seems, it must be said, to have met the difficulties which she has in prison with a remarkable degree of stoicism or fatalism.

Much earlier, English law had also been willing to make limited allowances for the needs of ethnic minority communities. Jews and Quakers have been exempted from the general marriage formalities since Lord Hardwicke's Marriage Act of 1753. They can perform their marriage ceremonies at any time, day or night, not necessarily in a registered building for the purpose of registration of marriages. Catholics and non-conformist dissenters were after the Marriage Act of 1836 allowed solemnisation of marriages according to their traditions (see in detail Hamilton, 1995). Recent statutory provisions such as the Marriage (Registration of Buildings) Act 1990 provided that buildings used for community activities and religious education can be used for marriage solemnisation and the trend has continued in more recent changes to the relevant law. All of this has increased the opportunity for ethnic minority communities to perform marriage ceremonies in familiar surroundings which are considered appropriate.

The harshness of the restrictive precedent in R v Bham, and the consequent non-recognition by English law of any ethnic minority form of marriage solemnisation in England itself, is partly alleviated by s. 1(1) of the Legitimacy Act, 1976 which confers legitimacy on children born in families where the parties did not validly solemnise their marriages according to the Marriage Acts.

In non-matrimonial matters, Sikhs appear to be the main beneficiaries of the accommodation that English law has made to the presence of various ethnic minorities. Sikh claims for the right to wear turbans have been recognised to a limited extent by Mandla v Dowell Lee (see chapter 3 above). Section 6 of the Motor-Cycle Crash Helmets (Religious Exemption) Act, 1976 states that s. 32(3) of the Road Traffic Act, 1972 shall not apply to Sikh motorcyclists, provided they are wearing turbans while riding motorcycles. This approach is reaffirmed by s. 16(2) of the Criminal Justice Act, 1988 under which Sikhs are now allowed to carry knives and daggers (kirpans) in public places for religious purposes. Earlier, the carrying of offensive weapons in public places without lawful authority or reasonable excuse was prohibited under the Prevention of Crime Act, 1953.

Muslims and Jews have benefited from limited legislative recognition of their religious needs regarding halal and kosher meat. The Slaughter of Poultry Act, 1967 and the Slaughterhouses Act, 1974 recognised the right of Muslims and Jews to slaughter animals according to their religious practices without stunning them first. Section 53(1) of the Shops Act, 1959 allowed Jewish traders to close their shops on Saturday, the Sabbath, provided they are open on Sunday.

Parental rights to withdraw children from sex education have now been recognised by new provisions in education law. Parents are not required to show cause as to why they want to withdraw their children from sex education (see Harris, 1995: 201). From the perspective of many ethnic minority parents, these are constructive steps because many parents think that sex education in schools, as well as multi-religious education, might be corrupting and harmful to their children's upbringing. Such concerns reflect a certain extent of self-segregation on the part of ethnic minority communities (see Ballard, 1994: 1-34) and shows that the legal system has been under constant pressure, for a very long time (see in detail Hamilton, 1995) to make allowances for particular ethnic minority needs.

Despite some glimpses of pluralist recognition, however, the English judiciary as well as Parliament appear to be imprisoned within ideologies which hinder the development of a comprehensive pluralistic legal system. We suggest that traditional restrictive thinking about family law issues should be reshaped, allowing the law to respect the cultures and personal laws of ethnic minorities to a larger extent. This may help to promote a more multi-cultural 'living law' which reflects the increasingly plural society of modern Britain more closely. At present, it seems, we are nowhere near a satisfactory situation.

Chapter 5

Parents and children

Family membership, functions and dynamics vary between different cultures and systems (Anwar, 1979: 50-57). Extended family systems predominate in Asia and Africa, and are quite different from the traditional West Indian family with strong ties through the female line and the British nuclear family of two parents and child(ren), a model itself changing towards the one-parent family. The weight and importance attached to the role and rights of children, and assumptions about appropriate standards of parenting, also vary between cultures, so provide a challenge for the domestic legal regimes that apply to parents and children from ethnic minorities in the UK today.

Family law should provide adjustive, protective and supportive functions (Eekelaar, 1984: 25). The law should be adjustive when deciding disputes between parents, and between parents and others, adjudicating on where a child should reside when parents separate, what control may be exercised over the child and by whom. Protective functions are mainly concerned with vulnerable family members. Supportive functions would include encouraging the continuity of relationships between adults and ensuring that responsibilities of the parent(s) to the child(ren) are fulfilled.

Courts tend to adopt dominant cultural views of childhood and of acceptable or unacceptable forms of parenting and welfare. Difficulties occur where the dominant cultural view is different from that of a particular minority. For example, support for the rights of the child may be inappropriate in a culture where the role of the parents or elders continues irrespective of the age of the child. The existence of different cultural views about parenting may create difficulties when certain practices are called into question.

In Australia, one role of the law is now seen as being to encourage the maintenance of cultural heritage within the context of the domestic law. The Australian Council on Multicultural Affairs has stated that all Australians 'should be free to develop, adapt and express elements of their individual cultural heritage within the unifying framework of a commitment to Australia, its law and institutions' (cited in Bates, 1992: 217). In this chapter, we consider to what degree English law has been successful in balancing the conflicting requirements of uniformity and plurality while providing an environment in which children from various ethnic minority cultures can flourish within the context of a national legal system. Before considering the approaches adopted by the courts, we provide a brief review of the basic principles of English child law relating to the welfare, placement and upbringing of children.

5.1 Child law concepts

The most important statute in this field is now the Children Act, 1989. The dynamics of the parent-child relationship centre around the concepts of parental rights and responsibility and the state's role in protecting vulnerable children by prescribing standards of parenting. The overriding criterion is that all decisions should be based on the child's best interests, the so-called 'welfare principle'.

The 1989 Act introduced comprehensive, radical reforms of the law affecting children, reforming both private and public law. In private law, the concept of parental rights was replaced with the concept of parental responsibility. Orders for custody and access are completely abolished and were replaced by residence and contact orders. Parenthood and guardianship are fully separated, the position of unmarried fathers is improved, as is the position of relatives and other non-parents. Custodianship, an idea to provide parenting between fostering and adoption, is abolished and is replaced with simplified procedures for obtaining access to the courts and to the new range of orders.

While the 'welfare principle' has long been a key concept of English child law; its role has been further strengthened. Where a court is considering the upbringing of a child or the administration of a child's property, the child's welfare is the court's paramount consideration. Decisions of carers and those with parental responsibility are judged as to whether they are in the child's best interests.

Section 1 of the Children Act, 1989 provided a new 'welfare principle', replacing s. 1 of the Guardianship of Minors Act, 1971. It reads:

1. Welfare of the child

   (1) When a court determines any question with respect to —

      (a) the upbringing of a child; or

      (b) the administration of a child's property or the application of any income arising from it, the child's welfare shall be the court's paramount consideration.

This is a linguistic change from the 'first and paramount' terminology of the 1971 Act. The statute now reflects the interpretation of the House of Lords in J v C [1970] AC 668. The new wording means that the welfare of the child should come before and above any other consideration in deciding whether to make an order (Lord MacKay LC, Hansard, HL, Vol. 502, 1990, col. 1167).

Of itself, the above section only provides a broad, undefined approach to the meaning of a child's best interest. Lack of specific guidelines in the previous legislation meant that decisions were subjective and arbitrary. The term 'best interests' is at best indeterminate (Mnookin, 1975) and at worst deeply ambiguous (Skolnik, 1975). The decision to provide guidelines was eventually rejected by the Law Commission (Working Paper 96, paras 6.34-6.39) and instead courts were provided with a list of matters which they should consider, with no indication of weight or importance attached to specific matters. The list is now found in s.1(3) of the Children Act, 1989. It aims to guide the courts and to achieve consistency across the country, as well as informing legal advisers and helping the parties to concentrate on the issues that affect the children. It states:

   (3) In the circumstances mentioned in subsection (4), a court shall have regard in particular to—

      (a) the ascertainable wishes and feelings of the child concerned (considered in the light of his age and understanding);

      (b) his physical, emotional and educational needs;

      (c) the likely effect on him of any change in his circumstances;

      (d) his age, sex, background and any characteristics of his which the court considers relevant;

(e) any harm which he has suffered or is at risk of suffering;

(f) how capable each of his parents, and any other person in relation to whom the court considers the question to be relevant, is of meeting his needs;

(g) the range of powers available to the court under this Act in the proceedings in question.

This checklist includes in (d) the potential to consider a child's ethnic background. We will return to that provision. Section 1(2) provides in addition that in any proceedings with respect to the upbringing of a child, the court shall have regard to the general principle that any delay in determining the question is likely to prejudice the welfare of the child. Further, in s. 1(5) a non-intervention principle is introduced, whereby if a court is considering whether or not to make one or more orders under the Children Act of 1989, the court shall not make any such order(s) unless it considers that doing so would be better for the child than making no order at all.

5.2 Child rights and parental responsibility

The common law rights of parents derive from their duties to the children. Parental rights exist to enable parents to perform their duties more effectively, and partly as a recompense for the faithful discharge of their duties towards the children. Such basic concepts were earlier interpreted to give the father an absolute discretion in deciding how best to fulfil his duty, illustrated in the infamous case of Re Agar-Ellis 10 ChD 49; 24 ChD 317, where a father was able to remove a young child from its mother even where the child was still being breast-fed. It was assumed that the father was always operating in the child's best interests. As Maidment (1984: 5) comments, '[a]s a general rule judges took the welfare of the child to lie with upholding the father's position in the patriarchal family'.

By the late 19th century this absolute view of rights was being questioned. The common law, under the wardship jurisdiction, began to question the views of fathers and now sought to determine whether a father was really acting in the best interests of the child according to an objective view of the child's interests. Thus, Lord Scarman said in Gillick v Norfolk Area Health Authority [1986] 1 FLR 224, at p. 249, that '...the parental right must be exercised in accordance with the welfare principle and can be challenged, even overridden, if it not be'. A similar view was already expressed by Kay LJ in R v Gyngall [1893] 2 QB 232, at p. 248.

Parental rights, then, exist only to further the interests of the child. There will come a time when the child will itself be able to decide what is in its own best interests. That age was originally set at 16 years by statute and was accepted to apply in other areas by Cockburn CJ in R v Howes (1860) 1 E&E 332, at pp. 336-337:

> We repudiate utterly, as most dangerous, the notion that any intellectual precocity in an individual female child can hasten the period which appears to have been fixed by statute for the arrival at the age of discretion; for that very precocity, if uncontrolled, might very probably lead to her irreparable injury. The legislature has given us a guide, which we may safely follow, in pointing out 16 as the age up to which the father's right to custody of his female child is to continue; and short of which such a child has no discretion to consent to leaving him.

More recently the Court of Appeal accepted the decline in parental rights in relation to the age of the child in Hewer v Bryant [1970] QB 357, where Lord Denning MR stated at p. 369:

> The legal right of a parent to the custody of a child ends at the 18th birthday; and even up till then, it is a dwindling right which the courts will hesitate to enforce against the wishes of the child, and the more so the older he is. It starts with a right of control and ends with little more than advice.

The difficulty caused by this rather vague summary of the law was highlighted by several writers (Hall, 1972; Maidment, 1981; Dickens, 1981; Eekelaar, 1984). The exact scope of rights of parental responsibility relating to the rights of the child was then discussed in Gillick v West Norfolk and Wisbech Area Health Authority [1986] 1 FLR 224. In 1974 the DHSS issued a Memorandum of Guidance on the family planning service in relation to giving advice on contraception, the medical examination of persons seeking advice, the treatment of such persons and the supply of contraceptives and appliances. Section G of the Memorandum related to children under 16 and, as amended in 1980, stated that special care was needed not to undermine parental authority; that it was hoped that a doctor or other professional worker would always seek to persuade the child to involve the parent and would proceed from the assumption that it would be most unusual to provide advice about contraception without parental consent; that it was widely accepted that consultations between doctors and patients were confidential; that some parents were unconcerned, entirely unresponsive, or grossly disturbed, and that in such exceptional cases the decision whether or not to provide contraception was for the clinical judgement of the doctor. Mrs. Gillick, a mother of five daughters, wrote to her local health authority seeking an assurance that they would not give contraceptive or abortion treatment to her daughters without her knowledge and consent. The plaintiff's aim in bringing the action was to establish the extent of parental rights and duties in respect of girls under 16. Lord Fraser stated, at p. 236:

> My Lords, I have, with the utmost respect, reached a different conclusion from that of the Lord Justice. It is, in my view, contrary to the ordinary experience of mankind, at least in Western Europe in the present century, to say that a child or a young person remains in fact under the complete control of his parents until he attains the definite age of majority, now 18 in the United Kingdom, and that on attaining that age he suddenly acquires independence. In practice most wise parents relax their control gradually as the child develops and encourage him or her to become increasingly independent... Moreover, the degree of parental control actually exercised over a particular child does in practice vary considerably according to his understanding and intelligence and it would, in my opinion, be unrealistic for the courts not to recognise these facts. Social customs change, and the law ought to, and does in fact, have regard to such changes when they are of major importance. An example of such recognition is to be found in the view recently expressed in your Lordships' House by my noble and learned friend Lord Brandon of Oakbrook, with whom the other noble and learned Lords who were present agreed, in Regina v D [1984] FLR 847, 858C. Dealing with the question of whether the consent of a child to being taken away by a stranger would be a good defence to a charge of kidnapping, my noble and learned friend said:

>> In the case of a very young child, it would not have the understanding or the intelligence to give its consent, so that absence of consent would be a necessary inference from its age. In the case

of an older child, however, it must, I think be a question of fact for a jury whether the child concerned has sufficient understanding and intelligence to give its consent; if, but only if, the jury considers that a child has these qualities, it must then go on to consider whether it has been proved that the child did not give its consent. While the matter will always be for the jury alone to decide, I should not expect a jury to find at all frequently that a child under 14 had sufficient understanding and intelligence to give its consent.

Lord Scarman summarised the matter at p. 251:

The underlying principle of the law was exposed by Blackstone and can be seen to have been acknowledged in the case law. It is that parental right yields to the child's right to make his own decisions when he reaches a sufficient understanding and intelligence to be capable of making up his own mind on the matter requiring decision.

We saw that the Children Act of 1989 introduced the concept of parental responsibility. Previous legislation, for example ss. 85 and 86 of the Children Act, 1975 and ss. 2, 3 and 4 of the Child Care Act, 1980 referred to 'parental rights and duties'. The use of the term 'parental responsibility' is an attempt to give statutory recognition to the change in emphasis from 'rights' to 'responsibilities', evident in the case law (see Hewer v Bryant above). Section 3(1) of the Children Act, 1989 now defines parental responsibility as 'all the rights, duties, powers, responsibilities and authority which by law a parent of a child has in relation to the child and his property'.

The search for a comprehensive list has produced only limited agreement. The lack of clarity in the Children Act, 1989 about parental rights and duties, caused by throwing parents and advisers back on the common law, is unsatisfactory. The position both before and after the Act has been highlighted by writers and law reform agencies (see Hall, 1972; Eekelaar, 1984; Maidment, 1981; Dickens, 1981; the Scottish Law Commission's Report on Family Law No. 135 (1992), para 2.18; see also s. 2 of the Children (Scotland) Act, 1995).

This new form of parental responsibility is conferred automatically on the mother of a child irrespective of her marital status. Whether the father also has parental responsibility depends on whether he was married to the mother at the time of the child's birth. A father who was married to the mother will have parental responsibility under s. 2(1) of the Children Act, 1989. A father not so married does not acquire parental responsibility automatically but has various options whereby he can acquire such responsibility, under either s. 4, s. 5, or s. 12 of the Children Act, 1989. It appears that in the debates about such issues, ethnic minority status has not played a significant role as a relevant criterion so far.

5.3 The role of the state

In addition to its adjustive and supportive roles, the law provides protection for vulnerable family members. Public opinion is regularly appalled by the death of an innocent child at the hands of an abusive parent, but also by the removal of a child from its family. This dilemma is dealt with by providing a sufficiently robust system to protect children who are considered vulnerable, whilst respecting the rights of individual family members, whether parents or children.

The White Paper on the law of child care and family services (1987, Cmnd. 62, ch. 2) proposed a unification of child care law and health and welfare provisions. The main principles upon which reform of the law was based can be summarised as being:

- the prime responsibility for the upbringing of children rests with parents;

- services to families in need of help should be arranged in a voluntary partnership with the parents;

- the transfer to the local authority of parents' legal powers and responsibilities for caring for a child should only be done by a full court hearing following due legal process;

- court processes affecting the child must recognise that, although the interests of the child are the primary concern, the parents' legal rights in relation to the child are also in issue;

- the application of emergency powers to remove a child at serious risk, which necessarily cannot be preceded by a full court hearing, should be of short duration and subject to court review; and

- where local authorities are caring for a child away from home their legal responsibility for the child should be clear.

The Children Act, 1989 repeals the grounds for compulsory care previously scattered between numerous statutes, including the Children and Young Persons Act, 1969 and the Child Care Act of 1980, replacing them with a single composite ground for care and supervision orders. The grounds are simplified, streamlined and extended. A court may now only make a care order (placing the child with respect to whom the application is made in the care of a designated local authority) or supervision order (putting them under the supervision of a designated local authority or a probation officer) if it is satisfied, as provided in s. 31(2) of the Children Act, 1989:

(a) that the child concerned is suffering or likely to suffer significant harm

and;

(b) that the harm or likelihood of harm is attributable to –

   (i) the care given to the child, or likely to be given to him if the order were not made, not being what it would be reasonable to expect a parent to give to him; or

   (ii) the child's being beyond parental control.

Both grounds (a) and (b) have to be satisfied to obtain a care order. In deciding which order to make, the court will then consider what approach is in the best interests of the child. The new composite ground to be satisfied for both of the above orders is an attempt to strike a balance between the need for state intervention and non-intervention. The key to the condition is the requirement of 'significant harm', later defined in s. 31(9) as being ill-treatment or the impairment of health or development. 'Health' is defined as physical or mental health, 'development' relates to physical, intellectual, emotional, social or behavioural development (see F v Suffolk County Council (1981) 2 Fam Law 208). Ill-treatment is defined as including sexual abuse and forms of ill-treatment which are not physical.

This ground is often described as the 'threshold criterion'. The threshold where the court may intervene by making a care order is the point at which the child is suffering or is likely to suffer 'significant harm' (s. 31(9) Children Act, 1989). This ground is qualified in s. 31(2), as cited above. As with the care proceedings under previous legislation, the applicants are restricted to any local authority or authorised person. An authorised person should consult with the local authority before making an application (s. 31(6)). Applications by the police, previously available under the offence condition, are now not allowed under this section.

The key issue, then, is one of degree: the harm needs to be 'significant'. This is further explained in s. 31(10) of the Children Act, 1989 which provides that, '[w]here the question of whether harm suffered by a child is significant turns on the child's health or development, his health or development shall be compared with that which could reasonably be expected of a similar child'.

There are no longer any alternative routes by which a local authority may acquire the care of a child: Criminal courts and the High Court in wardship are no longer free to make care orders. Care orders will automatically contain provisions allowing the child reasonable contact with parents and guardians. Local authorities are under a duty to endeavour to promote contact between children looked after by them and a wide range of family members and friends (Children Act, 1989, Sch. 2, para 15). Part IV also states the principles applicable to supervision orders and creates new 'education supervision orders' to deal with poor school attendees. In addition, the Act provides increased opportunities for participation in emergency and care proceedings. 'Place of safety orders' are replaced by 'emergency protection orders'. These last for eight days, can be extended for a further seven days, and are subject to review after 72 hours. Where an emergency protection order appears too draconian, but the court considers that enquiries into the welfare of the child are necessary, the half-way house of 'child assessment orders' is now available.

5.4 Child law and ethnic minorities

How far has English child law met the challenge to adopt pluralistic principles that allow ethnic minority customs to flourish and to operate alongside dominant customs and values? Or is this an impossible task?

It can be argued that the Children Act of 1989 is committed to cultural pluralism. It contains several references to the need to maintain, wherever possible, the child's religious, cultural or ethnic background. We already cited s. 1(3)(d) of the 1989 Act, according to which a court shall have regard in particular to a child's 'age, sex, background and any characteristics of his which the court considers relevant'. Other aspects relevant to the present discussion are indicated in s. 22(5)(c) of the 1989 Act, which states that when a local authority is making any decision in relation to a child, it shall give due consideration 'to the child's religious persuasion, racial origin and cultural and linguistic background'.

The guidance on interpretation of this section explains that this provision should be taken to mean that normally children should be placed with the same ethnic group. The departmental guidance on the Children Act (found in Guidance and Regulations, Vol 3, Family Placements, para 2.40-42) states:

> A child's ethnic origin, cultural background and religion are important factors for consideration. It may be taken as a guiding principle of good practice that, other things being equal, and in a great majority of cases, placement with a family of similar ethnic origin and religion is most likely to meet a child's needs as fully as possible and to safeguard his or her welfare most effectively.

As we saw, under s. 31(10), in deciding whether the harm suffered by a child is significant, the child's health and development shall be compared to the health and development of a similar child. This could be assumed to include cultural and ethnic similarities. However during the Parliamentary debates the Lord Chancellor stated only that 'similar' was to include physical, mental and emotional characteristics (Hansard, HL, Vol. 503, 1990, col. 354) but the Guidance (Vol. 1, para. 320) advises also to consider cultural background. According to s. 33(6)(a) of the 1989 Act, while a care order is in force with respect to a child, the local authority designated by the order shall not 'cause the child to be brought up in any religious persuasion other than that in which he would have been brought up if the order had not been made' (see also Children Home Regulations, SI 1991 No 1506, and Foster Placement (Children Regulations), SI 1991 No. 910, reg. 5(2)).

Other sections indirectly require consideration of a child's cultural background. In s. 1(3)(b) a child's needs and, as already indicated, in s. 1(3)(d) a child's background, are matters to be considered in determining what actions are in a child's best interests.

5.4.1 The meaning of 'best interests'

It is widely acknowledged that this concept, now found in s.1 of the Children Act of 1989, is at best indeterminate and at worst deeply ambiguous. Authoritative guidance on the earlier welfare principle was given by Lord McDermott in the House of Lords (see J v C [1970] AC 668). The case concerned the dispute over custody of a child born in 1958 to Spanish parents. At the time of the House of Lords hearing the boy was ten and a half years old and was living with English foster parents. He had not seen his parents for seven years and had only spent 27 months away from his foster parents. Lord McDermott, while dismissing the proposition that the welfare principle only applied to disputes between parents, stated at p. 710, interpreting the phrase 'first and paramount consideration':

> I think they [the words] connote a process whereby when all the relevant facts, relationships, claims and wishes of parents, risks, choices and other circumstances are taken into account and weighed, the course to be followed will be that which is most in the interests of the child's welfare as that term has now to be understood. That is the first consideration because it is of first importance and the paramount consideration because it rules on or determines the course to be followed.

Their Lordships, dismissing the appeal of the parents, decided that the boy should remain with the English foster parents. Plunging a child into what was for him now a foreign culture and country would, it was thought, injure the child's health and development. The phrase 'has now to be understood' is taken to mean how the English courts understand a child's welfare. They will consider the child's best interests in the light of common values of the majority, values that may therefore not be shared by ethnic minority cultures. In the above case the dominant culture favoured stability over the child's need to be brought up within his own culture. This reflects an absence of due consideration of cultural pluralism. As Brenan J commented in Secretary, Department of Health and Community Services v JMB and SMB, FLC 92-93 at 79, 191 [1992]: 'In the absence of legal rules or a hierarchy of values the best interests approach depends upon the value system of the decision maker'. The process was described by Balcombe J in C v C [1991] 1 FLR 223 at p. 230:

> In my judgement, he should start on the basis that the moral standards which are generally accepted in the society in which the child lives are more likely than not to promote his or her welfare. As society is

now less homogeneous than it was 100 or even 50 years ago, those standards may differ between different communities, and the judge may in appropriate cases be invited to receive evidence as to the standards accepted in a particular community, but in default of such evidence and where, as here, the child does not come from a particular ethnic minority, the judge is entitled, and indeed bound, to apply his or her own experience in determining what are the accepted standards (emphasis added).

This approach is by no means clear. If a child comes from an ethnic minority, is the judge to receive evidence of the standards of that community and ignore the standards of the dominant culture? Or should judges consider the standards of the ethnic minority community and then relate this to dominant standards? How is a judge to deal with any conflict between such standards? The following cases indicate that the value system of the dominant culture tends to prevail over the views of the minority culture. In Re A [1987] 2 FLR 429, Swinton Thomas J said at p. 437:

> In coming to a conclusion in this case, I must be guided by the provisions of s. 1 of the Guardianship of Minors Act 1971. It is of vital importance for all the parties, but particularly perhaps for the grandmother, who may find it difficult to accept, that, under the English law, the welfare of M must be the first and the paramount consideration.

In effect the criterion of the dominant culture, the paramount consideration of the child's welfare, is often adopted without recognition of alternative approaches. In this case the view of the grandmother was that the wishes of parents and others should be more important than the child's interests, but this was clearly not accepted.

The Children Act, 1989 gives more specific guidance to the meaning of welfare in an attempt to replace the 'rules of thumb' developed in a common sense approach to welfare. Courts are directed to the welfare checklist in s. 1(3) of the 1989 Act when considering cases that fall within s.1(4). The checklist derives from case law developed under the welfare principle and reflects English values, emphasising the child's wishes and needs apart from the importance of stability and continuity in relationships with persons whom the child considers to be the parent, in other words, the psychological parents rather than the biological parents. This shows a marked shift from upholding the predominant position of the father and the natal family in the child's life towards recognising theories of child development. Those most influential in promoting these shifts were John Bowlby (1969, 1972, 1980) whose work on attachment and separation dominated a whole generation, and Goldstein, Freud and Solnit (1979) who argued that children need to remain with their psychological parent and be free from conflict and inconsistent parenting.

The checklist under the 1989 Act serves to reinforce the dominant value system and thereby suppresses the values of ethnic minorities. The court is directed by s.1(3)(a) to consider the ascertainable wishes and feelings of the child concerned, in the light of the child's age and understanding. In addition, the 1989 Act contains provisions about seeking the views of the child and specifically grants the child a right to refuse medical examination or treatment. The importance given to the child's wishes is clearly reflective of a modern, Western view of the parent-child relationship which is also evident in Article 12(1) of the Convention on the Rights of the Child, 1989 which states that:

> States Parties shall assure to the child who is capable of forming his or her own views the right to express those views freely in all matters affecting the child, the views of the child being given due weight in accordance with the age and maturity of the child.

English law confines the parental right to circumstances where it is consistent with the child's best interest. The decision of the House of Lords in Gillick effectively reduces further the rights of parents, thus allowing a child, if competent, to make important decisions. This view of the rights of parents, children and courts may differ significantly from the views of ethnic minority parents. Goonesekere (1994) examines the interaction of parents and children in South Asia. She concludes that both Islamic and Hindu law mirror a concept of strong parental rights, similar to that evidenced in English common law. This is still true in many South Asian countries today. For example in Sri Lanka, child interests are still identified with the parental rights of the father or mother unless the parents are declared unfit by the court.

Before examining difficulties created by the differing perspectives, it is instructive to consider how English law has continued to develop after Gillick. We see that case law since Gillick appears to have retreated from the position that the children's views should be determinative. Courts have consistently overruled the wishes of a child if they consider the child not to be acting in its own interests. This is consistent with Gillick, if through age or incapacity the child is not competent to know its best interest, but in a series of cases which indicate a retreat from the position taken in Gillick, the courts have overruled the views of competent children.

This degree of control by the court is well-illustrated in the recent case of Sarah Cook (see Jones and Welhengama, 1996), where a girl who clearly expressed her wish to adopt another culture with the consent of her parents, found that the court was prepared to ignore the views of parents and child while imposing cultural norms. The court found itself in a difficult realm of the law, concerning this thirteen year old Essex school girl who, with her parents' blessing, or at least not their disapproval, had entered into a 'marriage' with an eighteen year old Turkish waiter in Turkey. Sir Stephen Brown, President of the Family Division, at the request of Essex County Council's Social Services Department, declared her a ward of court and ordered her return to England. As the case progressed, the tone of the court became more conciliatory. Sarah became a minor celebrity after the imprisonment of the young man in Turkey on charges of statutory rape. Claiming that she was bullied at school and felt ugly in England, in Turkey she acquired the status of the 'nation's daughter-in-law' and 'bride of the city'. After several weeks of undignified wrangling, Sarah was persuaded to return to England. Her return, she claimed, was prompted by a wish to save her parents from possible imprisonment.

The determination of the child's best interest in this case appeared to be based on a number of assumptions reflecting the court's value system. Sarah Cook, a minor white girl, wished to become a Muslim and live with her young husband in his country. Was it appropriate to apply the standards of the society in which this girl was raised or should an alternative approach be considered? How does English law deal with a marriage that may cut across communities and cultures? A marriage contracted in England is void if either party has not reached the age of 16 years. A foreign marriage involving a party under the age of 16 where either or both parties were domiciled in England would similarly be void, even if valid by the lex loci celebrationis of the lex domicilii of one of the spouses (Pugh v Pugh [1951] P 482). Arguments to make marriages of persons under 16 voidable rather than void were rejected by the Law Commission (Report on Nullity of Marriage, Law Comm. No. 33, paras 16-20). However child marriages entered into outside the jurisdiction will be recognised as valid, provided both parties have the necessary capacity to enter into such a marriage by the law of their domicile and the marriage does not seriously offend the conscience of the English court (Cheni v Cheni [1965] P 85 and Mohamed v Knott [1969] QB 1).

We have no difficulty in supporting the decision to invalidate a marriage on the grounds of one party's legal incapacity. Difficulties are caused by the implicit assumption that such a marriage is contrary to the child's welfare. Child marriages may be considered contrary to the interests of children as generally accepted in English society, but should such a view apply to a child who considers herself Muslim and clearly expresses the view that she desires to marry a particular foreign man? The ability to move between communities and cultures is accepted in cases where the child has been immersed in different cultures, but should this be the only way in which the child's dominant culture is deemed to change? Could not the child's express wishes enable the court to approach the case from an alternative perspective? Clearly the criteria listed in s.1(3) of the Children Act, 1989 require the court to take into account the wishes and feelings of the child. In addition the UN Convention on the Rights of the Child gives the child a right to freedom of thought, conscience and religion (Article 14) subject to appropriate parental guidance and national law.

The view of the English courts appears to be that as part of a number of factors the child's view cannot dominate. Wall J stated in B v B [1994] 2 FLR 489, at p. 498:

> His [counsel's] principal point, however, is that the judge elevated the single factor of the children's ascertainable wishes and feelings to paramountcy and made it determinative of the issue of care and control. That, says Mr. Forde, was an error of principle which vitiates the exercise of the judge's discretion, the more so because the wishes of the children were not in fact ascertainable; furthermore, to 'divine' the children's wishes and feelings from a few phrases contained in a court welfare officer's report more than one year old which itself does not make the children's wishes and feelings at all clear compounds the error. The judge's erroneous emphasis on a single aspect

of the 'checklist' under s 1(3)(a), submits Mr. Forde, meant that he did not consider the other aspects of s 1(3), all of which fell to be considered on the facts of the case.

In the Sarah Cook case the discussion ignored the cultural elements of the case, and the views of the child and her parents were completely disregarded. She had articulated her dislike for her life in England and her willingness to accept the community in Turkey. In that case the court had little discretion since the marriage was invalid. The child's welfare would normally suggest her return. We submit that judicial discretion should be exercised by considering the views of the parents and the child, and if such views as relate to cultural identity are considered valid within the context of the child's age and understanding, then the court should adopt those cultural norms in the application of the welfare principle.

The current trend in English child law appears to be not to adopt these cultural norms but to impose the dominant value system. In deciding a child's best interests, the courts will try to do so 'objectively' and will be guided, but not bound, by the wishes of the child. The views of the parents will only be of indirect relevance in that they may be best placed to meet the child's physical, emotional and educational needs (s.1(3)(b)). The effect is to replace the views of the parent(s) as to best interest with that of the court, in the process ignoring and showing little respect for ethnic minority cultures. We would not wish to question this in cases where cultural arguments continue to be used to justify the denial of children's rights, for example regarding female circumcision, now specifically prohibited by the Prohibition of Female Circumcision Act, 1985 (for details see Akers, 1994), or the non-education of lower classes and castes, or girls (Alston, 1994). What we do question, however, is imposition of the court's dominant value system, as reinforced through the checklist.

The willingness of the courts to impose their own view is particularly striking in cases involving the medical treatment of children. In Re O [1993] 2 FLR 149 the court was asked to authorise blood transfusions in a case where the parents refused their consent because of their religious beliefs as Jehovah's Witnesses. Johnson J in exercising the court's jurisdiction to authorise the transfusions commented at p. 155:

> Moreover when the State, in the form here of the legal system, is asked to override the views of parents such as those in the present case, then the system should ensure that so far as judicial ingenuity

can ensure, justice is seen, and felt, to be done. If nothing more, it is because of the gravity, every bit as much as the difficulty and sometimes complexity of the issues, that the parents are entitled to look for a decision to the High Court of Justice.

The parents wanted their view to be considered and weighed in an objective fashion. Thorp J explained their position at p. 150:

> J's parents are members of the sect known as Jehovah's Witnesses. The parents are devout believers in that faith. They are also deeply committed and loving parents. They want whatever is best for J. They do not want J to die but, for them, physical death is not the end of life and in considering what is best for J they are torn, desperately, between their passionate desire to preserve J's earthly life whilst at the same time wanting to avoid causing her the damage in her greater life that, in their sincere view, would come to her were she to be transfused with blood or blood products. Their dilemma is awesome.

The decision reflects the value basis of the Christian religion, as the parents' wishes appear to have no effect on the court's decision. The court, ostensibly acting as a reasonable parent, would allow the blood transfusion, but in relying on the concept of a reasonable parent is merely replacing one indeterminate proposition for another. The same dilemma arose in American cases. In the case of Prince v Massachusetts (1944) 321 US Reports 158, Justice Holmes said:

> Parents may be free to become martyrs themselves, but it does not follow that they are free in identical circumstances to make martyrs of their children before they have reached the age of full and legal discretion when they can make choices for themselves.

Such a view is compelling but does not explain those decisions in which the courts are prepared to ignore not only the wishes of the parents but also of a competent child. In Re R (A Minor) (Wardship: Medical Treatment) [1991] 4 All ER 177 and Re W (Wardship) (Medical Treatment: Court's Jurisdiction) [1992] 4 All ER 627, the judges relied upon some degree of incapacity evidenced by the child to justify their decision to overrule the child's wishes. However, in Re E (A Minor) (Wardship: Medical Treatment) [1993] 1 FLR 386 the court ordered medical treatment even on an intelligent and competent child of fifteen and three quarters. Ward J justified his decision at p. 394:

But I regret that I find it essential for his well being to protect him from himself and his parents, and so override his and his parent's decision... the welfare of A, when viewed objectively, compels me to only one conclusion, and that is that the hospital should be at liberty to treat him (emphasis added).

The wardship jurisdiction was instrumental in removing the child from the father's control, and placed the child under the supervision of a court whose value system may be significantly different from that of the child and its family. In the same case, the view of the reasonable parent was discussed by Ward J at p. 392:

It is an anxious question to answer – reasonable by whose standards? – in a case where the basis of the objection is religious, but in my judgment the approach I have to adopt is that urged by Lord Upjohn in the well-known decision of J v C [1970] AC 668 at p. 722 where he points out that:

The law and practice in relation to infants have developed and are developing and must and no doubt will continue to develop by reflecting and adopting the changing views as the years go by of reasonable men and women, the parents of children, on the proper treatment and methods of bringing up children, for after all that is the model which the judge must emulate, for he must act as the judicial reasonable parent.

The objective standard by which I therefore judge this case is the standard of the ordinary mother and father. In that sense it is wholly objective. In another sense, of course, it is subjective in that I am not looking at an ordinary child but I am looking at this particular child. I have, therefore, to apply that objective basis to this particular ward of court, given the question that is to be decided and given his own position as a boy of growing maturity living in the religious society that he does.

The court, again, is content to impose the values of the dominant culture, apparently without any reference to the values of either the parent or the child.

5.4.2 Placement of ethnic minority children

Another series of cases concern the placement of children from ethnic minorities. The most difficult decisions have been those in which the court is asked to decide whether an ethnic minority child should remain with white foster parents, with whom the child may have lived for a significant time, or whether the child should be placed with foster parents from his or her own ethnic group or even returned to the natural parents. Most relevant from the checklist in the Children Act, 1989 are s.1(3)(b) regarding the physical, emotional and educational needs of the child and s. 1(3)(c) about the likely effect on the child of any change in his or her circumstances.

Although these factors are not weighted or ranked in any way, the predominant view in the case law has been to maintain the stability of the present arrangements for the child, unless they can be shown not to provide for the child's needs. In this way, the needs of a child to have a well-developed sense of racial and cultural heritage are often subjugated to the requirement of stability. The importance of the natural parents and the consequent importance of culture and background are not always determinative of cases involving children. As we saw above, in J v C [1970] AC 668, the House of Lords refused to return a Spanish boy to his Spanish parents, because of the close links of the child with the foster parents and the need to maintain stability in the child's life. It is our contention that too often the values attached to the role of psychological parents and to stability outweigh considerations of cultural and ethnic needs.

In a common case, a black child may have lived with white foster parents for some time. Those arguing that this child should be moved either back to the natural parents or to foster parents from a similar ethnic background are required to argue against the in-built assumption that the status quo should be maintained and are forced to show that the present arrangements do not meet the child's needs. At its simplest, the court is required to discard the benefits of stability and continuity and accept that a white family cannot meet the needs of a black child and that these needs outweigh other matters, so that the child should be moved. In many cases courts have not accepted this view. Their value system has not allowed them to appreciate the importance of being brought up with a strong cultural identity. English judges have not been able to accept that the cultural 'need' is sufficient to justify moving a child from a stable environment. That children need a strong cultural identity has also been supported by the British Agencies for Fostering and Adoption, as quoted in Re N [1990] 1 FLR 58, at p. 62:

> Over and above all these basic needs, children need to develop a positive identity, including a positive racial identity. This is of fundamental importance since ethnicity is a significant component of identity. Ideally such needs are met within the setting of the child's birth family. Historically black people have been victims of racism for centuries. This has manifested and continues to manifest itself in many forms. Racism permeates all areas of British society and is perpetuated through a range of interests and influences, including the media, education and social service policies and practices. Negative and stereotypical images and actions can have a major impact on black children through the internalisation of these images, resulting in self-hate and identity confusion. Black children therefore require the survival skills necessary to develop a positive racial identity. This will enable them to deal with the racism within our predominantly white society.

The courts have either not been able to appreciate the needs of ethnic minorities or have allowed the status quo requirement to dominate. A number of cases are illustrative of this. In Re A [1987] 2 FLR 429, Thomas J said at p. 437:

> Of course, her family are important to her. However, M undoubtedly has had and will continue to need stability, love and security. I do not in any way underestimate the loss to a degree of M's Nigerian culture and background and her own family if she remains with Mr. and Mrs. N. However, I am quite sure that to remove M now from the family with whom she has lived for, in her life, many years, would have a quite devastating effect on her. I do not believe that Mrs. A, perhaps naturally, has any real insight into the problems that would be caused to this young girl by removing her now from Mr. and Mrs. N.

In consequence the importance of the child being brought up within her own culture was subjugated to the need to provide her with continuity and stability. This again was the decision in Re P [1999] 3 All ER 734. Whilst not questioning the veracity of the Court of Appeal's decision did it have top go to such lengths to dismiss the importance of the child's cultural heritage? A child born of Orthodox Jews had been placed with Christian foster parents. The child suffered from Down's Syndrome and the natural parents had doubted their ability to raise the child. After several years the natural parents applied to vary the residence order so that the child could be brought up in the Jewish faith. The Court of Appeal, we believe, correctly refused to move the child. Commenting on the balance between religion and other welfare factors Butler-Sloss LJ said at p. 746: 'But N's religious and cultural heritage cannot be the overwhelming factor in this case, for the reasons set out by the judge nor can it displace other weighty welfare factors'. More worryingly, Ward LJ commented at p. 757: 'In other words in the jurisprudence of human rights, the right to practice one's religion is subservient to the need, in a democratic society, to put welfare first.'

The inherent indeterminacy of the concept of welfare leaves open the possibility of the Court inserting whatever current welfare factor is in vogue in order to displace religions and cultural factors. Welfare as presently viewed – leaving a child with foster parents and refusing contact – increases stability and security but has the effect of damaging the child's sense of identity.

Some cases have appreciated the importance of the need to establish a strong cultural identity. In Re M [1995] 1 FLR 546 the Court of Appeal remitted for further consideration a case where the magistrates had refused contact for a black father to his child where the child's white mother had, following the break-up of the relationship with the father, married a white man. Butler-Sloss LJ said at p. 550:

> Whether in the future this father will have any contact at all, frequent contact, infrequent contact or indirect contract, will be a matter for the judge rehearing the application. He or she will have to consider the significance of race and the hostility of the maternal family towards the father and place those and all the other factors for and against the father having contact to the child in the balance in coming to the decision on contact. But the child's racial origins and the concerns of the court welfare officer have to be carefully considered and it is for those reasons that I felt this appeal had to be allowed.

Similar views were expressed in Re P [1994] 2 FLR 374. In this case the parents were not married and a child was born in 1988. The parties separated in 1989. The mother was granted custody with reasonable access to the father, and an order was made granting the father parental rights and duties. Access continued on a fortnightly basis until 1991, when it was prevented by the mother who had refused to disclose her address to the father. The father made an application for renewed contact, which the mother opposed. The justices ordered direct contact. In dismissing the mother's appeal, Booth J said at p. 379:

> The father is West Indian; the mother is partly West Indian and partly English. This was a factor, among others, which led the welfare officer to conclude that there was a particular need here for the child to know his father; and that he should have the awareness of, as he said, his racial origins, background and traditions from his father and not just from the maternal side of his family.

The decision of the Court of Appeal in Re M [1996] 2 FLR 441 may be viewed as recognition of the child's cultural background and needs by stating that a child should, all things being equal, be brought up by the natural parents. In Re M, the child P was born in South Africa to Zulu parents in 1986. P's mother worked as a nanny and housekeeper for the appellant, living with P in the house of the appellant. The appellant and P became close. In 1992 the appellant returned to England taking P with her. The details of this arrangement were disputed by the parties. In 1994 the appellant applied to adopt P, while P's parents claimed that the boy should be returned to South Africa. The Court of Appeal ordered that P should be returned to South Africa at Easter 1996. The child's development should be as a Zulu and not Afrikan or English.

The decisions in such cases can be explained not by ascribing an appreciation of cultural needs of children but based on an affirmation of pre-eminence of the role of the natural parent. Cretney (1997: 167), in categorising the case of Re M as one where greater weight is given to the natural parent's wishes, makes no mention of any cultural issue in the case. Are we to imply that the courts are accepting a cultural need that can obviously be met by the natural parent? Or are natural parents favoured for their ability to provide less tangible needs? Lord Templeman in Re KD (A Minor) (Ward: Termination of Access) [1988] AC 806 said at p. 812:

> The best person to bring up a child is the natural parent. It matters not whether the parent is wise or foolish, rich or poor, educated or illiterate, provided the child's moral and physical health are not in danger.

However, there are evidently many cases, such as Re A [1987] 2 FLR 429, in which the position of the non-white natural parents was not favoured. The need to research this particular issue in more depth is evident. At this stage, there is no clearly discernible pattern to reassure us that the concerns of ethnic minority parents – or indeed of ethnic minority children – are systematically taken into account by the courts.

5.5 Adoption

The political and personal opinions of individuals who make decisions about the welfare of children in Britain has been a particularly obvious factor in cases relating to mixed-race adoptions, or interracial adoptions, where the need to maintain a child's cultural links is arguably an important consideration. There is, however, no specific requirement for courts or adoption agencies to consider the child's racial origins or cultural background (compare this with the duty placed on local authorities under s. 22(5) of the Children Act, 1989, referred to above). Some local authorities and agencies operate policies allowing children to be adopted only by parents of a similar ethnic background. The approach was based upon the need to strengthen the child's self-esteem, to educate the child in racial self-perception and to foster positive and frequent contacts with the respective community. Adoptive parents not from that ethnic group were seen as unable to meet the needs of the child. This approach was not accepted without criticism (see Hayes, 1995; Tizard and Phoenix, 1993). A substantial groundswell of opinion developed following a number of cases where children were wrenched from loving foster parents because they were of a different ethnic background than the child.

Blanket policies of refusing adoption in cases of mixed race would be contrary to the adoption welfare principle under s. 6 of the Adoption Act, 1976. The Secretary of State commented in 1989 that local authorities or agencies who operated such policies might risk losing their approval. Guidance was then issued and a review of adoption law in 1992 also included a review of the literature on children of ethnic minorities. The White Paper (Adoption: The future, Cmnd 2288, 1993) considered what guidelines should be given to all those concerned in the adoption process and stated in para. 2.6 that such guidelines should emphasise the need for:

> ...skilled professional assessment and for common-sense human judgements reflecting the value placed on traditional parenting and

the need for stable and secure relationships between parents and between them and their children...common-sense values in such matters as to the age of adoptive parents and issues of race and culture in considering the best options for the child.

On the appropriateness of the adoptive parents, the White Paper stated:

4.32 The Chief Social Services Inspector has emphasised that ethnicity and culture are amongst the issues to be considered but that they should not necessarily be more influential than any other.

4.33 There is no conclusive research which justifies isolating such questions from other matters needing assessment; or which supports the proposition that children adopted by people of a different ethnic group will necessarily encounter problems of identity or prejudice later in life.

Guidance has now been issued along these lines and the effect has been to reduce the significance of the cultural needs of the child. Rather than strengthening mechanisms to provide for the cultural needs of ethnic minority children and providing more comprehensive guidance to avoid the previous blanket approaches, the effect is that one form of narrow ideology has replaced another. As a result, children are more likely to find themselves lost culturally. The problem is graphically illustrated in Re B (Adoption: Setting Aside) [1995] 1 FLR 1. In this case the adoptive child, born in 1959, was adopted in the year of his birth. His natural mother was an English Roman Catholic, and his natural father was a Kuwaiti Muslim. The parents never married and the father left the country without knowing of the pregnancy or birth. The adoptive parents were Jewish. The little boy was brought up as a Jew. The adoptive parents were led to believe that the child was Jewish but in 1968 they were told that he was not Jewish. After the discovery, the adoptive parents took steps to ensure that he was formally introduced to the Jewish faith and confirmed in it. He now had considerable difficulty, being asked to leave Israel, yet was prevented from travelling to Kuwait to see his natural father because of his previous travels to Israel. The court, in dismissing the application to have the adoption order set aside, found no procedural irregularity on which to found such a claim. The only cases where adoption orders had been set aside were those where there was a procedural irregularity. There are no statutory provisions for the annulment or revocation of an adoption order in the circumstances of Re B. As a result the court had no power to set aside or purport to nullify the order which was made in July 1959.

How have the courts reacted to this problem? In deciding on an adoption, the court must give first consideration to the need to safeguard and promote the child's welfare throughout his childhood. Section 6 of the Adoption Act, 1976 states:

6. Duty to promote welfare of child –

In reaching any decision relating to the adoption of a child a court or adoption agency shall have regard to all the circumstances, first consideration being given to the need to safeguard and promote the welfare of the child throughout his childhood; and shall so far as practicable ascertain the wishes and feelings of the child regarding the decision and give due consideration to them, having regard to his age and understanding.

Bush J in Re N [1990] 1 FLR 58 appeared to dismiss the need to have special rules for children from ethnic minorities when he commented, at p. 63:

He and his children will make their own way in the world because of intelligence and flair. To suggest that he or his children need special help because they are black is in human terms an insult to them and their abilities.

The courts, in a series of cases, seemed at best ambivalent to the policy of some agencies to encourage positive cultural identities. In some cases, the judges seemed unable to move away from the practice in custody disputes of reviewing a list of factors, weighing culture as one factor, along with requirements of stability and continuity. In Re Lancashire ex parte M [1992] 1 FLR 109 the Court of Appeal refused an application for judicial review of a local authority's decision to place a mixed-race child for adoption. The applicants were white short-term foster parents who had brought up the child for the first two years of his life. They had shown a willingness to adopt the child. The local authority decided not to place the child with them. The local authority social worker's report highlighted the unambiguous support for cultural values necessary in such a case, as cited at p. 113:

The applicants' attitude has been one of 'colour-blindness'. They do not accept that colour is significant and do not see D as a different race/colour. However much they may choose to ignore this issue, it may not be too long before D's colour becomes important to him. Whilst [the female applicant] has said that members of the extended family are of mixed race, [the applicants'] general attitude does not bode well for them coping with issues of cultural and racial identity as D grows older.

The prospective other adopters were felt more able to address the cultural needs of a mixed-race child, as stated at p. 113:

It is felt that the prospective adoptive family recently identified could meet all... these needs [of D]. The female applicant does not work and has plenty of time to devote to a young child's needs. They have already adopted two children who are half black/Afro-Caribbean. These children are aware of their backgrounds and origins and this has been openly addressed. They appear to be happy and well-adjusted. The extended families have accepted the children whole-heartedly. D would benefit from the attention he needs and the company of siblings. This family do not live in the...area [where the mother lives].

Balcombe LJ seized on the criticism coming from the government and advised caution in accepting too rigid a policy. With reference to recently issued guidelines from the Social Services Inspectorate he said, at p. 111:

They were issued by the Social Services Inspectorate of the Department of Health on 29 January 1991, in the light of, what I think is now generally known, considerable public concern about the policy of placing mixed-race children with families of the same ethnic background.

The relevant sections of the guidelines quoted below are as given by Balcombe LJ, at pp. 111-112:

There may be circumstances in which placement with a family of different ethnic origin is the best choice for a particular child. In other cases such a placement may be the best available choice. For example, a child may have formed strong links with prospective foster-parents or adopters or be related to them...

...Planning is of vital importance... Children should not be removed from placements which are otherwise satisfactory solely because the

ethnic origin of the foster-parents does not accord with the requirements of general policies.

Whilst allowing the child to be moved to a family more able to deal with
his cultural needs, the court gives no indication of any enthusiasm for this
result. The application was for a judicial review of the local authority's
decision, so the court was constrained to judge only the reasonableness of
that decision. Balcombe LJ said at p. 113:

> What I do know is that it does seem to me that no court, in the light
> of that evidence, could say that this local authority had acted in such
> a way that no reasonable local authority could so have acted.

Woolfe LJ expresses similar sentiments in the same case, which is very
different from those cases in which the court has to make the decision
itself on the basis of the child's welfare. One may speculate on whether
the court would have moved the child, had the court been asked to apply
the welfare principle as they understood it. Similar ambivalence was
evident in Re P [1990] 1 FLR 96 where a child of mixed race was removed from short-term foster parents and placed with black adopters. In
that case, at first instance, as quoted by Balcombe LJ in Re Lancashire ex
parte M [1992] 1 FLR 109, it had been emphasised that it was desirable
for a child of mixed race to be brought up by a black or mixed-race
family. While the Court of Appeal dismissed the case of the white foster
parents, the judgments point to some reservations about the decision to
remove the child. Balcombe LJ said in Re P [1990] 1 FLR 96, at p. 101:

> The advantages of bringing up a child of mixed race in a black family
> may be less obvious to those without practical experience in this
> field, but the judge had, as he said, evidence of those advantages to
> which he was entitled to give such weight as the circumstances of the
> particular case required. Whether we would have reached the same
> decision as the judge we do not know, but we did not have the
> advantage which he did of seeing and hearing the witnesses over a
> period of 3 days. We are quite unable to say he was plainly wrong.

Where the courts are applying the welfare principle, they are able to
revert to the importance of stability over the ethnic needs of the child. In
Re JK (Adoption) 1991 2 FLR 340, the female child concerned was three
years old and born to a Sikh mother who, at the time, was seeking a
divorce. The child was illegitimate and the mother freely placed her for

adoption at birth. The child was immediately placed with short-term foster-parents who had two children aged 6 and 12, and with whom she had remained. The child had become very attached to the family who had always been considered by the local authority as adequate short-term foster-parents. The local authority intended the placement to be short-term only, so that in accordance with its policy the girl should be placed for adoption with a suitably matched family from a similar racial background. However, the local authority found two main obstacles in placing the child for adoption, since adoption in the Sikh community was very rare, even more so where the child was illegitimate. The local authority also became concerned that the child was bonding with the foster mother and therefore took steps to remove the child. This prompted the foster parents to issue wardship proceedings, seeking an order for the child to remain a ward during her minority and asking to be granted her care and control. The view of the child psychiatrist was that the child would suffer irreparable damage if she were to be moved from the only home she had known in her life. The issue for the court was whether the child should be left in her present home, and adoption procedures for the existing foster-parents should be commenced, or whether because of her different racial and cultural background she should be moved to an as yet unidentified family. The court held that the child should continue to be a ward of court and remain with the present foster parents with a view to them adopting the child. The decision is based on the court's view that the child had a secure home, a factor that evidently outweighed the child's needs for a positive cultural identity. As the headnote states at p. 340:

> The foster-parents were tolerant, wise people, capable of loving children of whatever race, and they would assist the child to follow her own Sikh traditions and culture and to seek assistance if necessary.

The court's reasons for leaving this child with the white foster parents are not made clear. Two reasons seem to be given, the impossibility of finding a suitable adoptive home and the bond between the child and the foster parents. Sir Stephen Brown said, at p. 342:

> The problem in this case is that it has not been possible to find such a family. The evidence before me has been quite clear and specific that adoption in the Sikh community is very rare indeed, save in cases where a blood relative is concerned. Furthermore, it is even more rare in cases where the child is illegitimate. It has not been possible for

the social services department to find a Sikh family which would answer the requirements of an adoptive family. They tried no fewer than 63 agencies before this wardship summons was issued. That indicates very starkly the very considerable lengths to which they went to find a suitable adoptive family.

This seems to imply that if an adoptive home had been found, the child would have been moved, yet later the reasoning shifted to the bond between the child and the foster parents. It was held at p. 346:

I have listened very carefully to a wealth of evidence in this case. I have read, I think, twenty-two affidavits and the various reports which have been given to me. I note that there is no conflict about the principles which should apply in general in approaching the placement of children of certain racial backgrounds but, as I have already observed, the core of this matter is: what is to be done for this child? I am satisfied that she is happy, well looked after and well integrated into this family. She has a secure home, loving foster-parents and also a loving family in the form of a 'brother' and 'sister', that is to say the foster-parents' son and daughter.

There is no ambiguity, however, when the court comes to the view of the child's needs, in what is at best a simple view of the cultural needs of the child and of the foster parent's ability to meet this need. Sir Stephen Brown commented, at p. 346:

I have the evidence of the supervisor at the play-group that she now attends, that she is a normal well-balanced child, just like the other children. I bear in mind that it is the foster-parents' proposal that she should go to the same school as is attended by their own two children, where there are children of mixed race, including Asian children. They have been thoroughly successful, so it seems to me, in preserving this child from any racial problems thus far. For 3 years they had Asian neighbours; these have now moved to another area. There is no hint of racial feeling of any kind on the part of the foster-parents.... Whilst they are not of an advanced intellectual standard which can assimilate easily the finer details of different races and religions, they have been making a very praiseworthy attempt to help the little girl in this respect: They take her weekly to a Sikh temple in the area. One of the features of the area is that there are these facilities there, and the area is one which has become well accustomed to various racial groups, and they say, and I have every reason to believe them, that if the child remains in their care they will see to it that her contact with her own background is followed up and that they will seek assistance in order to be able to deal with this matter. I am perfectly certain that in this area there is available such assistance. The schools have to deal with children of all racial backgrounds, particularly Asian backgrounds, and I have no doubt that there are other facilities readily available.

The court's lack of appreciation of the impact of discrimination and the importance of the Sikh culture is obvious. Attending a mixed school, living next door to an Asian family and visiting the Sikh temple once a week are simply assumed to give the child the survival skills necessary to develop a positive racial identity.

In a similar vein, Re N [1990] 1 FLR 58 involved a child born of unmarried Nigerian parents. Three weeks after the baby's birth, the mother placed her with white foster-parents by way of a private fostering arrangement. Apart from one visit to the child in England in 1985, the mother remained in the USA. The father took an interest in the child from her birth and eventually made an application for wardship to enable the child to live with him in the USA. The court held that the doctrine that black children should never be placed with white foster parents derived from the political approach to race relations in the USA in the 1960s and 1970s. The court was not prepared to accept this approach without question. Bush J stated, at p. 61:

> I have also been bombarded by a host of theories and opinions by experts who derive their being from the political approach to race relations in America in the 1960s and 1970s. The British Agencies for Fostering and Adoption forcefully expressed the view that black children should never be placed with white foster-parents. That that part of the approach was politically inspired seems clear from reading the summary to a practice note, the date of which is not clear. Nevertheless, it is an approach which due to the zeal of its authors has persuaded most local authorities not to place black children with white foster-parents... As Dr B, an eminent and experienced child psychiatrist with consultancies attached to Great Ormond Street and the Royal Free Hospital pointed out – and this was accepted by a

consultant social worker, Mrs. E (to whom I shall refer in a minute) there seems little real evidence, save anecdotal, to suggest that black-white fostering is harmful. Indeed, Dr B says that her experience, particularly at Great Ormond Street, indicates to the contrary, namely, that the placement of black children with white foster-parents works just as well as black foster-children with black foster-parents, and the real problem, of course, is that black foster-parents are in short supply in this country.

The guardian ad litem, as quoted at p. 66, had adopted the view that welfare is best served by stability and continuity, rather than cultural interests:

> N is emotionally bonded with Mr. and Mrs. P. They are her psychological parents. She needs them because she has had no other family. Whilst in Nigerian culture the needs of the child would not be more paramount than those of the parents, N has been raised in a western society. It is impossible to draw a curtain over her initial years of emotional and physical development.

Not only did the court choose to downgrade the cultural values of the Nigerian parents but it imposed the westernised construct of psychological parent to justify its conclusion that separation from the foster parents would be cruel; wardship was granted with care and control to the foster parents. However, the court did make reference to the positive role of the father, refused the adoption application by the foster parents and gave the father reasonable access. Bush J concluded at p. 66:

> The later harm that may arise in her teens when she wishes to seek out her cultural roots can best be dealt with by sympathetic understanding and education, upon which the Ps have already embarked, and it can also hopefully be met by the father continuing his interest and having access to N. It can only be helped if the father accepts the situation and enjoys access not on the basis of an expected rehabilitation but on the basis of a contact access designed to keep N in touch with her origins.

In Re O [1995] 2 FLR 597, there are a number of factors that could be seen to justify the adoption of a black Nigerian child by a white couple. It is instructive how little the court referred to the problem of transracial adoption. This may be due to the peculiar facts and the poor calibre of the experts and professionals in this case. Thorpe J said, at p. 607:

It seems to me that the placement of R as a black Nigerian 7-year-old was a particularly difficult placement, particularly in a rural county. Mrs. W had the attraction at least of having been raised in a family where Nigerians had been successfully fostered. Both Mr. and Mrs. W offered to take on this child unconditionally. Both of them have made a heavy investment in rooting her psychologically within the family, both as child to themselves and also as sibling of their older adopted children.

Having decided to allow the adoption application and to dispense with the consent of the parents, the court then turned to the cultural needs of the child. In the peculiar circumstances of the case, the court felt that the only way in which these needs could be met was by allowing contact with the birth mother. Thorpe J said at p. 610:

The second consideration is that she is being brought up in a family and in a locality where it is very difficult to buttress her Nigerian heritage and identity. Obviously if she had contact with her mother there would be through that relationship immediate exposure to Nigerianness.

Can the cultural needs of a child be met by occasional contact with her mother? There may be overriding considerations in this case that prevented the child from being re-united with her natural parents but these factors are not present in many cases where either the child's adoption by white parents is allowed or the child is allowed to remain with white foster parents with at best some contact with the natural parents and their culture (see further Re B (Adoption: Child's Welfare) [1995] 1 FLR 895).

It would, however, be wrong to conclude that all courts have shown such ambivalence to the cultural needs of children from ethnic minorities. In Re J (A Minor) (Wardship: Adoption: Custodianship) [1987] 1 FLR 455, the court held that the mother of a West Indian child was reasonable in withholding consent to adoption by a white Jehovah's Witness couple. Sheldon J commented at p. 460:

There are, however, a number of other factors which the mother is entitled to have taken into account which, considered individually, might not justify her refusal but which collectively, in my view, point to that refusal not being unreasonable. Of these, three relate to or arise out of the boy's origin and character. Thus, although the first is a matter of no significance whatever to the applicants, the facts are that he is coloured in appearance and that, as I accept, he is far more boisterous in nature and behaviour than the applicants themselves or their children. I agree, therefore, that the possibilities exist that as he gets older they may find his liveliness difficult to understand and to handle, and that if he seeks or wishes to seek his friends and companions from among others of like nature, particularly others of similar ethnic origin, he will be either inhibited from so doing for fear of offending the applicants, or will cause them distress by seemingly turning away from them to others of a different hue. If, in those events, his link with his mother has been broken by an adoption order, he might have no other obvious person to turn to for guidance; on the other hand, if no such order were to be made, even if no more than contact access had been maintained with her, she could be a help to him in such a situation.

It remains our view, and is now reinforced by government guidelines, that in the majority of cases the courts have refused to consider the needs of ethnic minority children by insisting on the use of a 'best interest' concept which places greater emphasis on a Westernised view of the parent-child relationship than on the cultural needs of the child. Allowing contact with birth parents or encouraging foster parents to attempt to relate to the child's culture are poor substitutes for the immersion of a child in a particular cultural heritage. In failing to adopt a pluralistic stance, solutions to the problem have only been addressed from the possibility of adoption and fostering techniques, common within the dominant community but often unknown and resented within ethnic minority communities. The Children Act, 1989 provides a range of options that could be considered and that may fit better into the culture of certain ethnic minorities. There is, however, little evidence from the cases that such strategies have been considered.

5.6 Parenting in ethnic minority communities

We turn now to the intervention of the state into the lives of families, with particular reference to questions about acceptable levels of parenting in ethnic minority communities. The state will interfere in the family where the behaviour of carers falls below a pre-set level. This level is often indeterminate, raising the problem of how such a level or threshold is to be judged. Decisions prior to the Children Act, 1989 lacked clarity and some courts adopted the standards of the dominant population, in others the standards of the ethnic minority community were at least seen as relevant.

In Re JT [1986] 2 FLR 107, a mother gave birth to her elder child when she was fifteen years old. In 1980 the mother became a Rastafarian and in 1983 she formed a relationship with Mr. J and became a member of his extended Rastafarian family, over which he exercised total control. On 14 November 1983 the elder child was admitted to hospital. He was clinically dead on arrival, but was revived after intensive care. He was found to be suffering from hypothermia, malnutrition, and extensive injuries over most parts of his body. The injuries were non-accidental and had been inflicted over a period of time. The mother was convicted of wounding the child and sentenced to two years imprisonment. A care order was made and the local authority placed the child with the grandmother. In July 1984 the mother gave birth to Mr. J's baby, 'the younger child'. That child was removed from the mother at birth. A place of safety order was obtained and the younger child was placed with foster-parents. The local authority began care proceedings in a juvenile court and interim care orders were made. The Family Division held that because of the dominant position of Mr. J and his apparent indifference to the suffering of the elder child, wardship should continue in respect of the younger child, and in addition the child should be committed to the care of the local authority and placed with long-term foster-parents with a view to adoption. Butler-Sloss J, commenting on the standard to be applied, stated at p. 118:

> The group is, in general, anti-white. They recognise black superiority. Views that they are, subject to modern legislation, perfectly entitled to hold, but such views, together with an anti-authoritarian approach, are highly relevant to any future effective co-operation with social workers... What I am saying, in effect, so that the father understands it, is that the views of his group, when they operate on their own, are their own business, but if they have to work with predominantly white social workers their views and their approach have to be considered in the light of how they will cope with the way that, for instance, social services will require them to cope.

This view is similar to the approach taken in R v Derriviere [1969] 53 Cr App R 637, a case concerning the use of excessive force by the defendant in disciplining his 12 year old son. Derriviere was prosecuted for assault and battery arising from excessive disciplining of his son. English law permits parents to apply reasonable force to their children for the purpose of punishing the child, but the force and its manner of application must be reasonable. Derriviere, a West Indian man, argued that his own customs allowed more severe punishment to be used. He was found guilty and sentenced to six months imprisonment. On appeal Lord Widgery CJ admitted that these kinds of cases raised difficult questions and stated, at p. 639:

> The court fully accepts that immigrants coming to this country may find initially that our ideas are different from those upon which they have been brought up in regard to the methods and manner in which children are to be disciplined. There can be no doubt that once in this country, this country's law must apply; and there can be no doubt that, according to the laws of this country, the chastisement given to the boy was excessive and the assault complained of was proved.

Continuing this trend in Re KR (A Minor) (Abduction: Forcible Removal) [1999] Times June 16, the Family Division suggested that pressure brought to bear on children to conform to religious and cultural norms could in some circumstances constitute significant harm.

A different approach is evident in a case involving a Vietnamese family, In Re H [1987] 2 FLR 12. Two children, now wards of court, were born of a North Vietnamese mother after the family had escaped from North Vietnam. The mother, the father of one and possibly both wards, and the children made their way to England in 1980. They lived first in Cumbria, then (after the father left the family) in Lancashire, and finally in London. In Cumbria, in 1981, the children were placed on the child abuse register, after which the family had the support of professional agencies. There were repeated incidents of neglect, ill-treatment and bizarre cruelty on the part of the mother. She frequently hit the children with sticks. They were disturbed and unhappy, and the little girl demonstrated some strange sexual behaviour. The mother rejected outside help and reacted violently to the social workers. She claimed the right to inflict punishment on the children, including hitting them with sticks across the head and shoulders. The mother's behaviour was eventually judged un-acceptable in her own culture. Judge Callman commented, at p. 22:

> Dr Lau recognises that hitting children with sticks is fairly common chastisement in some levels of Chinese society, but this is usually controlled, reasonable and ritualised, and relates to specific issues, and it would not be used in such a way as to cause marks and bruises. More to the point and quite specific, Dr Lau said hitting in the face would not be sanctioned by the mother's own wider community, and the doctor said that the mother's baffling behaviour is consistent with her own early childhood of having herself received severe beatings.

It was held that where the court in the discharge of its parental duties was dealing with children of foreign ethnic origin and culture, it must con-sider the situation against the reasonable objective standards of that cul-ture, so long as they did not conflict with our minimal acceptable stan-dards of child care in England (p. 17). In this case the mother's cruelty and neglect of her children had been grossly excessive by any standard and it would be in the children's best interests to remain in a family setting with long-term foster-parents. Judge Callman held, at p. 17:

> Let me say immediately that this type of case presents exceptional factors because one is here dealing with a wholly different culture from that which is our culture, or even western culture; but the basic responsibility of the court remains, as it must do, that which is enshrined in the law of England. That, where wards are concerned, the courts have parental duties and these duties must be exercised on the basis of one criterion only, that is the welfare and best interests of the children concerned. The court is only interested in promoting their welfare and future. It is their right to have as beneficial a future as can be applied to their circumstances. The court is not concerned with the wishes or desires of parents if they conflict with the welfare and best interests of the children. In exercising this jurisdiction the court in a case of this kind is faced with a contention that cultural background should be given special weight. The issue to be faced is whether that should be given more weight than in an ordinary western type of case. There could well be circumstances where a society from where the wards come lays down standards of conduct that wholly offend against the canons and principles accepted by our society.

I consider, and find, that in this case I must consider the case against the reasonable objective standards of the culture in which the children have hitherto been brought up, so long as these do not conflict with our minimal acceptable standards of child care in England. There is evidence before me that in Chinese culture, as applied to the lower social and cultural levels of society, in some rural based societies, such as North Vietnam and perhaps some parts of China, chastisement with sticks, of a nature and degree which is not acceptable in western society, is practised. Such conduct may wholly offend the more educated Chinese society, as it does other sections of western society. In my judgment, I apply first the reasonable objective cultural standards of the society from which the mother comes.

The Children Act, 1989 seems not to have provided definitive guidance one way or the other. The threshold criterion is the level at which the state may interfere in the family to protect the vulnerable members (usually children) by obtaining a court order, either giving the local authority parental responsibility which may be used to remove the child or by a supervision order. In cases of emergency, an emergency protection order may be sought under s. 44 to allow removal of the child for seven days. Given that views of parenting standards may vary between cultures, are the concept of significant harm and the quality of parental care to be judged by the standards prevailing in the ethnic minority community or by the standards of the dominant population? Concern was expressed during the Parliamentary debates on the Children Bill that the wording would lead to ethnic minority parents being judged against white middle class standards (Lord Banks, Hansard, HL, Vol. 503, col. 1525, Children Bill Report Stage). As finally drafted, section 31 of the 1989 Act, discussed above from various angles, still lends itself to that interpretation.

The court in Re O [1992] 2 FLR 7 explained the meaning of 'similar child', in this case in the context of a child truant from school. Ewbank J held at p. 12:

In relation to whether the harm is significant, on behalf of M it is said that the comparison which has to be made is with a similar child under s. 31(10), and that there is no evidence that she has suffered harm compared with a similar child... In my judgment, in the context of this type of case, 'similar child' means a child of equivalent intellectual and social development, who has gone to school, and not merely an average child who may or may not be at school. In fact, what one has to ask oneself is whether this child suffered significant harm by not going to school. The answer in my judgment, as in the magistrates' judgment, is obvious.

Could this concept of a similar child be considered to allow a court to view the cultural background of the child and conclude that the harm is not significant within the context of a particular culture? This approach seems to be encouraged by the Guidance and Regulations (Vol. 1, Court Orders, 1991), provided under the Children Act of 1989, to the effect that the meaning of 'similar' in such cases would require judicial interpretation, but may need to take account of environmental, social and cultural characteristics of the child. This view was supported by Freeman (1983) and seems consistent with the stated aim of the 1989 Act in terms of accepting cultural pluralism. The contrary view is put by Bainham (1993: 389) who suggests that section 31 sets 'minimally acceptable limits of behaviour towards children' (see further Bainham, 1991: 99). As such, society has a right to expect everyone from whatever cultural background to comply with these minimum standards. Bainham suggests that cultural considerations should be relevant only at the final stage of the care proceedings where the child's welfare is considered. This raises an additional difficulty, summarised by Barton and Douglas (1995: 138):

> It seems open to two possible meanings, one that better standards of care are legally available for, and only for, children from 'better' backgrounds; or two, an uncomfortable admission that our legal standards are indeed 'minimal' – an equally low safety net for all.

The assumption being made here, and by a number of other commentators, is that the standards of parental care of ethnic minorities are lower than those of the 'white middle class'. Such views are reinforced by research into punishment of children. In an unpublished paper on 'The extent of parental physical punishment in the UK', presented by Newson and Newson in 1976 to the Children's Legal Centre seminar on 'Protecting children from parental physical punishment', parents of African-Caribbean origin were shown to punish their children more frequently and severely than white parents. The conclusion of the authors was that such approaches to punishment derive from the historical system of beating slaves. A parallel study by the same authors purports to show that parents in Panjabi households hardly ever hit their children. Such findings may only tell us that parental care differs between cultures. An appreciation of cultural views within a pluralistic legal framework would focus on views from within an ethnic minority culture about parental care. Evidence of such standards would allow courts to determine whether such parenting was acceptable within that cultural context.

What of the place of the dominant culture's view of a minimum acceptable standard? Judge Callman (see In Re H [1987] 2 FLR 12 above) appears to have suggested that these would operate as a form of exception to be applied instead of considering ethnic minority values in their own right. This is mere tolerance and is not the same as operating within a pluralistic framework. If ethnic minority values are viewed within the context and from the perspective of the values of the dominant culture, this is a process of comparison rather than appreciation. Since the first question is always what a white English parent would do in the same situation and in view of general assumptions that ethnic minority standards are somehow lower than those of the majority, we note lack of depth in the courts' understanding and application of ethnic minority values. Since these are never tested in their own right, but always measured against dominant standards, we suggest that this is not real pluralism that can take care of the 'best interests' of children from ethnic minority backgrounds. Non-compliance with dominant standards is bound to be punished or otherwise criminalised, and will therefore run the risk of working to the detriment of ethnic minority parents and children. To what extent this is possibly another example of 'unwitting', indirect discrimination should be further researched.

Chapter 6

Conflict of obligation systems and blasphemy

In 1988, Salman Rushdie published his controversial book, The Satanic Verses, which deeply offended many Muslims, exposing the strength of the commitment among British ethnic minorities towards their traditional belief systems and normative values (see Ballard, 1994: 1-34). The 'Satanic affair' highlighted the continuing failure of English law to accommodate the multi-religious and multi-cultural aspects of contemporary British society, and created new doubts about the adequacy of English blasphemy law. Through a number of legal actions, the willingness of British Muslims to challenge the existing legal ethos and norms of English law became evident.

Starting from a discussion of the 'Satanic affair' and its consequences, this chapter further explores to what extent the presence of ethnic minorities in Britain challenges dominant value systems and legal norms, showing how conflicts of obligations for members of ethnic minorities have arisen. Through our analysis of how the English judiciary has responded to Muslim sensitivities about religion, we explain why and to what extent Muslims were prepared to challenge English law with regard to freedom of religion and blasphemy.

6.1 Protests against The Satanic Verses

The Satanic Verses, published by Penguin/Viking consists of different stories with no central theme. The book is difficult to read even for an educated person and has had a limited readership. The central character of Mahound (a derogatory name used by medieval Christians for the Prophet Muhammad) is depicted as a shrewd, dishonest man and is described in a

179

negative light, mainly through a chain of dreams. The poet portrays the Prophet, Abraham, and Muhammad's wives and disciples as clumsy and silly individuals who live in sin and cheat on their followers. The Satanic Verses thus appears to challenge the purity and divinity of the Qur'an, portraying it as a set of 'revelations of convenience'. Not surprisingly, this clashed with Muslim perceptions of the Prophet as a perfect person, whom every Muslim tries to emulate and whose every action is considered a 'perfect embodiment of the will of God' (see Rippin, 1990: 40-44). Muslims consider the Prophet 'more dear than their parents' (Qureshi and Khan 1989: 12) and felt insulted by Rushdie's book.

Within the Muslim community, educated individuals like Shabbir Akhtar, a Cambridge-educated scholar based at Bradford, embarked upon the difficult task of reading Rushdie's book to educate ordinary Muslims about the alleged derogatory passages. Akhtar was mandated by religious leaders of the Bradford Council of Mosques to read the text and share his findings. So Bradford, the Mecca of Britain or the Islamabad of Europe, a city renowned for having the largest mosque in the Western world, became the centre of the campaign against The Satanic Verses.

The given task was probably painful for Dr. Akhtar; other Muslims who attempted to read Rushdie's book allegedly collapsed and fainted. Dr. Zaki Badawi, then Headmaster of the Ealing Muslim School, and a leading scholar of Muslim affairs in Britain, described the reading as 'like a knife being dug into you – or being raped yourself' (The Guardian, 27 February 1989, cited in Ruthven, 1991: 29; see also Akhtar, 1989: 42-43).

Why did Muslims feel so insulted and vilified by The Satanic Verses? After all, it is merely a novel, not a scholarly historical analysis of Islam. At one level, the book was seen as a 'calculated attempt to vilify and slander the Prophet of Islam' (Akhtar, 1989: 1), thus undermining the religious authority of the faith, and criticism came from fundamentalists and liberal scholars alike. Shabbir Akhtar, prominent throughout the campaign, gave the arguments a philosophical touch. In his view, The Satanic Verses was literary terrorism, attacking Muslims and their whole way of life (see details in Akhtar, 1989, ch. 2). He was in no doubt that The Satanic Verses was blasphemous.

Dr. Mughram Al-Ghamdi, convenor of the UK Action Committee on Islamic Affairs (UKACIA), alleged that the book grossly distorted Islamic history and betrayed the Prophet Muhammad, the Prophet's wives and his companions (Sunday Telegraph, 9 October 1988, cited in Appignanesi and Maitland, 1990: 58-60). He saw a deliberate attempt by the enemies of Islam to collude in ridiculing Muslims and concluded that 'this is the most offensive, filthy and abusive book ever written by any hostile enemy of Islam and deserves to be condemned in the strongest possible way' (Ruthven, 1991: 93).

In echoing the universal condemnation by Muslims, Tariq Modood, a renowned Muslim scholar of race relations, argued that one need not be a militant or fundamentalist to be offended by The Satanic Verses. Modood (1990: 154) wrote:

> Virtually every practising Muslim was offended by passages from the book and shocked that it was written by a Muslim of whom till then the Asian community were proud.

Modood (1990: 154) further noted that Muslims were unashamedly determined to revolt against the book and its author, seen as 'Satan's son'. Indeed, many Muslims reacted with private and public fury. Shabbir Akhtar (1989: 39) describes how the Bradford Muslims organised their campaign:

> ...in all major British cities with Muslim populations, outraged Muslims met, argued, discussed and went back home frustrated. They met again and again. At the Bradford Council of Mosques, we burnt the midnight-oil every night....While Muslim groups and organisations met regularly to form committees that would formulate long-term strategies, Muslim writers on both sides of the Atlantic began to offer detailed critiques of The Satanic Verses.

Initial strategies to get the book banned through the Saudi king as the guardian of Mecca and Medina failed. The Saudi royals, still reeling from the 'Death of a princess affair', were reluctant to use their influence to persuade the British authorities to ban the book. The campaigners turned more successfully to mass demonstrations and meetings. After book burning incidents, first in Bolton and later in Bradford, protesting Muslims converged on London, where thousands gathered to express their anger. They came from all walks of life, the well-bred mixed with those from more modest backgrounds, young and old, scholars as well as workers, fundamentalists as well as moderates (Ruthven, 1991: 1; Modood, 1990: 149).

Rushdie professed surprise and tried to argue that a novel could hardly be responsible for inciting race riots. He attempted to shift responsibility onto politicians and fundamentalists who, he alleged, had joined the protests to further their own agendas. In a letter to The Observer (22 January 1989) he claimed that the campaign was 'whipped up by Mullahs' for their own political aims and rejected the theory that his book was a Zionist plot or an attempt to ridicule Muslims or their religion.

Rushdie was able to muster some support. One of the leading liberal commentators on the affairs, Malise Ruthven, agreed with Rushdie, pointing out that The Satanic Verses was being used by politicians, particularly in Iran, India and Pakistan, to raise their own profiles. The affair was turning into a 'political football', used by hard-line Muslim sects and individuals to pursue their own personal goals (Ruthven, 1991: 152). Even Akhtar (1989: 54) reluctantly admitted that a small section of the Muslims in the UK used The Satanic Verses for ulterior motives. Professor Akbar S. Ahmed, the distinguished Muslim anthropologist of Cambridge University, pointed out that some leaders of different British Muslim sects vied with each other in expressing anger. Having dis-covered the power of the media, they sought to command attention (Ahmed, 1992: 171-173). The Iranian journalist Amir Taheri (cited in Appignanesi and Maitland, 1989: 92-95) described how the Ayatollah Khomeini intentionally stirred the poor and illiterate masses, waving Rushdie's novel to strengthen his power base in the Muslim world against Saudi Arabia and Pakistan. Many ordinary Muslims were thus persuaded to defect from the path of religious moderation towards a form of extremism which had previously held no attraction for them (Webster, 1990: 34).

The range and severity of the reactions against Rushdie's novel are partly explicable because the book itself exists at so many levels. The Satanic Verses was not simply a novel. To uncover its underlying messages, one must explore Rushdie's background. He studied history at Cambridge, concentrating on the life of the Prophet Muhammad. His views were a product of his Western upbringing and the aim was, as in Grimus and Midnight's Children, to attack corrupt political systems controlled by post-independence politicians, especially in the Indian sub-continent. The Satanic Verses also attacked oppressive regimes and tribal gangs based on extremist fundamentalist cults. Interviewed by Madhu

Jain, an Indian journalist, Rushdie unambiguously emphasised that The Satanic Verses represented a challenge to fanaticism and fundamentalism (India Today, 15 September 1988, cited in Appignanesi and Maitland, 1989: 39).

Rushdie saw the political implications of extremist fundamentalism as damaging to a democratic environment and treated the corrupt regimes of Iran, Pakistan and India as betraying the people's trust. He witnessed how his mother country (Rushdie considers both India and Pakistan as his mother countries) had deteriorated as a result of a series of corrupt regimes. Rushdie said in a Bandung File programme (reprinted in Appignanesi and Maitland, 1989: 29):

> I have seen what the Mullahs have done in Pakistan over the past 11 years – the level of oppression instituted there by Islamisation. I've seen, too, how almost all the poets in Pakistan were in exile in England during that period.

He had witnessed how, in the name of God, both Iran and Pakistan had been engaged in Islamisation of all aspects of human behaviour. He observed how little room was left for individuals to regulate their social intercourse, as rules derived from God were now used to control human behaviour. Rushdie's despair is evident in the book itself.

Condemnation of the book and its author spread to other Western countries. The late Kalim Siddiqi saw a Western plot behind the book, linked the large advance paid to Rushdie and the non-stop praise of Western media and literati and declared that the book was the result of a conspiracy against Muslims and their religious way of life (Ahmed, 1992: 172). The book was also seen as supporting Zionism, with the assistance of American money, against the Prophet Muhammad, Allah and Islam.

Many Muslims passionately believed that The Satanic Verses represented the 'latest battle in a long history of religious and cultural tensions between Muslims and European civilisation' (Webster, 1990: 37) and saw reflections of the Crusades and other historical evidence of Muslim suppression worldwide (Appignanesi and Maitland, 1989: 85). Richard Webster (1990: 37) writes:

> Hostility was so deep because it was based on a real power struggle for control of Europe. The Arab invasion of western Europe was stopped only at the battle of Tours in 712. But the military and

political threat which Islam posed to Christendom remained under Turkish rule. Christian fears of Islam, then, were based in part on a real perception of its military, political and cultural strength. But the tendency of Christians to dominate their enemies meant that realistic fears of Islam were increasingly overlaid by demonological fantasies in which Muslims in general, and Muhammad in particular, were seen as Satanic beings.

Thus, Rushdie's fictional adaptations of ancient stereotypes are not simply hatred, 'but the long terrible, triumphalist hatred which the west has had for Islam almost since its beginning' (Webster, 1990: 40). The anti-Muslim warriors' part has been played by the so-called literati and the media (Akhtar, 1989: 8-9; Ahmed, 1992: 223). Akbar Ahmed saw the hand of the Western media in a secret contract to destroy Muslims in postmodern societies, a plot that was more dangerous than gunpowder or modern weapons. He was in no doubt that the Western media wanted to achieve what the great enemies of Islam could not accomplish during the past two centuries.

In the eyes of millions of Muslims, Rushdie's novel represented the turning point of a contemporary campaign against Islam. Webster (1990: 41) states that 'it is little wonder that they feel that their own future existence, security and safety in the west is threatened'. Tariq Modood saw this campaign also as a form of agitation over a rightful place for Muslim minorities in Europe and spoke of 'a Muslim crusade' (Modood, 1990: 143).

Shabbir Akhtar (1990: 7) frankly admitted that, in a sense, the uproar over The Satanic Verses had 'nothing to do with Rushdie or his book'. Muslim leaders seized the chance to conduct a sustained campaign on many unresolved issues, including modest demands on small matters and renewed calls for introducing Muslim personal law in Britain. The conflict was perceived by Muslims as a spiritual confrontation, a clash of civilisations, even as a declaration of war (Appignanesi and Maitland, 1989: 85).

From the perspective of Muslims, there were valid reasons for a militant stance in the search for a new religious and political identity for Muslims in Britain. The memories of great Muslim Empires in many parts of Europe and Asia are recollected with pride and reverence. Recent experience as 'second class citizens' in the UK and elsewhere leads

Muslims to believe that they are unwanted strangers in British society (Ahmed, 1992: 174). Many British Muslims, in particular Bangladeshis and Pakistanis, finding themselves at the bottom of socio-economic structures, have developed a siege mentality while racial harassment and racial discrimination against Muslims have continued to be rampant.

British Muslims have also been much concerned about the Western influence on second-generation Muslims and negative effects on traditional family concepts, community life and culture. Marital breakdown, increasing marginalisation of elderly people and lack of respect for elders, teachers, preachers and religious leaders, alcoholism and drug abuse, disintegration of family life and a general deterioration of values are perceived as worrying factors. Present Western civilisation, in the view of many Muslims, represents only evil, from which Muslims are deliberately seeking a way out without being corrupted. Global developments seem also to be going against Muslims and have been causing anxiety. Such matters have regularly been on the agenda of Friday khutba' sermons (Ahmed, 1992: 196-197).

In reacting against such forces, Muslims began to isolate themselves deliberately from the wider society. For example, Bradford Muslim parents protested against multi-faith religious studies and began to withdraw their children from such classes. Their point of view was that multi-religious lessons only contribute to the corruption of youngsters. Muslim children should, from primary education onwards, only be taught Islam and the Muslim way of life. Many Muslims see it as their historical duty to fight against secularisation (Ahmed, 1992: 37). Inspired by assumptions of the supremacy of Islam and all that goes with it, Muslim leaders in the UK were and are using their institutions to organise their communities for their cause. Mosques are increasingly becoming 'barometers for politics' in the struggle against the 'wild west' (Ahmed, 1992: 157; see also Lewis, 1994).

6.2 Western reactions

The reactions of Muslims were often identified with fundamentalists and fanatics. Mashuq Ally complained that leading Muslim organisations such as the UK Islamic Mission are compared to terrorist organisations such as the IRA (Lewis, 1994: 112). Hijacking, kidnapping, execution of opponents on Fridays and cruel treatment of females are seen as tragic consequences of Muslim fundamentalism. Memories survive of how John Macarthy, Jackie Mann, Terry White, Brian Keenan and Terry Anderson were kidnapped and kept captive by Muslims in inhuman conditions for many years. The British way of life was being threatened by 'Muslim fundamentalism' working behind the scenes 'to engulf the achievements of Western European culture' (Parekh, 1995: 266; Rath, Groenendijk and Penninx, 1995: 101-114). Such views were also evident in Germany, France, the USA and other Western countries. The former editor-in-Chief of The Observer, Conor Cruise O'Brien, wrote in The Times in May 1989 (cited in Webster, 1990: 43):

> Muslim society looks profoundly repulsive... It looks repulsive because it is repulsive... A Westerner who claims to admire Muslim society, while still adhering to Western values, is either a hypocrite or an ignoramus, or both. At the heart of the matter is the Muslim family, an abominable institution... Arab and Muslim society is sick, and has been sick for a long time...

The 'big guns' of the British literary world and the media (Ahmed, 1992: 177) and the 'gutter press' (Akhtar, 1989: 40) also seized the opportunity to attack Muslims for burning the book and supporting the Ayatollah's fatwa. Without any hesitation, they knew what side to support. The Daily Star (21 February 1989) took Muslim fundamentalists to task:

> Isn't the world getting sick of the ranting that pours non-stop from the disgusting foam-flecked lips of the Ayatollah Khomeini? Clearly this Muslim cleric is stark raving mad. And more dangerous than a rabid dog. Surely the tragedy is that millions of his misguided and equally potty followers believe every word of hatred he hisses through those yellow stained teeth. The terrifying thing is not that a lot of these crackpots actually live here among us in Britain, but that we are actually becoming frightened of them. The whole thing is crazy. And it has to stop.

Such comments could only contribute to greater divisions. Some individuals were even demanding a ban on Islam. The creation of a Muslim Parliament in Britain, the campaign for separate voluntary-aided schools for Muslim children and readiness to obey the fatwas of Iranian Mullahs, were all alarmingly evil developments for many native whites. Threats, such as those from Kalim Siddiqi, who demanded a special Muslim citizenship or Muslim local and national government (for details see Nielsen, 1992), accentuated the gap between 'natives' and Muslims. Unsurprisingly, some white British commentators began to perceive Islam as the next major enemy after communism (Ahmed, 1992: 37).

6.3 Conflict of obligation systems: English law and *shari'a*

This shadow boxing between the two civilisations raised a number of important issues, not least the rights surrounding freedom of expression and freedom of religion. We now turn specifically to some of the legal issues in the debate. To understand this conflict of obligation systems better, we first need to take a closer look at the nature of Muslim laws.

6.3.1 The nature of *shari'a* law

The 'Satanic affair' posed a particular type of conflict between the predominantly secular English law and Islamic shari'a. There are major differences between the two systems. In character, English law is or purports to be secular, though some principles of common law have been shaped by the Christian ethos. The Queen in Parliament enacts the law; in reality it is the members of the House of Commons and the House of Lords who actively engage in the law making process. The influence of the dominant religion is less direct, its protagonists persuade and lobby within the Parliamentary process of law making.

In the view of some observers, the contrast with shari'a law could not be greater. In religious terms, all shari'a law derives from God, therefore administrators, rulers or members of state assemblies are not, in the eyes of orthodox Muslim law, empowered to make laws in that sense. The divine shari'a law is immutable, and the process of interpretation and adaptation is held to have been completed in the past (the so-called 'closing of the gates of ijtihad'), although this concept is certainly not unquestioned (Hallaq, 1984).

Muslim observers of the processes of English law making have sometimes made fun of them. A Muslim visitor to the British Parliament in the 19th century professed to be surprised at seeing laymen shouting 'like a pack of parrots', engaged in enacting laws without divine blessing. He wrote that unlike in Muslim countries, the British did not accept any divinely revealed holy law to guide them and regulate their civil, criminal, ritual and dietary matters. Instead they pass laws 'in accordance with the exigencies of the time, their own dispositions, and the experience of their judges' (see Lewis, 1994: 1).

Views similar to the above are still voiced by Muslim jurists. Brohi (1982: 63-66) argues that law without divine intervention is illogical. The late Ayatollah Khomeini, a Shi'a Imam, bluntly rejected any law making role for legislative assemblies. In his view, parliamentary functions should be limited to oversee implementation, as 'laws themselves are divine or deducible from the Qur'an and the hadith' (Fischer, 1983: 169).

Shari'a law as a religious law is undoubtedly based on revealed laws, but Muslim law is in practice a combination of revealed laws (the Qur'an and the sunna of the Prophet Muhammad, found in the hadith) as well as man-made laws, customs and human interpretations. Customs and interpretations are, in cases of conflict, subordinate to the revealed laws. In addition there may be certain laws enacted by rulers in Islamic states or territories (dar-ul Islam); these are referred to as 'regulations'. As they are enacted by rulers or a legislative assembly, they are inferior to shari'a law. In classical Muslim law, rulers are treated as having been given delegated authority by God to introduce rules and regulations (Brohi, 1982: 66). The delegation of such powers allows believers to administer their own culture-specific rule systems and to continue the state's activities under the umbrella of shari'a law.

The scope of shari'a law is in marked contrast to English law, which only governs one's relationship to the state and to other human beings, while shari'a law governs one's relationship with God, in addition to the state and fellow human beings. Rippin (1990: 74) comments:

> Law... is a far broader concept than that generally perceived in the English world. Included in it are not only the details of conduct in the narrower legal sense, but also minute matters of behaviour, what might even be termed 'manners', as well as issues related to worship and ritual; furthermore, the entire body of law is traditionally viewed as the 'revealed will of God', subject neither to history nor to change.

The law is thus 'Islamic' through and through (Rippin, 1990: 77; Lewis, 1994: 1). Therefore, in an Islamic state, there is supposed to be divine authority behind every legal principle and rule. This divine power makes shari'a law authoritative and, theoretically, this authority seeps into every nook and cranny of Islamic society. Islam without law or law without Islam is unimaginable for orthodox Muslim societies. The law in all its details is divine, not human, revealed not enacted.

There are limitations, however. Muslim law, too, applies only to those who submit to its authority (Lewis, 1994: 1-2). It is therefore a matter of individual conscience and belief. More substantially, the practical limitations of traditional Muslim theories are virtually impossible to operate within a large and complex state, and do not operate in non-Muslim countries. Even in most Muslim states, the gap between traditional Muslim theory and legal reality is wide, since the traditional Muslim orthodoxy does not prevail over secular political and legal authorities. In effect, the divine shari'a law co-exists with other forms of Muslim law, so that the workings of the state and the judicial system look to an outside observer as similar to Western models.

6.3.2 Blasphemy in shari'a law

In publishing The Satanic Verses, Salman Rushdie was alleged, according to shari'a law, to have committed recantation, blasphemy and treason. The matter was considered by Ayatollah Khomeini under verse 36 of chapter (sura) 5 of the Qur'an, which lists the following three offences:

- declaring war against God and his disciples, treason;

- becoming an apostate (murtadd), which occurs when a person born as a Muslim

- abandons his faith and crosses over to the enemies of Islam (recantation); and

- creating 'mischief through the land' by engaging in corruption (fasad).

It is a fundamental element of Islam that the religious and legal authority of the Qur'an and of the Prophet Muhammad exist as a fact and cannot be questioned. Most Muslims are prepared to be broad-minded about most things but not about anything that touches on essentials of their faith. 'Better that I be dead than see Islam insulted', said Ayatollah Majlisi in the last century. An Arab proverb, cited in Appignanesi and Maitland (1989: 92), says: 'Kill me, do not mock my faith'. If someone slandered or vilified the Prophet, the Qur'an or Islam in public, they would be punishable for treason or high treason.

Salman Rushdie was said to have committed treason by creating mischief, which in turn amounts to a declaration of war on Allah, the Prophet and the Qur'an. This most serious offence, challenging the roots of

Muslim existence, is treated as punishable by death. Sura 5, verse 36 of the Qur'an, translated by Ali (1946: 252-253), speaks of the following punishments:

> The punishment of those
> Who wage war against God
> And His Apostle, and strive
> With might and main
> For mischief through the land
> Is: execution, or crucifiction,
> Or the cutting off of hands
> And feet from opposite sides,
> Or exile from the land:
> That is their disgrace
> In this word, and
> A heavy punishment is theirs
> In the Hereafter.

Rushdie was found guilty, in his absence, on all the above counts and the Ayatollah Khomeini imposed the death penalty. Rushdie had not only insulted the Prophet, the Qur'an and Islam, but had done this on the world stage. According to Khomeini, anti-Islamic materials should not be allowed to be written, published or preached (Fischer, 1983: 152). The Ayatollah Khomeini, in his capacity as a mujtahid, a person recognised by Shi'a tradition as qualified to interpret the divine sources, issued an edict (fatwa) on 14 February 1989 against Rushdie and the publishers of The Satanic Verses (for details see Fischer and Abedi, 1990: 388), urging all dutiful followers of Islam, wherever they live, to carry out the fatwa (cited in Ruthven, 1991: 112; Appignanesi and Maitland, 1989: 84):

> I would like to inform all the intrepid Muslims in the world that the author of the book entitled The Satanic Verses, which has been compiled, printed and published in opposition to Islam, the Prophet and the Koran, as well as those publishers who were aware of its contents, have been declared Mahdur el dam (i.e. those whose blood must be shed). I call on all zealous Muslims to execute them quickly, wherever they find them, so that no one will dare to insult Islam again. Whoever is killed in this path will be regarded as a martyr, God willing.

There is no doubt that the fatwa was taken by many Muslims as an authoritative statement of law because Khomeini acted as a mujtahid and Imam on behalf of God (Yapp, 1989: 97). Putting to one side the issue of guilt, was such a punishment for blasphemy valid or justified? The Qur'an does not prescribe any punishment for blasphemy per se. However blasphemy by a 'believing Muslim' against God, the Prophet or the Qur'an may be considered a serious criminal offence, amounting to apostasy. For example, the orthodox and highly respected Muslim jurist Ibn Taymiyya stated in 1905 that vilification of the Prophet and insulting Muslims was a very serious criminal offence (Ruthven, 1991: 51). Akhtar (1989: 71) writes that the Qur'an does not refer to such a scenario, but he points to isolated incidents where execution has been used or threatened. The Literature Nobel Prize winner of 1988, the Egyptian writer Nagib Mahfouz, was made the subject of a fatwa for writing a book that displeased the authorities (Ruthven, 1991: 116). A Lahore bookseller was executed in 1924 by two Muslim youths for publishing blasphemous material in a book, The merry Prophet, as reported by Ruthven (1991: 87), who refers to several other examples. A prominent Muslim figure, Yusuf Islam (cited in Qureshi and Khan, 1989: 9), has remarked that 'the Qur'an makes it clear that if someone defames the Prophet, then he must die'. Muslim loyalty, ultimately, belongs to God, not to any secular laws.

Liaquat Hussain, the General Secretary to the Council of Mosques in Britain, asserted that under Islamic law Rushdie's crime was punishable by death. He further stressed the point saying that 'we cannot denounce that... it would be difficult for any Muslim leader to condemn anyone who carried out the Ayatollah's sentence' (Telegraph and Argus, 20 February 1989, cited in Qureshi and Khan, 1989: 10). Musharaf Hussain was equally serious, saying that Rushdie should not be allowed to escape without punishment, since '(i)t is like someone walking on the third lane of a motorway and expecting to be saved' (Qureshi and Khan, 1989: 14).

When a believer crosses to the enemy line, turning his back on divine guidance, it is considered a crime in Shari'a law. In Akhtar's opinion, the Qur'an contains no specifically prescribed penalty for such an offence but envisages punishment after death through the journey to hell. However, if a believer persistently attacks the lives of Muslims or their property, or engages in warfare against Muslims and Islam after recantation, this warrants capital punishment (Akhtar, 1989: 72).

Hence, a Bengali father in Birmingham killed his daughter for apostasy a few years ago. The alleged offence was her conversion to Jehovah's Witness. Contemporary Muslim scholars did not object to such punishment and capital punishment was approved 'even for a privately committed apostasy' (Akhtar, 1989: 73). Akhtar also observes that internationally reputed Muslim jurists in Egypt and Pakistan have in the recent past approved capital punishment for apostasy, particularly for male apostates, unless they were severely mentally retarded or of a tender age (below 12 years). This view is supported by many Muslim jurists and scholars in Iran, Pakistan, India and Bangladesh.

However, there is certain Sunni school of thought which is more liberal. Muslim jurists in Egypt do not normally approve of hudood punishments for apostates. Akhtar (1989: 76) thus concluded that,

> ...by and large, Muslims who privately commit apostasy are not harassed by the Islamic establishment. However, if an individual became an apostate or, like Rushdie, publicly insulted the Prophet Muhammad or launched abusive attacks on the contents of the Koran and the derivative Islamic tradition, he is almost always taken to task for it.

In Rushdie's case, shari'a law in the Shi'a tradition was applied as a deterrent punishment, a combination of retribution and incapacitation. The desire of vengeance reflected in this penal policy is not generally given priority in Western democratic countries (Faruqi, 1988: 60). Rehabilitation seems irrelevant in the tariff for blasphemy and high-treason.

The issues in the case became more complex as doubts began to be expressed whether Rushdie could be convicted of treason and what, if any, was the effect of his alleged apology. Once Salman Rushdie had become the subject of a fatwa, the lack of a trial, or an admission of guilt, began to be questioned. Yapp (1989: 97) wrote:

> A Mujtahid gives an opinion on a point of law. It remains an opinion even when it is regarded as authoritative. Before it can be applied to a case under Islamic criminal law, there must be a trial under proper procedure. Here there is something of a puzzling discrepancy between Khomeini's two reported statements. In the first he seemed to be delivering an opinion in the traditional manner, although many took it to be verdict and sentence against Rushdie as well. But in his

second statements about the futility of Rushdie' repentance he seemed to be adopting the role of judge.

As the crisis progressed, a further twist occurred when Rushdie offered a form of apology for the distress caused by the book. Such an expression of regret may have been considered an admission of responsibility (Appignanesi and Maitland, 1989: 97). Those seeking a compromise now seized their chance. If offering an apology could be considered as admission, then could it also be used for a reduction in the severity of the punishment, leading to the withdrawal of the fatwa? The initial response was that Rushdie's statement was not an apology. Rushdie had by way of explanation described himself as 'a pretty secular Muslim'. This attempt to move himself away from the religious controversy was instantly ridiculed. A secular system detached from Islam is virtually unknown in Islamic tradition. Akbar Ahmed (1992: 173) asked sarcastically: 'A secular Muslim. What sort of gobbledygook, what kind of literary conceit, is this?'.

Muslim organisations in the UK took a similar view and questioned the probity of the apology. The Bradford Council of Mosques stated it was 'not a sincere apology but a further insult to the Muslim community' (The Sunday Times, 19 February 1989). Khomeini characteristically dealt with the issue head on: 'Even if Salman Rushdie repents and becomes the most pious man of all time, it is incumbent on every Muslim to employ everything he has got, his life and his wealth, to send him to hell' (cited in Appignanesi and Maitland, 1989: 122). This implies that a fatwa is irrevocable but authorities differ on this. The view that the fatwa is un-challengeable was expressed in the Muslim Parliament in 1996 by Kalim Siddiqi, who confirmed that a fatwa, once issued, could only be withdrawn by the person who issued it. However when Rushdie's apology was referred to Ayatollah Motaheri, his interpretation differed from that of Ayatollah Khomeini. If the apology were sincere and genuine, Motaheri would have been prepared to pardon Rushdie and withdraw the fatwa. As reported by Yapp (1989: 97), he stated:

> If they attacked Islam openly, they should be answered in the same way, book against book, opinion against opinion. Only if they attacked deceitfully, intending to mislead the believers, should they be dealt with violently. Even then, if the attackers sincerely repented they should be forgiven.

This opinion was shared by President Ali Khomeini of Iran who said that if Rushdie apologised, 'this wretched man might yet be spared' (Appignanesi and Maitland, 1989: 118). The Egyptian Mufti Sheikh Tantawi said, referring to Rushdie's trial, that even a convicted criminal could ask the court or tribunal for clemency and forgiveness (Ruthven, 1991:115-116). The view that a fatwa can be withdrawn appears to be supported by verse 37 in sura 5 of the Qur'an. Thus, if one were to assume Rushdie's genuine repentance, he could on the balance of authority be pardoned by a mujtahid. However, at the time of writing there is no evidence of true repentance by Rushdie.

6.3.3 The 'fatwa' and conflicts of law

How should the validity of the fatwa be considered in the light of the fact that Rushdie was domiciled in England? We have already seen that, from the Iranian point of view, the fatwa was valid irrespective of domicile: the Ayatollah Khomeini, as a Shia Imam, had acted on behalf of God (Yapp, 1989: 97). The Imam is the constituted authority to supervise and arbitrate human affairs (Rippin, 1990: 114). His power to make judicial decisions and to impose penalties is enormous in classical Shi'a law. His obligation is to ensure that believers are obeying God's laws and the sunna of the Prophet. Khomeini was a rare combination of sovereign, imam and mujtahid. In the light of classical Qur'anic law, Khomeini could not be challenged for punishing someone who betrayed Islam and insulted God's authority by slandering the Prophet. The fatwa has a divine and sovereign authority as far as Shi'a Muslims are concerned. Such Muslims are, however, a minority among British Muslims. The fatwa was therefore challenged on three counts:

- the encouragement to kill for money rather than for Islam;

- due process had not been followed (see Fischer and Abedi, 1990: 388);

- it is questionable whether an Iranian religious authority could issue a fatwa against a person abroad, living in non-Islamic territory (dar-ul harb).

A £1 million reward was offered for killing Salman Rushdie in compliance with the fatwa and some Muslims argued that this conflicted with the Qur'an. The Secretary General of the fundamentalist 'Renaissance Movement' in Tunisia, who refused to recognise the validity of the punishment, saw the fatwa as an 'impious outrage contrary to the spirit of Islam' (Ruthven, 1991: 116). Islam, he argued, does not encourage anyone to kill individuals simply because they are alleged to have committed a crime.

As to the second possible challenge, due process, Salman Rushdie had not been provided with the opportunity to defend himself. When the trial took place, he was in hiding. The evidence against him was allegedly provided by Iranian officials in London and the Ayatollah gave his verdict in Rushdie's absence. Due process, as understood in English law, requires that individuals should be given the opportunity to defend themselves before an impartial judge. Parties should be heard before being tried, in line with the principle of audi alteram partem (see Ridge v Baldwin [1964] AC 40, HL). No such rule exists in classical Muslim law, so that judges can decide cases based on what is presented to them (Rippin, 1990: 84). Khomeini followed these traditional Islamic legal procedures. The witnesses were his officials, including diplomats working in London, whose statements, based on presumptions of classical shari'a law about proper witnesses as truthful and honest people, were taken as the truth. This approach fitted well with Khomeini's own style and view of the process. He was alleged to have preferred deterrent and summary execution, arguing that a criminal needs no lawyers. Procedural laws were, in his reign, commonly neglected to secure convictions (Fischer, 1983: 168). Once, Khomeini was reported to have issued a fatwa, at a public meeting, against anyone who dared to insult or joke about Muslims. 'Their wives shall be forbidden (haram) to them, their property shall be seized and distributed, and their blood may be wasted' (cited in Fischer and Abedi, 1990: 173). It is hardly surprising, therefore, that no explanation was sought from Rushdie before the imposition of the death penalty against him.

Other Islamic jurists, however, invoke principles similar to the procedural rules of English law. The Egyptian Mufti Sheikh Tantawi considered that before an author such as Rushdie may be given the death sentence, 'the court must ask the writer to explain his intentions and not be limited by misreading and misunderstanding' (Ruthven, 1991: 116). Tariq Modood also argued that no person can be sentenced to death without a proper trial and concluded that the Teheran fatwa was a cruel and unjust order which was against the moralist aspect of Shari'a law

(Modood, 1993: 69). Khomeini was criticised for manipulating shari'a law for his own sake, even interfering with the relationship between man and God (see Fischer and Abedi, 1990: 168).

The third challenge relates to jurisdiction. Muslim law normally only applies to Muslim territory (dar-ul Islam), the 'house of Islam'. When Muslims live in a country which does not come under Muslim law or is not governed by a Muslim ruler, that country is considered dar-ul harb, the 'house of warfare', a country belonging to infidels. The initial publication of The Satanic Verses took place in the UK, thus in dar-ul harb territory. There is a view, held by some UK Muslims, that when there is a sizeable Muslim population in a particular dar-ul harb, that country can be considered dar-ul Islam. Despite the fact that Islam is now the second largest religion in the UK and that there are well over one million Muslims and more than 1,000 mosques in Britain, Islamic law does not prevail over the indigenous norms (Raza, 1991: 159; Shaikh, 1992: 261; Joly, 1995, ch. 4). The UK must therefore be considered dar-ul harb.

The view of the Sunni tradition of Islam was that Khomeini's fatwa did not apply to Muslims domiciled in dar-ul harb. This was in contradiction to the Iranian position, which holds that Muslims are subject to shari'a law wherever they live. This view accepts that the Ayatollah was entitled to exercise his judicial power over the universal Muslim brotherhood (the ummah). How such an edict would be carried out in practice is another matter.

The problem of the fatwa was indicative of a more general problem facing Muslims living in dar-ul harb. Britain is neither under Muslim rule nor are Muslim laws officially recognised by the English legal system. In theory dar-ul harb remains a land of warfare until it is con-quered by Islam. In the view of Khadduri (1955: 171-172), Muslims in a non-Muslim territory are under no obligation to submit to the law of the non-believers' territory, but neither are they expected to engage in hostile action against any individuals in that territory. Khadduri (1955: 172) emphasised that 'Muslim law, as has been repeatedly stated, is binding on the Muslim regardless of the territory he lives in'. Should a Muslim find a conflict between the law of the land and his own law, there is no doubt as to what his choice must be (see Khadduri, 1955: 171; also Lewis, 1994: 13).

A minority were more conciliatory. Mughram Ali Al-Ghamdi said, as cited in Appignanesi and Maitland (1989:113):

> We are a minority living in this country and we do intend to fully abide by the law. We are not above the law. We do not condone violence of any kind by anybody under any pretext... Britain is not a Muslim country. Islamic laws do not apply here... Only courts and governments can deal with offending authors.

The potential legal irregularities did little to reduce the support of fundamentalist, pro-Iranian groups for the fatwa. Iqbal Sacranie, a member of the UK Action Committee on Islamic Affairs, was uncompromising, insisting that 'death, perhaps, is a bit too easy for him... his mind must be tormented for the rest of his life' (cited in Appignanesi and Maitland, 1989: 100). Some Muslims in other countries adopted a similar view. Yet the question remained whether Muslims who were British citizens could implement such an edict, issued by a leader of a foreign country. Scholars and commentators appeared to be uncertain as to the possible consequences of carrying out such orders.

At the same time Muslims seemed to be trapped by a 'loyalty test'. Islam teaches that it is the responsibility of true Muslims to propagate good and to combat evil. Muslims who see wrong being done and do nothing to stop it become a partner in that crime (Appignanesi and Maitland, 1989: 93). According to this rationale, since The Satanic Verses embodies a crime in the eyes of the ordinary Muslim, its author should be killed. While for Sunni Muslims, dicta issued by an Iranian imam are not binding in terms of Muslim law, Shi'a Muslims faced no such theological or legal barriers. After the Imam of Iran had issued the fatwa, it was their religious duty to protect the honour of God and the Prophet, and to uphold God's law. Muslims in both traditions were therefore ready to implement the fatwa, if and when an opportunity arose, preferably in secret.

Musharaf Hussain reminded British Muslims of their obligation to stand up for their faith: 'If someone offends or attacks them, they have every right to respond without fear – no matter where they are in the world' (Evening Post, 7 March 1989, cited in Qureshi and Khan, 1989: 14). Shabbir Akhtar's opinion was that a fundamentalist approach was necessary to respond to such a provocation (Lewis, 1994: 159). Professor

Syed Ali Ashraf, Director General of the Islamic Academy in Cambridge University, writing to Impact International (28 October 1988: 10, cited in Appignanesi and Maitland, 1989: 59-60), asked:

> Should not the Muslim community have the right to condemn this man for blasphemy because he is using a thin veil of fiction in order to vilify the Prophet and all that they hold dear to them? As he is not interested in presenting his own realisation of any truth, as he is preaching an anti-Islamic theory in the guise of a novel, his liberty as a writer ends and he should be treated as anyone producing blasphemous writings is treated.

What would be the response of the English legal system? Even among faithful campaigners, the practicability and legality of implementing the fatwa raised a number of questions. It appears that, for the majority of British Muslims, Rushdie was seen as a criminal. Some British Muslims had asked the Ayatollah Khomeini to issue a fatwa, submitting a petition to him directly via the Islamic Embassy in London. Khomeini had been deliberately chosen in preference to other authoritative figures, as the Ayatollah most likely to provide the severest punishment (Appignanesi and Maitland, 1989: 96). In addition, South Asian Muslims in Britain knew very well that those who insulted Islam and the Prophet during the British Raj in India were often brutally killed.

But how was English law to view the fatwa? There is no doubt that the views of the Muslim elders were shaped by and based on the jurisprudence of India and Pakistan (Lewis, 1994: 155). In both Pakistan and India, blasphemy against Islam, the Prophet and the Qur'an is a criminal offence. In July 1986, the Pakistan National Assembly enacted the Criminal Law (Amendment) Bill. It provides, as cited by P. Lewis (1994: 155):

> Whoever by words, either spoken or written, or by visible representation or by any imputation, innuendo or insinuation, directly or indirectly defies the sacred name of the Holy Prophet... shall be punished with death or imprisonment.

The Indian colonial administration had introduced a new section 295A into the Indian Penal Code of 1860 in 1927, following the Lahore events surrounding the murder of an allegedly blasphemous author, referred to at p. 191 above. The section reads:

Whoever, with deliberate and malicious intention of outraging the religious feelings of any class of citizens of India, by words, either spoken or written or by signs or by visible representations or otherwise, insults or attempts to insult the religion or the religious beliefs of that class, shall be punished with imprisonment of either description for a term which may extend to three years, or with fine, or with both.

It seemed obvious to many Muslim elders, therefore, that English law should also provide some redress against the vilification of Islam. Dr. Al-Ghamdi advised Muslims in a UKACIA publication of 28 October 1988 (cited in Appignanesi and Maitland, 1989: 59-60):

We are exploring... all possible legal action. We will keep you informed of all developments. Please try to approach your local M.P.s and police chiefs and tell them that the publication of the book has angered and outraged Muslims enormously and they should take up the matter with Scotland Yard to prosecute the publisher/author under criminal law, i.e. Public Order Act or Race Relations Act.

It seems that Muslims were arguing to themselves that Rushdie's offences against Islam and Muslims should be taken care of by the English legal system. The obvious remedy would be to use the official legal channels, rather than lobbying and protests on the streets or in publications.

6.4 Challenges in the British courts

At first sight, it would appear that The Satanic Verses falls foul of the English blasphemy laws. The book did, after all, ridicule and insult God and Abraham, holy figures for Christians and Muslims. Abraham was referred to as a bastard, and some Muslim lawyers appeared confident that there was a case to answer under English law. In the now famous London Hyde Park rally, Al Mohammed Azhar, a barrister, announced that papers had been filed with Bow Street Magistrates' Court and said that, '[w]e believe the book infringes the blasphemy laws. We are prepared to go all the way to the European Court. My duty is to see that my faith is protected' (see Appignanesi and Maitland, 1989: 77-78).

Such optimism was rudely shattered. Subsequent events showed the profound ignorance of some Muslims about how English law operates within a democratic and secular environment. They were soon to be in conflict with English law. In urging them to follow Muslim law, the Secretary to the Bradford Council of Mosques, Sayyid Abdul Quddus, indicated his organisation's support of the fatwa and provoked the then Home Secretary Douglas Hurd and Home Office Minister John Patten to remind Muslims of their legal obligation to uphold the rule of law (see Qureshi and Khan, 1989: 8).

In Britain such extra-judicial order, a request to kill someone residing in Britain, amounts to a criminal offence, i.e. incitement. A person who made such request is an inciter, defined as 'one who reaches and seeks to influence the mind of another to the commission of a crime' (Smith and Hogan, 1996: 273). The same authors comment (id.) that 'mere incitement of another to commit an indictable offence is a common law misdemeanor, whether the incitement is successful in persuading the other to commit, or to attempt to commit the offence or not'. An inciter could be charged and prosecuted under s. 4 of the Offences Against the Person Act, 1861 (as amended by the Criminal Law Act, 1977) if he proved to be incited, solicited, encouraged, persuaded, or endeavoured or proposed to any person to murder any other person (Race Relations Board v Applin [1973] QB 815, CA, at p. 825). Not only those who issued orders to kill someone, but also those who supported, solicited, aided, tried to carry out or carried out the offence could be prosecuted. Punishment is prescribed in Schedule 2 of the Criminal Law Act, 1977, which replaced s. 16 of the Offences Against the Person Act, 1861 and reads as follows:

> A person who without lawful excuse makes to another a threat, including that that other would fear that it would be carried out, to kill that other or their person shall be guilty of an offence and liable on conviction on indictment to imprisonment for a term not exceeding ten years.

The crime occurs when an alleged threat is communicated and reaches the persons who are to be influenced. Whether that person's mind was influenced is irrelevant. The courts would not accept arguments that the accused were ignorant of the English legal system or that their religion obliges them to follow shari'a law in preference to 'man-made' British law. In R v Barronet and Allain [1852] Dears CC 51, at p. 58, Lord Cambell CJ pronounced that, 'persons who fly to this country... must obey the laws of the country, and be content to place themselves in the same situation as native born subject'.

In consequence of such possible criminal liability, the Council of Mosques issued a press statement saying that members of Mosques did not support violence, nor did they wish to incite Muslims to break the law of the country in which they live. As an independent Muslim organisation, the Council of Mosques wished to clarify that it did not take directives from any institutions or government abroad and that it would urge Muslims to respect English law (Ruthven, 1991: 120). Nevertheless the West Yorkshire police sent details to the Crown Prosecution Service to consider prosecution of those who incited or supported the fatwa.

The support for the fatwa formed only one part in the campaign against The Satanic Verses. Salman Rushdie's books were burnt in major cities in December 1988 and January 1989 and a Penguin bookshop in London was bombed, allegedly by Muslims. Apart from that, there remained only the legal option of attempting to have the book banned, and to prosecute Rushdie and the publishers. Since the Public Prosecutor and the police had refused to act, the Muslim campaigners launched a two-pronged legal attack when two separate actions were initiated before the Chief Metropolitan Stipendiary Magistrate at Bow Street and before the Horseferry Road Metropolitan Stipendiary Magistrate. The parties in both cases appear to have acted in concert, aware of each other's position in advance.

The first case, instituted by Abdul Hussain Choudhury on behalf of the Muslim Action Front, tried to establish that the law of blasphemy at common law covers all three major religions, Islam, Christianity and Judaism. Mr. Choudhury applied for the criminal prosecution of Salman Rushdie and Viking for publishing The Satanic Verses, on the ground that the publication was a blasphemous libel against God Allah, Islam, Abraham, the Prophet Muhammad, his wives and his companions. The action was an attempt to revive the pre-17th century interpretation of English blasphemy laws. It raised the issue of whether it is justifiable to exclude religions of ethnic minorities in Britain today from the protection of the law of blasphemy. The second case, initiated by Sayid Mehdie Siadatan, an Iranian living in Britain, argued that if The Satanic Verses were allowed to be distributed, it would provoke unlawful violence contrary to s. 4(1) of the Public Order Act, 1986.

The law of blasphemy had become almost moribund, or as Webster (1990: 20) said, remained a 'kind of legal appendix.'. Historically, most

English legal principles and tenets are based on the Christian ethos and developed 'under the shadow of Solomon's throne supported by lions on both sides' (Lester, 1993: 270). Since 1688, when King Solomon's throne was succeeded by the communicants of the Church of England, 'the court of King's Bench began to treat criminal libel including blasphemies...as misdemeanors at common law' (Feldman, 1993: 686).

In the English common law system, the law of blasphemy was taken to apply only to Anglican Christianity. This was confirmed in R v Gathercole [1838] 2 Lew CC 237, 168 ER 1140, where the position of English law was expressed as follows:

> A person may, without being liable to prosecution for it, attack Judaism or Mohomodinism, or even any sect of the Christian religion [save the established religion of the country]: and the only reason why the latter is in a different situation from the others is, because it is the form established by law, and is therefore a part of the constitution of the country, like manner, and for the same reason, any general attack on Christianity is the subject of criminal prosecution, because Christianity is the established religion of the country.

The public importance of the Christian religion was so great that no one was allowed to deny its truth (Smith and Hogan, 1983: 737). Since Christianity is the religion of the land, any scurrilous attack on Christianity is an attack on the establishment because it is part and parcel of the laws of England. This interpretation was confirmed in a number of early cases. The offence of blasphemy also required that the statements in some way affected the stability of the state. An attack on Christianity was assumed to involve an attack on the integrity and stability of the state. In R v Taylor [1676] 1 Vent 293, 86 ER 189, the oldest case in common law in the area of blasphemy, Hale CJ observed that 'blasphemous words were not only an offence to God and religion, but a crime against the laws, state, and government and therefore punishable in the court'. In Bowman v Secular Society [1917] AC 406 Lord Sumner, with some reluctance, still affirmed this view. Thus any attack on the state's religion was presumed to undermine the stability of the state.

However, already by the mid-19th century, the mood had begun to change and sober, rational and serious discussions about religious beliefs and traditions were found not to be blasphemous. For a successful prosecution it was now necessary to show that the attack on a religion was such that it would be an attack on the stability of society. Lord Sumner stated in Bowman v Secular Society Ltd [1917] AC 406 that the judiciary is more worried about whether any act of blasphemy would 'shake the fabric of society generally'. Lord Scarman in R v Lemon [1979] AC 617 at p. 658, summarising the legal position, said that 'the offence belonged to a group of criminal offences designed to safeguard the internal tranquillity of the kingdom'. An attack on a religion that affects the sensibilities of individuals or group of individuals is, as such, insufficient to constitute an offence.

Within this context, Mr. Azhar as the barrister representing Mr. Choudhury and the Muslim Action Front had to show that in publishing The Satanic Verses, Rushdie and his publishers had also attacked Christianity and that such an attack had affected the stability of society (see R v Chief Metropolitan Stipendiary Magistrate, ex parte Choudhury [1991] 1 All ER 306). Thus it was argued that the book had vilified and insulted God and the Prophet Abraham. Azhar's argument was partly based on an old case (R v Williams [1797] 26 St Tr 653), where the defendant was found guilty after attacking the Old Testament. It was argued that since the New Testament is based on the Old Testament, any attack on the latter amounts to an attack on Christianity. Could an attack on Islam be taken as an attack on the Old Testament? This line of argument failed, the court finding that Islam is based on the Qur'an, not on the Old Testament.

Mr. Azhar then attempted to challenge directly the requirement that Christianity must be the subject of the attack. He argued that the court should interpret common law offences in the light of changing demography in contemporary Britain. An attack on any religion that led to social instability should amount to blasphemy. Relying on R v Gott [1922] 16 Cr App R 87, it was argued that an indecent and offensive attack on scriptures, sacred persons or objects with a view to injuring the feelings of the general body of the community would amount to both blasphemy and sedition. Mr. Azhar argued that 'scriptures' goes beyond Christianity and would undoubtedly cover both Judaism and Islam. If this were accepted, there was strong evidence that The Satanic Verses had already caused much damage to community and property; people taking part in protests and demonstrations had lost their lives in many parts of the world. However, Watkins LJ rejected this argument, indicating that Mr. Azhar had misunderstood the ratio decidendi of R v Williams.

Mr. Azhar then argued that if there was no judicial remedy available in the area of blasphemy for religious groups other than Anglican Christians, the judiciary should correct such irregularity by extending the law of blasphemy to other religions. He emphasised, at p. 318, that 'it is anomalous and unjust to discriminate in favour of one religion', thus questioning the legitimacy of preferential treatment for a state's religion. This was the first time in British legal history that non-Christians questioned and challenged the legitimacy of the state's religion.

In support of his contention, Mr. Azhar turned to Articles 9, 10 and 14 of the European Convention on Human Rights of 1950. In particular, Article 14 of the ECHR seemed relevant. It reads:

> The enjoyment of the rights and freedoms set forth in this Convention shall be secured without discrimination on any ground such as sex, race, colour, language, religion, political or other opinion, national or social origin, association with a national minority, property, birth or other status.

As a signatory to the ECHR, he argued, the UK should ensure that there was a mechanism in English law to protect individuals on an equal footing irrespective of racial or religious differences. 'If the law of blasphemy', argued Mr. Azhar at p. 319, 'is designed to protect Christianity alone, it means that other religions have been left unprotected ever since the Convention was signed in [the] 1950s'. Such a position would be in violation of the Convention obligations. Interpreting Article 14 together with Article 9, Mr. Azhar further argued that if the right to freedom of religion for Muslims was not protected from sacrilegious attack and blasphemous libel, Muslims would be denied the rights guaranteed by both articles (p. 319). This is a compelling argument. Here is a case where English law is differently applied in respect of Christians and Muslims, with the latter being discriminated against on the grounds of religion. Preferential treatment in respect of one set of individuals is not prohibited by international law if it is designed to correct past injustices and applied only on a temporary basis. This is not so in this case, for it was the Muslims who are alleged to have been discriminated against.

Anthony Lester QC, appearing for Viking Penguin, stressed that the UK was not in breach of the ECHR. Answering the questions raised by the applicant, Lester admitted that the obligation imposed on the UK by the Convention are a relevant source of public policy where the common law is uncertain. He maintained, however, that the 'common law of blasphemy is, without doubt, certain' (p. 320). Therefore it was not necessary to pay any regard to the Convention in the given case. Lester argued further that if the court decided to convict Rushdie and his publishers, it would violate the author's rights as guaranteed by Articles 7 and 10 ECHR. Article 7 deals with retroactive offences and provides:

(1) No one shall be held guilty of any criminal offence on account of any act or omission which did not constitute a criminal offence under national or international law at the time it was committed. Nor shall a heavier penalty be imposed than the one that was applicable at the time the criminal offence was committed.

(2) This article shall not prejudice the trial and punishment of any person for any act or omission which, at the time when it was committed, was criminal according to the general principles of law recognized by civilized nations.

Clearly, in the light of article 7, Rushdie or his publishers could not be punished for the alleged offence, simply because it was not a criminal offence when the book was published. In the eyes of English law, Rushdie did not attack Christianity or any of the institutions of the British government or try to incite individuals against Her Majesty's government. On the other hand, as Lester argued at length (pp. 320-324), Rushdie exercised his freedom of expression as guaranteed by Article 10 of the ECHR by publishing a book which was acclaimed by the literary world as a distinguished novel. Article 10 ECHR reads as follows:

(1) Everyone has the right to freedom of expression. This right shall include freedom to hold opinions and to receive and impart information and ideas without interference by public authority and regardless of frontiers. This article shall not prevent States from requiring the licensing of broadcasting, television or cinema enterprises.

(2) The exercise of these freedoms, since it carries with it duties and responsibilities, may be subject to such formalities, conditions, restrictions or penalties as are prescribed by law and are necessary in a democratic society, in the interests of national security, territorial integrity or public safety, for the prevention of disorder or crime, for the protection of health or morals, for the protection

of the reputation or rights of others, for preventing the disclosure or information received in confidence, or for maintaining the authority and impartiality of the judiciary.

Lester argued that the freedom of expression guaranteed by Article 10 ECHR prevented the court from restricting Rushdie's right to hold opinions and to receive and impart information and ideas (pp. 320-322). These rights shall be guaranteed, in the view of the defence, without interference by any public authority. Even though article 10(2) ECHR allows restrictions to be placed, in the given case, Lester's opinion was that Rushdie and Viking Press had not committed offences which could be considered under the exceptions contained in Article 10. Therefore, he proposed, neither the British government nor the judiciary could interfere with Rushdie's rights.

Lester further observed that the freedom of expression was a sine qua non in a democratic and secular society, in which civil liberties are jealously guarded. Any interference with a well-founded right to freedom of expression, argued Lester at p. 321, would be a fatal blow to the basic structure of free democratic societies and their value system. This argument is indeed logical in terms of freedom of expression, but it failed to take into account the detrimental impact of such an unlimited right. Should there not be a limit to guarantee the rights and beliefs of other communities and religious sects against unjustifiable attack?

Lester's arguments won the day. The court refused to fill a vacuum by creating new legal remedies and encroaching upon the territory of the legislature. The court found at p. 318:

> We have no doubt that as the law now stands it does not extend to religions other than Christianity. Can it in the light of the present condition of society be extended by the courts to cover other religions? Mr. Azhar submits that it can and should be on the grounds that it is anomalous and unjust to discriminate in favour of one religion. In our judgment, where the law is clear it is not the proper function of this court to extend it; particularly is this so in criminal cases, where offences cannot be retrospectively created. It is in those circumstances the function of Parliament alone to change the law... The mere fact that the law is anomalous or even unjust does not, in our view, justify the court in changing it, if it is clear. If the law is uncertain, in interpreting and declaring the law the judges will do so

in accordance with justice and to avoid anomaly or discrimination against certain classes of citizens; but taking that course is not open to us, even though we may think justice demands it, for the law is not, we think, uncertain.

The court hit the mood of both Western liberal intellectuals and human rights lawyers who had been shocked to hear of demands to restrict freedom of expression. Richard Webster (1990: 45) writes that freedom of expression is 'as precious to the West, almost, as the Koran itself is to Islam'. The UNESCO's Director General expressed his deep anxiety about the campaign against The Satanic Verses (Appignanesi and Maitland, 1989: 125). Anthony Lester, one of the most distinguished and respected human rights lawyers in Britain, vigorously resisted the claims of Azhar. He said 'what the applicant seeks to do is to interfere with a well-founded right to freedom of expression, a kind of interference never at any time foreshadowed by the common law of this country' (p. 321). The campaign, with its militant and violent demonstrations and book burning incidents, seemed to have alarmed and shocked members of the judiciary. Granting leave to appeal against the decision of the Stipendiary Magistrate at Bow Street, Nolan J took the opportunity to warn Muslim activists (see R v Chief Metropolitan Stipendiary Magistrate, ex parte Choudhury [1991] 1 All ER 306, at p. 309):

> Whatever the outcome of these proceedings may be,the fundamental rule of English law is that the peace must be preserved. I know that this is fully understood by your own very responsible clients. It would be a great tragedy if the continuation of this argument in court were taken by others as a sign that demonstrations and the like, which might lead to breaches of the law, would give assistance; in fact they will be counter-productive.

In the second case, R v Horseferry Road Magistrate, ex parte Siadatan [1991] 1 All ER 324, the argument was focused on whether publishing and distributing The Satanic Verses would result in 'immediate violence' within the meaning of s. 4(1) of the Public Order Act, 1986. This section provides:

> A person is guilty of an offence if he
> (a) uses towards another person threatening, abusive or insulting words or behaviour, or

(b) distributes or displays to another person any writing, sign or other visible representation which is threatening, abusive or insulting,

with intent to cause that person to believe that immediate unlawful violence will be used against him or another by any person, or to provoke the immediate use of unlawful violence by that person or another, or whereby that person is likely to believe that such violence will be used or it is likely that such violence will be provoked.

Watkins LJ, who had delivered the main judgment in ex parte Choudhury, concentrated on technical aspects of the phrases 'such violence' and 'immediate unlawful violence'. Mr. Siadatan's application appears to be based on stronger and sounder legal arguments than ex parte Choudhury. Laying information before the Horseferry Road Metropolitan Stipendiary Magistrate, Mr. Siadatan complained that the distribution of the book was 'an act whereby it was likely that unlawful violence would be provoked' (p. 326). The magistrate's view was that the applicant had failed to include in the charge sheet that immediate violence would occur if the distribution of The Satanic Verses was allowed.

Counsel for the applicant, Mr. Geoffrey Nice, appearing before the Queen's Bench Division, argued that s. 4(1) should be read in conjunction with s. 6(3) of the Public Order Act, 1986 to determine whether Salman Rushdie had published the book knowing that his words were threatening, abusive or insulting, or that he was aware that it may have been perceived as threatening, abusive or insulting. His principal argument was that Salman Rushdie intentionally or maliciously published materials prohibited by the above provision, knowing that it would provoke violence. Therefore, Rushdie 'should not escape criminal liability under s. 4(1) simply because the violence which the written words are likely to provoke will not be immediate' (p. 327). Mr. Nice also stressed that giving a narrower interpretation to s. 4(1) of the 1986 Act would defeat what Parliament intended to achieve when passing the Act, namely to protect certain groups from racially motivated attack or publication of materials which insult racial groups or invite violence against such groups. He also argued that an individual's right to freedom of expression is limited by s. 4(1) and s. 6(3). 'Such rights', it was argued, 'do not include a freedom to insult or abuse other persons in such a way that it is likely that violence will be provoked' (p. 327). Watkins LJ did admit that the arguments appeared to be 'intricate and persuasive', but the claim for judicial review was nevertheless rejected.

6.5 Remedies under European human rights law

Mr. Choudhury, a determined Muslim campaigner against The Satanic Verses, proceeded to petition the European Commission of Human Rights. He complained to the Commission that the UK had failed to protect the British Muslims against blasphemy under Article 9 of the ECHR (Application No. 17439/90, Choudhury v UK, cited in Vol. 12 No. 4 [1991] Human Rights Law Journal, p. 172). He argued that British Muslims, their religion, Islam and their spiritual leader, the Prophet Muhammad, were subjected to abuse and scurrilous attack. Without protection against such abuses, British Muslims would not be able to enjoy the freedom of religion guaranteed by Article 9 ECHR. The Commission found that the applicant's claim was not covered by the ECHR, holding that legal remedies are not guaranteed by Article 9 in respect of such scurrilous abuse. Refusing the application, the Commission also held that both points raised by the applicant were incompatible within the meaning of Article 27(2) ECHR.

Feldman (1993: 696) agreed with this decision and argued that 'there is no warrant for extending such a principle to cases in which an applicant is asserting a right which is not recognised within the Convention'. However, he does not state the legal implications which may arise if an individual abuses Article 9 rights so as to insult the religious feelings and beliefs of others. By necessary implication, Article 9 imposes 'a duty on all of us to refrain from insulting or outraging the religious feelings of others' (per Lord Scarman in R. v Lemon [1979] AC 617, at p. 658). If an irresponsible individual attacks or insults the religious faith of others, then Article 9 should surely provide for a judicial remedy for those individuals who allege to have suffered.

It was held in a number of judgments (Marckx v Belgium [1979] 2 EHRR 330 and Johnston v Ireland [1987] 9 EHRR 203) that the ECHR should be interpreted in the light of present-day developments rather than the ideas prevalent when the ECHR was drafted. It is imperative that the contracting parties shall secure to everyone within their jurisdiction for both aliens and nationals the enjoyment of the rights contained in Article

1 ECHR without any distinction as to race, religion, nationality, or other similar grounds. Thus the underlying purpose of Article 9 together with Article 14 is, inter alia, to remove all differential treatment between members of different religious communities to whom these rights have been guaranteed on an equal footing. It is therefore surprising that the European Commission on Human Rights did not discuss the extent to which The Satanic Verses raises issues in the context of European human rights jurisprudence.

The reluctance of the judiciary to take positive steps in enhancing the scope of law of blasphemy invites some criticism. There are some judicial precedents to suggest that in the recent past the judiciary has taken progressive step on certain issues when radical changes were required in the development of common law principles. For instance, in R v R. [1991] 4 All ER 481, the House of Lords reversed the 250 years old judicial position in respect of marital rape. The common law, it was said, is capable of evolving in the light of changing social, economic and cultural developments. Strictly speaking, the judiciary does not have enormous difficulty in according new interpretations to the existing common law principles where these are not suitable in view of modern socio-legal developments. Thus, the argument that only Parliament can change laws, employed to counter Muslim claims for changes in the law, is not always used. It appears to have been employed in the Muslim blasphemy cases to protect the domestic law from Muslim claims for equal treatment which arose, at that time, in a rather agitated fashion.

We argue here that unlimited right to freedom of expression would surely disturb relations between different ethnic and religious communities. Particularly in multi-ethnic and multi-religious societies, freedom of expression should be enjoyed with restraint. It is therefore neither desirable nor sensible to allow unlimited right of freedom of expression without paying due regard to all members of the community. These rights are closely related to freedom of thought, conscience and religion, as guaranteed by Article 9 ECHR. Both Article 9 and Article 10 have frequently been considered together, and both have a limitation clause. The Article 10 right is subject to derogation, so that the exercise of these rights and freedoms carries with it duties and responsibilities and is subject to conditions, restrictions or penalties as prescribed by law and necessary in a democratic society in the interest of, inter alia, morals and the reputation of others. Thus, it is obvious that freedom of expression is not an absolute right which individuals can enjoy at their whim and pleasure.

The limitation of Article 10 rights and the wider supervisory power which the European human rights mechanism is allowed to use were discussed in a number of cases by the European Court of Human Rights. For example, in Handyside v UK [1979-80] 1 EHRR 737, the petitioner argued that the legal action taken against himself and The Little Red School Book in the English Courts was in breach of his right to freedom of thought, conscience and belief under Article 9 of the Convention. But it was held by 13 votes to 1 that the restrictions imposed upon Mr. Handyside's freedom of expression in publishing the book were prescribed by law and necessary in a democratic society for the protection of morals in accordance with Article 10(2). The judgment clearly placed emphasis on the responsibilities of individuals when enjoying such rights (p. 738).

It is true that freedom of expression constitutes one of the essential foundations of a democratic society and is one of the basic conditions for its progress and for each individual's self-fulfilment (The Observer and the Guardian v UK 14 EHRR 153; Lingens v Austria 8 EHRR 407). Nevertheless, this right is subjected to a number of exceptions. Interference by domestic institutions in freedom of expression is warranted by Article 10(2) ECHR if such a restriction is justified by a pressing social need and if it is 'necessary in a democratic society in the interest of national security and for the protection of the reputation or rights of others' (Sunday Times v UK [1991] 14 EHRR 229, para 59). In the Choudhury case, both before the English courts and the European Commission, the main argument appeared to be that by publishing The Satanic Verses, Salman Rushdie had intentionally insulted and ridiculed the Muslim community, Islam and the Prophet Muhammad, putting security at risk, as was evident from the subsequent events. For some reason, however, Mr. Choudhury's arguments fell on deaf ears.

The Article 10 right is distinguished from other rights contained in the ECHR. An individual exercising freedom of expression undertakes certain duties and responsibilities when doing so. This allows the state to impose restrictions on freedom of expression when it appears that individuals are exploiting such rights for their own interests. As argued in Choudhury, that was exactly what Salman Rushdie did, in good faith or not, in publishing his novel. Therefore interference with such cases is prescribed by law and is legitimate under Article 10(2). Otherwise the basic structure of a democratic society cannot properly be maintained. There seems to be no reason why restrictive measures could not be adopted in both the domestic courts and Parliament in matters such as The Satanic Verses.

In conclusion, if the common law of blasphemy allows one section of the population or their religious faith to be attacked by an irresponsible person, such a position cannot find any justification in the context of modern human rights laws. More so when the existing domestic laws are inconsistent with or contrary to the ECHR, it is the responsibility of Parliament to make necessary legislative amendments in accordance with the ECHR, even though it used to be the position that, strictly speaking, neither Parliament nor the judiciary are legally obliged to follow the European human rights laws (Drzemczewski, 1983: 323). Moreover, not only judicial organs but also the contracting states must ensure that their domestic legislation is compatible with the Convention (van Dijk and van Hoof, 1990: 9-11).

Chapter 7

Turbans and beards in English courts

Building on our discussion in chapters 2 and 3 regarding the evidently discriminatory treatment of various ethnic minorities in Britain under the provisions of the Race Relations Act of 1976, we concentrate here on the effects of such discrimination in employment law, with particular reference to Sikhs.

Many immigrants in the 1950s and early 1960s treated Britain as a temporary home and developed a 'myth of return' (Anwar, 1979). Staying at most for a few years, they were intent on saving money and returning home (Banton, 1985: 51). David Pitt, later Lord Pitt, the prospective Labour party candidate in the 1970 by-election in Clapham, was told by an old West Indian lady: 'Me, came here to get some milk... not to try and take the cow!' (cited in Banton, 1985: 66). Such immigrants showed little inclination to confront inequities and discrimination in British society and tended to take a subservient stance. Many adopted the lifestyle of the native white population and sought to assimilate. Some strove to 'obey...and prove ourselves good citizens' (Banton, 1985: 58). Doing so, they chose to ignore what they saw as the repulsive features of English culture, which in the view of many immigrants had been irreparably corrupted (Ahmed, 1992; Akhtar, 1989; Ballard, 1994: 1-34).

Gradually realising that they had to compete with whites not only to survive but also to win their rights as citizens, non-white immigrants began to protect their ethnic and religious identity more consciously by continuing and reconstructing their customs and traditions (see Menski, 1993 for Asians). In the early 1950s, direct clashes with native whites were avoided and survival plans were cautiously laid out. Conflict was inevitable if the immigrants were to stick to elements of their culture that marked them out as 'the other', quite apart from their skin colour.

Sikh immigrants in Britain claimed early on that they found it difficult to discard their customs and religious ethos. In East Africa, Sikhs had also been concerned not to let go of Sikhism (Bhachu, 1985: 49). Early immigrants had tried to find ways of practising their customs without arousing hostility, emphasising their loyalty to the British Empire as soldiers and in many other ways, but without much success. Gradually, conflicts between this ethnic minority group and the white establishment led to disputes. Foremost among the contested issues were Sikh demands to be allowed to wear religious symbols, especially turbans and beards, at work. This shows that the imagined division between the supposedly private sphere of religion and the public sphere of the workplace could not be maintained. The disputes involved students, lawyers and police officers as well as scores of Sikh employees in the food industry. Initially, these demands were vigorously resisted because they were seen as attempts to impose an alien culture on the indigenous community. The official stance was that immigrants should assimilate to local standards, with only limited recognition of pluralism and cultural diversity.

We argue here that the responses of politicians and the judiciary, although ostensibly impartial, detached and objective, did not result in satisfactory solutions. The ongoing dispute over Mrs. Inderjit Kaur's right to wear a steel bangle (kara) at work in a food processing factory in Leicester (see e.g. Asian Times 18 August 1998) illustrates that the English legal system and its network of rules continue to exert pressure on British Sikhs today to abandon cultural traditions and to conform to so-called national norms, which are influenced by Christian standards. Mrs. Kaur rightly emphasised that the right of her Christian co-workers to wear a wedding ring had never been challenged, confirming that official assumptions about the nature of uniform standards are not culture-free and value-neutral. While we could have chosen to write about Muslims in this context, too, the present chapter focuses more or less entirely on legal issues raised by British Sikhs who have made Britain their home and are engaged in the process of reconstruction of their new socio-cultural environment to suit their own needs (see Ballard, 1994: 1-34). Before we turn to the legal issues, we reflect briefly on major cultural aspects of Sikhism.

7.1 Sikhs and Sikhism

Sikhism has its origins in the writings of Guru Nanak (1469-1539 AD), the founder of this new religion (see Cole and Sambhi, 1978; McLeod, 1968; Singh, 1969; Singh, 1963; Singh, 1939). The succeeding nine leaders or Gurus developed Sikhism into one of the major religions of the Indian subcontinent. From its traditional base in the Panjab, especially Amritsar and Lahore, Sikhs and their religion have gradually spread world-wide and are today a typical transnational community (see Singh and Thandi, 1996). Archer (1946: 2) argued that Sikhism started as a result of attempted reconciliation of Hinduism and Islam. Some Sikh writers dispute this popular assertion, arguing that Sikhism is not a blend or reproduction of earlier religions, but a new revelation altogether (Sikh Missionary Centre, 1990: 3). The term 'Sikh' was derived from the Sanskrit word for 'disciple' (shisya), as noted by Lord Denning in Mandla v Dowell Lee [1982] 3 All ER 1108, at p. 1113. Cole and Sambhi (1978: 169) defined a Sikh as 'any person whose faith is in one God, the Gurus and their teaching and the Adi Granth'. Followers must believe in the necessity and importance of initiation (amrit) and should not adhere to any other religion.

As a monotheistic religion, Sikhism requires the worship of a formless God with no equals or rivals. In the Sikh temples (gurudwaras) poems are sung in the glory of the Lord. Sikhs do not belong to a separate racial stock (James, 1974, ch. 2). Guru Nanak himself was brought up as a Hindu and more than half of the Sikhs are descendants of Jats, the main traditional farming community of the Panjab. Rajputs, aristocratic Hindus, are prominent among Sikhs in terms of numbers and influence. Sikhism is essentially a mixture of temporal and spiritual aspirations and is not detached from worldliness, its main concern being life before the 'thereafter'. It has been described as the most materialistic of Indian religions (Cole and Sambhi, 1978, ch. 1), an assessment confirmed by vigorous Sikh involvement in political and religious matters. Sikhs have never been afraid to fight for their religious identity, particularly against their traditional arch rivals, the Muslims. Gobind Singh (1666-1708 AD), the last recognised Guru of Sikhism, created a new, separate identity for Sikhs, which is at once non-Muslim and non-Hindu (Archer, 1946: 2). Male Sikhs were given the name Singh ('lion'), while women received the title Kaur ('princess').

7.2 Conflicts over turbans and beards

Religious beliefs and a particular outward appearance are essential for a person to be recognised as a true disciple of Sikhism (Hiro, 1992: 126; Archer, 1946: 196). Guru Gobind Singh, at the Anandpur festival in 1699, requested his followers to wear five symbols which start with 'K' (Sikh Missionary Centre, 1990: 200):

- Kesh. Uncut long hair, often tied into a knot on the head. This demonstrates the natural appearance of sainthood;

- Kanga. A comb, worn in the hair behind the knot, used to clean the hair twice a day;

- Kara. A steel bracelet usually worn on the wrist of the left arm. It is a symbol of dedication to the divine;

- Kachha or kachch. Long underpants, or a pair of shorts which must not reach below the knee. This signifies chastity;

- Kirpan or khanda. A sword or a two-edged dagger. This can be used for self-defence and symbolises dignity, power and unconquerable spirit.

The first requirement is most conspicuous and is considered most important by the majority of Sikhs (Banton, 1985: 54). It has been an ethnic marker from the start but took on new meanings once Sikhs migrated all over the world. While there is nothing unusual about women wearing long hair, male Sikhs tie their hair in a top-knot (jura) and the kanga is placed behind the knot. The long hair should be covered with a turban, which became the most distinctive symbol of Sikhism.

As far as English law is concerned, it has been recognised that turbans and beards provide a sign of Sikh communal identity (per Lord Fraser, Mandla v Dowell Lee [1983] 1 All ER 1062 at p. 1064) and are a source of pride (Bhachu, 1985: 51; James, 1974: 50). Disapproval is reserved for those Sikhs, patits or lapsed Sikhs, who break the communal Khalsa discipline, typically by cutting their hair and beard (Shackle, 1986: 8). In addition to its religious significance, the turban has important social functions. When a person is born, married or has died, exchange of turban lengths is a prominent custom among Sikhs.

There are many different ways, traditional and modern, of wearing a turban. Those worn by British Sikhs do not have any one particular shape or colour. Sikhs of Indian origin usually wear turbans which do not have a point at the top (Bhachu, 1985: 51), while Sikhs from East Africa often wear white turbans with a point. However, many young Sikhs from an East African background prefer to wear turbans with light colours, such as navy blue, red, maroon, grey or even black (James, 1974: 48).

Most early Sikh migrants in Britain, mainly Jats from the Panjab, chose not to wear turbans. Many Jat Sikhs cut their hair and shaved their beards, believing this would enhance their employability and indicate their acceptance of a new lifestyle. Yet there were a significant number of Sikhs who did away with beards and turbans with much reluctance. For them the choice was between cutting their hair and finding a job or not compromising on their traditions and returning home. Hiro (1971: 128) described one man's dilemma:

> When faced with this situation, Trilok Singh Dhami, a newcomer to Wolverhampton, booked a passage home. But relatives and friends prevailed upon him to reconsider. He went through an agonising re-appraisal of his religious identity. Reluctantly, he cut his hair. 'Afterwards I felt less than a man', he later recalled. 'I didn't want to go out in the street: I didn't want to be seen by people. It was like I had got a scarred face overnight'.

The arrival of the East African Ramgarhia Sikhs during the late 1960s and early 1970s was instrumental in changing the relaxed attitude towards external appearance. Parminder Bhachu (1985: 50) was told by one Ramgarhia Sikh of East African origin:

> When I first came to this country, there weren't any Ramgarhia families around. We used to live like the Jats because they were the only Sikhs we knew. We used to work with them, we went to the pubs with them, we drank heavily, we started to talk like they did, and we cut off our hair because they had done so. Also, because it was difficult for turbaned men to get jobs. Since the East Africans have arrived, we have associated with them and have started to go to the temple.

The recourse to traditional values led to conflicts in the workplace. Two early Sikh immigrants, Tarsem Singh Sandhu of Wolverhampton and G. S. S. Sagar of Manchester, championed the right to wear beards and turbans to work. Mr. Sagar had applied to the Manchester Transport

Authority (MTA) to be a bus conductor. He was told that he would be offered the job provided he cut his hair and removed his turban. Otherwise, MTA were prepared to offer him a job in the garage, hidden from public view! Mr. Sagar did not accept this offer and challenged MTA's decision for seven years, from 1959 to 1966. Ultimately, his demands were accepted by MTA and he was allowed to wear a turban and a beard at work (Banton, 1985: 55).

Mr. Sandhu in Wolverhampton was one of those early bus conductors who had cut his long hair and shaved his beard in order to obtain employment. Once he fell ill for three weeks and began to wonder if this was divine retribution for his lack of faith. He let his beard grow and began to wear his turban again. When he returned to work, his employers refused to allow him to take up his job as a bus conductor, arguing that this would offend the native whites. Mr. Sandhu's community took up the cause, organising protest meetings and petitions, with no obvious effect. Mr. Sohan Singh Jolly, a leader of the local Sikhs and president of the Shiromani Akali Dal, an umbrella organisation for the religious affairs of British Sikhs, threatened to burn himself in public if Mr. Sandhu was not allowed to wear his beard and turban. He was joined by many other Sikhs in Britain, while thousands of Sikhs marched to the British High Commission in India threatening that if Jolly and others committed suicide, the lives of British citizens in India would be in danger. British politicians took the matter seriously enough to advise the Wolverhampton authority to climb down. The case, which never went to court, made many clean-shaven Sikhs more aware of their ethnic and religious identity. In Wolverhampton alone, 200 Sikhs decided to wear turbans and beards again in a baptism ceremony organised by the local Sikh activists. Another 135 clean-shaven Sikhs in Manchester underwent a religious ceremony and returned to beards and turbans at a local Gurdwara (Hiro, 1971: 155).

Starting in the 1970s, several cases of discrimination in relation to employment eventually reached the courts. We now turn to those cases to examine the attitudes of members of the judiciary towards the wearing of beards and turbans.

7.3 Beards and turbans in English courts

The case of Singh v Lyons Maid Ltd [1975] IRLR 328 was determined before the enactment of the Race Relations Act, 1976. Gurdev Singh, an orthodox Sikh, had been a production worker at the Lyons Maid ice-cream factory since 1969 and until the end of January 1975 he had remained clean-shaven. Rule 6 of the company guidelines stated that beards may not be worn by staff working on the production floor, and that policy was strictly implemented by the respondent company. To avoid any health hazards, bearded visitors were required to wear beard masks. Mr. Singh signed this document when he joined, knowing that under no circumstance would beards be allowed in the production area of the factory. The respondent company, as was revealed in the Industrial Tribunal proceedings, was concerned to avoid bacteriological infection of its products from hair, especially facial hair.

Between January and February 1975, Mr. Singh underwent a spiritual revival and decided to adhere to the requirements of the Sikh religion regarding uncut hair. On his return to work, he was told that he would have to shave off his beard. When he refused, he was dismissed. The dismissal notice, cited at p. 329, stated:

> Further to your interview on the 30.1.75, with regard to your returning to work wearing a beard. At that time you agreed to remove it, as it was contravening the conditions of employment with relation to production floor work. Since 30.1.75 you have been sick and on your return you still have a beard. As you do not wish to remove your beard and there is no alternative employment on site thus on 18.2.75, this note records that your conduct is considered of such a nature as to justify dismissal and you are therefore dismissed under the terms of the Contracts of Employment Act 1963, as amended 1971, and the company's disciplinary procedure.

Mr. Singh's complaint was brought under the Trade Union and Labour Relations Act, 1974, para 4 of Schedule 1, which stipulates that employees should not be unfairly dismissed. Para 6(1) of the Schedule to the Act states that in case of dismissal of an employee, it is the responsibility of the employer to show the reasons for the dismissal. According to para 6(1), the employer has to show that he acted reasonably having regard to equity and the substantial merits of the case.

Mr. Singh's counsel, Mr. Dogra, asked the Industrial Tribunal to consider whether the 'no beard rule' in the ice-cream factory was justifiable, given that the condition operated to the detriment of Mr. Singh. The Tribunal held, at pp. 329-330, dismissing the complaint:

> Mr. Dogra on Mr Gurdev Singh's behalf reminded us that such a requirement acted to the detriment of members of the Sikh community who were required by their religion to wear beards. We do not think it either necessary or relevant in the present circumstances to decide such a general issue, nor do we think it is relevant to enquire into what rules apply in other branches of the food production industry. What is important is that the rule was a condition of Mr. Singh's contract of employment with the respondent company. We are not prepared to hold that it was an unreasonable one...We can see nothing unreasonable in a dismissal which is based on a refusal by the employee to comply with a term of his contract. It was a term which his employers regarded as fundamental and which appears to us to be not unreasonable. Accordingly the complaint of unfair dismissal must fail.

In Panesar v Nestlé Co Ltd [1980] IRLR 64 CA, Mr. Panesar, an orthodox Sikh, had applied for a job in the Nestlé Company at Hayes. He wore a turban and a beard. At the interview he was told that unless he was prepared to cut his beard he could not be employed because of the company's rule that beards and excessively long hair were forbidden in their factory, in the interest of public health. Mr. Panesar complained to the Industrial Tribunal that the company had discriminated unlawfully against him in violation of the Race Relations Act, 1976.

Panesar argued that he should be allowed to wear a beard and unshorn hair at work, since uncut hair was a requirement of his religion. The conditions imposed by the respondent company, argued Mr. Panesar, amounted to indirect discrimination against Sikhs in violation particularly of s. 1(1)(b)(ii) and s. 4 of the Race Relations Act, 1976. We already cited the relevant provisions of the Race Relations Act, 1976 in chapter 2.4 above (see pp. 36-37). The relevant provision on indirect discrimination in s. 1(1)(1)(b) is, in essence, that a person discriminates against another if, he applies to that other a requirement or condition which he applies or would apply equally to persons not of the same racial group as that other but –

(i) which is such that the proportion of persons of the same racial group...who can comply with it is considerably smaller than the proportion of persons not of that racial group who can comply with it; and

(ii) which he cannot show to be justifiable irrespective of the colour, race, nationality or ethnic or national origins of the person to whom it is applied; and

(iii) which is to the detriment of that other because he cannot comply with it.

Since Mr. Panesar's argument was that the company had imposed a condition on him as a Sikh in breach of the above provisions, the question was whether the respondent could show this to be justifiable under s.1(1)(b)(ii). Panesar was to fall at the first hurdle, since there were 24 clean-shaven Sikh workers in the factory who had not objected to the condition, thereby weakening his assertion that the proportion of Sikhs who can comply with the condition is considerably smaller than the proportion of persons not of that group who could comply. It is worth mentioning that the company did admit to having some workers who were allowed to wear moustaches, whiskers and sideburns. The company had banned only beards and long hair. It was argued, at p. 65, that this alleged prohibition was imposed in the interest of hygiene and safety:

As a factory concerned with the production of food, it is necessary that our employees, in the interest of hygiene and safety, comply with certain essential regulations. Hair must be adequately covered and men must be 'clean shaven.' Beards and excessively long hair styles are forbidden.

The respondent company called a series of experts to show how important it was that beards should not be worn in their factories, where chocolate was produced. Dr. Moss of the Quality Assurance Department gave evidence that human hair harbours bacteria. This was supported by another expert witness and the court accepted the necessity of the alleged condition on the basis of such scientific evidence. The respondent's position was therefore seen as justifiable, because 'the prohibition against the wearing of beards was essential in a factory making chocolate in order that it should not be contaminated by bacteria' (p. 65). Thus, the Court of Appeal found no reason to change the decision, Lord Denning stating at p. 65:

> I would like to pay tribute to the careful and full inquiry made by the Industrial Tribunal. They heard a lot of evidence in the case. The judgment covers 15 closely-typed pages, reasoning the matter out in an excellent manner. I can see no error in point of law in this case... I would refuse this application.

While accepting the view of the scientific evidence in relation to beards, it is difficult to see the rationale for not including other facial hair within the prohibition. Are not moustaches also a source of bacteria? It is difficult not to draw the conclusion that the restriction was aimed at a particular group, the Sikhs. Yet the courts were prepared to accept the restriction as being valid without considering difficulties which Sikh employees would have to face. It seems that Lord Denning felt great sympathy for the respondent when he admitted the validity of the no-beard campaign of the Nestlé company.

In Singh v Rowntree MacKintosh Ltd [1979] ICR 554 EAT, the courts moved one step further in their discriminatory approach to Sikhs. The facts of this case are almost identical to those of Panesar. It was alleged that the MacKintosh Company at Edinburgh, which produced confectionery, had not offered a job to Mr. Ragbir Singh because of his refusal to shave off his beard. Mr. Singh had been told that he would be offered employment only if he was prepared to remove his beard in compliance with company health and safety rules. Mr. Singh, an orthodox Sikh, had refused and subsequently complained to the Industrial Tribunal alleging racial discrimination under s. 54 of the Race Relations Act, 1976. The respondent company prohibited workers wearing beards in its factory on grounds of hygiene. As noted in the EAT by Lord MacDonald, this 'automatically rules out more Sikhs than non-Sikhs' (p. 555). However, as revealed in the industrial tribunal proceedings, the company had not imposed this condition in its other factories, only in Newcastle and Edinburgh.

At the industrial tribunal proceedings, the respondents summoned several expert witnesses, a dermatologist, a bacteriologist and an experienced food and drugs officer to testify that the alleged requirement was justifiable in maintaining hygiene in food. Further, the respondents argued that the controversial condition was applied to everyone regardless of race or ethnicity; there was therefore no element of racial discrimination. The Industrial Tribunal found for the respondents on the ground that the complaint was not well-founded.

On appeal to the Employment Appeal Tribunal, Mr. Singh argued that only a small proportion of Sikhs could comply with the requirement, which therefore amounted to indirect discrimination under s. 1(1)(b)(ii) of the Race Relations Act, 1976 because the imposed requirement could not be complied with by the majority of Sikhs. The burden, which is a heavy one, was therefore on the respondents to show that the condition was justifiable. Lord MacDonald found that the respondent company had justified the condition, dismissing the appeal by saying that 'an employer must be allowed some independence of judgment as to what he deems to be commercially expedient in the conduct of his business' (p. 557).

Is such an interpretation based upon commercial expediency sustainable? The Shorter Oxford English Dictionary defines 'justifiable' as 'generally equitable and reasonable in an objective sense' and this definition was adopted both by the Industrial Tribunal and the Employment Appeal Tribunal. The appellant had argued relying on dicta in Steel v Union of Post Office Workers [1977] IRLR 288 that this is too narrow an interpretation in the context of the Race Relations Act. In Steel it was held that in deciding whether a requirement is 'justifiable', it is not sufficient merely to take into account the needs of the enterprise or company, but it is necessary to look at all the circumstances including the discriminatory effect of the requirement or condition if it is permitted to continue. It was revealed in Singh v Rowntree MacKintosh Ltd that in six other factories belonging to the respondent company, workers were allowed to wear beards. If, as suggested, 'justifiable' requires the respondent to show that the restriction was necessary, it would have been difficult (if not impossible) for the respondents in this case to show that what was unnecessary in six factories was necessary in a seventh. The judiciary, however, focused particularly on the justifiability of the requirement in contention. Both Lord Denning in Panesar and Lord MacDonald in Singh v Lyons Maid held that the employer must be allowed some degree of independence of judgement in deciding what is expedient in the conduct of his own business. These cases were instrumental in changing the more favourable interpretation developed and initiated in Steel.

The above cases proceeded on the assumption that Sikhs are a racial group within the meaning of the Race Relations Act, 1976. That question was not fully considered until Mandla v Dowell Lee [1982] 3 All ER 1108 CA (see ch. 2.4 above). In Mandla, the wearing of turbans arose in a rather different context when Mr. Mandla insisted that his son be allowed to wear a turban at school. The headmaster of a school had refused a Sikh boy admission on the ground that allowing an exception from the rules about school uniform might have a negative impact on discipline in the school. The immediate effect of the headmaster's refusal was to put pressure on a Sikh individual to abandon the religious symbols of uncut hair and turban.

There were five Sikh boys in the school who had all cut their hair. In the Court of Appeal, the matter came before Lord Denning MR, Kerr and Oliver LJJ. Apart from the question whether Sikhs are a racial group within the meaning of s. 3 of the Race Relations Act, 1976, the issue was whether the prohibition of turbans amounted to indirect discrimination. The Court had the opportunity to look at the arguments put forward in Panesar and Singh v Rowntree MacKintosh. Lord Denning was unhappy with the Sikhs' insistence on wearing turbans and wrote at p. 1110:

> How far can Sikhs in England insist on wearing their turbans? A turban is their distinctive headgear. They do not cut their hair but plait it under their turbans. Some of them feel so strongly about it that, when they are motor cyclists, they do not wear crash-helmets: and when they are barristers they do not wear wigs.

Oliver LJ made lengthy references to turbans, too and referred to historical developments. He thought that the turban was adopted not so much as a symbol of religious faith but as a mark of political protest (p. 1119). It seemed to Oliver LJ that wearing turbans was no more than a custom, and he observed that a substantial proportion of British Sikhs chose not to follow it. Kerr LJ considered the importance of turbans slightly differently. In his view, stated at p. 1119, the turban had also become a symbol of Sikhism:

> In the field of employment generally, even where turbans conflict with the prescribed headgear for particular occupations, the right of Sikhs to wear turbans has been widely recognised out of respect for their beliefs. Thus, Sikhs wear turbans in the armed forces, in the

police, as traffic wardens; Sikh barristers do not wear wigs; and the crash-helmet regulations for motor cyclists have been expressly relaxed for them. It is only when their beards have caused problems in employment, for instance in the processing of food, that it has been held justifiable to object to these.

However it was held that Sikhs could not insist on the right to wear turbans, because, 'Sikhs are Indians, and in particular Punjabis' (per Kerr LJ, at p. 1122) and not a racial group within the meaning of the Race Relations Act, 1976. Not cutting one's hair and wearing a turban was held to be a religious practice, which was not protected by the 1976 Act. Kerr LJ explained this more fully at pp. 1120-1121:

> To that extent the right not to be discriminated against must give way to the beliefs and free will of others. If persons wish to insist on wearing bathing suits, then they cannot reasonably insist on admission to a nudist colony; similarly, people who passionately believe in nudism cannot complain if they are not accepted on ordinary bathing beaches. Further, as with religion and religious or other social customs, the 1976 Act is not concerned with politics. It operates only in the field of 'race', and only on the basis of the definition which Parliament has given to this word.

Kerr LJ also found – without relying on any empirical research – that the wearing of turbans is prevalent only among 'strict or orthodox Sikhs' and stated that a very large number of Sikhs cut their hair and do not wear turbans or beards (p. 1122). The Court of Appeal therefore held that the Sikhs were not a racial group as defined by s. 3 of the Race Relations Act, 1976.

We saw that this judgment was reversed by the House of Lords in Mandla v Dowell Lee [1983] 1 All ER 1062, which considered turbans as one of the main characteristics of Sikh cultural and religious identity. As such the prohibition on turbans was discriminatory and in conflict with s.1 of the Race Relations Act, 1976 and the House of Lords recognised the right of Sikh schoolchildren to wear a turban, while in places of employment, on account of concerns about hygiene and public health, different rules continued to prevail.

After the Mandla judgment in the House of Lords, many British Sikhs thought that the turban issue had been satisfactorily resolved. The matter was again called into question in the employment context in Kuldip Singh v British Rail Engineering Ltd [1986] ICR 22 EAT. The company rules required safety headgear to be worn in designated areas of British Railway premises. In 1982, a new production controller became concerned about the possibility of injuries to Sikh employees who did not wear headgear. In March 1983 he declared the area where Mr. Singh and another 24 workers ('scotchers') worked as a 'hard hat area', requiring that every worker should wear a hard hat or bump cap.

Mr. Singh objected to the requirement on religious grounds and complained to the Southampton Industrial Tribunal that this 'hard hat rule' constituted unlawful indirect discrimination, on several grounds: It was a condition with which he could not comply, it was unjustifiable, and such a condition was to his detriment. At the Industrial Tribunal proceedings, it was accepted by both sides that it was a condition with which he could not comply and that this was to his detriment. The hearing therefore centred on whether the 'hard hat rule' was justifiable on grounds of safety. The complainant argued that in considering whether the condition was justifiable, the Tribunal should take into account the discriminatory effect of the condition with which he could not comply as a devout Sikh. However, the Tribunal held that it was not entitled to take into account a discriminatory effect of the requirement on the complainant within the meaning of s.1(1)(b)(ii) of the 1976 Act, on the ground that the requirement in question was justifiable irrespective of colour or race of a person concerned. It was held that even if the discriminatory effects of the requirement were taken into account, the requirement remained justifiable.

At the Employment Appeal Tribunal, the main argument centred around the concept of 'justifiable.' Mr. Goudie QC, appearing for the Sikh appellant, argued at p. 27:

(a) when inquiring whether a particular requirement is justifiable, all the circumstances should be taken into account including the discriminatory effect of the requirement and the practical effect of that discrimination upon the complainant; and

(b) discriminatory effect had to be weighed against the need for the requirement.

He also argued that the law required the Tribunal to take the view that a justifiable reason does not extend to insisting on a requirement for the employer's own benefit when the employee for good reason cannot comply with the requirement, and when the employee will otherwise be dismissed. He further argued that there was no realistic possibility of British Rail ever incurring any liability in permitting Mr. Singh to work without protective headgear. The Employment Appeal Tribunal did not agree and the appeal was dismissed. It was stated at p. 27:

> We find these submissions startling. It seems to us that it would be remarkable if conscientious employers, aware of a real risk to their employee in the place of work they provide for him, and aware that they can eliminate or reduce that risk by insisting on a safety requirement, are precluded by law on such insistence. But we find ourselves unable to say that there is only a fanciful (to use Mr. Goudie's term) possibility that BR will be held liable in the particular circumstances that it has knowingly exposed as employee whom it itself believes to be inadequately protected to a real risk known to it.

The EAT chose to ignore the significant exemptions already granted by Parliament to allow Sikhs to retain their identity and stated, at p. 27:

> Mr. Goudie drew our attention to the fact that during the war Sikh soldiers wore no helmets and at the present time Sikh police officers are allowed to wear turbans and not police helmets. But because of the special need to recruit and retain Sikhs in the war-time services and in the police today this fact seems to us to provide little assistance on the question of the justification of a requirement by an employer for its employees to wear protective headgear. Nor do we derive help on that question from the enactment by Parliament of a special exemption for Sikhs from the statutory requirement that motor cyclists should wear helmets. Parliament has not specifically enacted what employers can or cannot do in relation to Sikh employees or Sikh applicants for employment who refuse to wear protective headgear.

It is evident from the above judgment that in the conflict between the requirements of health and safety law and potentially discriminatory practices the EAT allowed the interests of the former to prevail and thereby chose to ignore the issue of indirect racial discrimination.

More recent cases have followed the same line. In S. S. Dhanjal v British Steel General Steels (unreported, Case No. 50740191, delivered on 16 December 1993), the Industrial Tribunal held that a Sikh worker employed by the steel factory was not entitled to wear a turban as of right if an employer refused to allow this on the grounds of public safety and health. The case once again raised the uncertainty of the issue and the concerns of British Sikhs (see Welhengama, 1994).

Mr. Dhanjal brought an action against his employer alleging unlawful discrimination on the ground that he had been made redundant due to his refusal to wear a hard hat. As an orthodox Sikh, Mr. Dhanjal strongly believed that his soul would suffer 'eternal damnation' if he failed to wear a turban at all times. A Sikh priest, who was called as a witness for the applicant, emphasised that according to Sikhism it was necessary for male Sikhs to wear turbans. Mr. Dhanjal therefore argued that the rule imposed by the company was discriminatory and in breach of s. 1(1)(b) of the Race Relations Act, 1976. On the other hand, the employer argued at the tribunal hearing that the Health and Safety at Work etc. Act, 1974 would not allow anyone an exemption in safety matters, whether on religious or other grounds. This Act imposes upon employers statutory obligations to take safety and protective measures to avoid possible accidents to employees.

The Industrial Tribunal, agreeing with the respondent, concluded that the employer's insistence on 'no turbans' was justifiable because it was the employer who had the duty to comply with the requirements of the Health and Safety at Work etc. Act. It further stated that in the absence of any specific exemption from the Act for steel workers, similar to the one granted to Sikh workers on construction sites in the building industry, the requirements guaranteeing safety and health must prevail over the non-discrimination requirements of the Race Relations Act, 1976. This means that a chance was missed to extend the exemption granted to construction workers by the Employment Act, 1989, which recognises Sikh construction workers' right to wear turbans at work. Section 11 of the Employment Act, 1989 states:

> (1) Any requirement to wear a safety helmet which (apart from this section) would, by virtue of any statutory provision or rule of law, be imposed on a Sikh who is on a construction site shall not apply to him at any time when he is wearing a turban.

(2) Accordingly, where -

(a) a Sikh who is on a construction site is for the time being wearing a turban, and

(b) (apart from this section) any associated requirement would, by virtue of any statutory provision or rule of law, be imposed-

(i) on the Sikh, or

(ii) on the other person,

in connection with the wearing by the Sikh of a safety helmet, that requirement shall not apply to the Sikh or (as the case may be) to that other person.

This provision provides exemption from safety helmet requirements only for Sikhs who wear turbans. 'Construction site' covers not only buildings or works of engineering construction, but also similar works in relation to any steel or reinforced concrete structure. Thomas, in Current Statutes Annotated, 1989, (ch. 32-40/38-26) concludes:

The exemption in the present section is a wide one. Subs. (1) set aside the statutory requirement on a Sikh who is on a construction site (whether or not at work). Sub- section (2) provides that any associated requirement connected with the wearing, provision or maintenance of safety helmets, which would otherwise be imposed on a Sikh or any other person shall not apply. So, for example, it set aside any liability which might otherwise be imposed upon an employer who fails to ensure that all his workers wear safety helmets on site. The section also seeks to address some relevant issues which follow on from the grant of the safety helmet exemption, in particular the effect of such an exemption on liability in tort, or, in Scotland, an action for reparation...The Government have estimated that there are as many as 40,000 Sikhs employed in the construction industry in the UK (Minister of State, Hansard HC Vol. 159, col. 1106, 8 November 1989). For religious reasons, an orthodox Sikh is unable to wear anything other than a turban on his head in public, and consequently the introduction of a compulsory requirement to wear safety helmets at work might have forced many Sikhs to choose between their religion and their job. By granting the exemption, which was opposed by the Building Employers Confederation, the Government have accepted that the objective of improving health and safety on construction sites should give way to the deeply held religious beliefs of one section of the community. There is of course a precedent for such a decision, in that turban-wearing Sikhs are exempt from the requirement to wear protective headgear while driving or riding on motor cycles (Road Traffic Act 1988, s.17, re-enacting the Road Traffic Act 1972, s.32 (2A), as inserted by the Motor-Cycle Crash-Helmets (Religious Exemption) Act 1976, s.1). There is no exemption for other individuals or groups who may have personal, religious or cultural reasons for not wearing a safety helmet (for example Rastafarians)...The exemption in the present section is a wide one. Subs. (1) sets aside the statutory requirement on a Sikh who is on a construction site (whether or not at work – subs. (8)) and is wearing a turban. Ss. (2) provides that any associated requirement connected with the wearing, provision or maintenance of safety helmets which would otherwise be imposed on a Sikh or on any other person shall not apply.

Mr. Dhanjal's case was dismissed. The decision failed to focus attention on the above exemptions, nor did it properly analyse the extent and effects of sections 11 and 12 of the Employment Act, 1989 on the Sikhs.

The Industrial Tribunal's statement that the safety requirements prevail over the non-discrimination requirements of the Race Relations Act, 1976 needs to be questioned. As Lord Fraser stated, 'the main purpose of the 1976 Act is to prohibit discrimination against people on racial grounds' (Mandla v Dowell Lee [1983] 1 All ER 1062, at p. 1064). This requirement cannot be defeated by another Act unless it is expressly or impliedly provided for. Under s. 4 of the Race Relations Act of 1976, it is unlawful for an employer to discriminate either against an applicant for a job or against one of his employees, whether in relation to his treatment during employment or in his dismissal. S. 1(1)(b) in conjunction with s. 4 prohibits indirect discrimination being practised by employers. Indirect discrimination consists of treatment which at first sight seems to be necessary or justifiable, but in practice operates to the detriment of a person or group of persons to whom it is applied. In S.S. Dhanjal, the requirement that every employee should wear a hard hat appeared to be justifiable and it was applied to everyone. In practice, Mr. Dhanjal found it extremely difficult to observe that requirement since it conflicted with his religious beliefs. Thus, if he was compelled to wear a hard hat, giving up his turban, this would amount to indirect discrimination under the Race Relations Act, 1976 on the basis that the proportion of Sikhs who 'can comply' with such a rule in practice would be considerably smaller than the proportion of non-Sikhs who can comply with it.

It seems that S. S. Dhanjal gives employers a wider margin of discretion in deciding whether Sikhs should be allowed to wear turbans in their factories as of right. Sikhs had believed that the issue had been resolved by the exemption made for them in the Employment Act, 1989. However the effect of S. S. Dhanjal reinforces the restrictive jurisprudence of Kuldip Singh, Panesar, and Singh v Rowntree MacKintosh. More recent cases, some of whom involve Sikh women like Mrs. Inderjit Kaur, who has been prohibited from working in a food factory because she is wearing a steel bangle (kara), show that even the basic legal issues in this field have remained contested and unresolved, thus keeping Sikhs in Britain under the constant threat of discrimination. From the evidence in this field, too, it appears that the English legal system has become more negative than in the 1960s towards recognising the needs of ethnic minorities.

7.4 From liberalism to conservative judicial intervention

We have seen that Sikhs are now both a religious and a 'racial' group and that religion is not a relevant criterion under the 1976 Act. However, if a religious group is recognised as a 'racial group' for the purposes of the Race Relations Act of 1976, then their religious practices should be covered against discrimination (Bradney, 1993: 111). The Code of Practice for the Elimination of Racial Discrimination and the Promotion of Equality of Opportunity in Employment, 1994 also emphasised that religious practices should be given proper consideration when conditions are laid down in respect of a group which is legally recognised as a racial group. This has not been considered in sufficient depth by the judiciary, as the above cases show. It is our contention that the case law concerning Sikhs and requirements to remove beards and turbans, or to shorten hair, has erred in adopting the wrong criteria in deciding whether employers have been guilty of indirect discrimination for the purposes of s. 1 of the Race Relations Act, 1976. The main focus of our attention in this respect is the 'can comply' test.

As is evident from S. S. Dhanjal, Kuldip Singh, Panesar and Singh v Rowntree MacKintosh, many orthodox Sikh employees have vigorously opposed the rule of 'no turbans or beards,' arguing that it is a rule with which they cannot comply without being in breach of their cultural and religious beliefs and practices. There is no doubt that if 'can' is interpreted literally, Sikhs like anyone else 'can' refrain from wearing turbans or beards while they are at work. However it should be remembered that the term 'can' is not intended to have the meaning of ability to 'carry on physically'. Here one has to analyse whether a member of the Sikh community 'can actually' or 'can in practice' follow a particular condition or requirement imposed by his employer upon him without deviating from or violating his religious and cultural tenets. Of course, if they are under constant pressure to give up their turbans and beards, there is no doubt that Sikhs may comply with such demands, albeit with great difficulty. Nevertheless, it is evident from the above cases that Sikhs cannot comply with such requirements without being in breach, at the same time, of most revered cultural and religious beliefs.

In Price v Civil Service Commission and another [1978] 1 All ER 1228 EAT, it was held that the term 'can comply' in s. 1(1)(b)(ii) of the Sex Discrimination Act, 1975 (which is identical to s. 1(1)(b)(ii) Race Relations Act, 1976) was not to be construed as meaning 'physically possible to comply'. Phillips J held at p. 1231:

> 'Can' is defined (Shorter Oxford English Dictionary) as 'to be able': to have power or capacity. It is a word with many shades of meaning, and we are satisfied that it should not be too narrowly, or too broadly, construed in its context in s. 1(1)(b)(i). It should not be said that a person 'can' do something merely because it is theoretically possible for him to do so: it is necessary to see whether he can do so in practice...

Lord Fraser took a similar view in Mandla v Dowell Lee, [1983] 1 All ER 1062, at p. 1069:

> It is obvious that Sikhs, like anyone else, 'can' refrain from wearing a turban, if 'can' is construed literally. But if the broad cultural/ historic meaning of ethnic is the appropriate meaning of the word in the 1976 Act, then a literal reading of the word 'can' would deprive Sikhs and members of other groups defined by reference to their

ethnic origins of much of the protection which Parliament evidently intended the 1976 Act to afford to them. They 'can' comply with almost any requirement or condition if they are willing to give up their distinctive customs and cultural rules... The word 'can' is used with many shades of meaning. In the context of s.1(1)(b)(i) of the 1976 Act it must, in my opinion, have been intended by Parliament to be read not as meaning 'can physically', so as to indicate a theoretical possibility, but as meaning 'can in practice' or 'can consistently within the customs and cultural traditions of the racial group'.

Both Lord Fraser and Phillips J, in Mandla and Price respectively, correctly in our view, stated that 'can comply' has a wider meaning; it is to be identified against an environment of specific cultural and religious backgrounds.

'Can comply' should also be interpreted in conjunction with 'justifiable'. However, as Lord Fraser concluded in the House of Lords case of Mandla (at p. 1069) the term 'justifiable' raises more problems than the term 'can comply'. His Lordship held that a person who imposed a condition or requirement should be able to show that it is justifiable in the relevant sense, in this case of business necessity. 'Justifiable' was also explained in Griggs v Duke Power Company 401 US 424 [1971], at p. 431:

Congress has now provided that tests or criteria for employment or promotion may not provide equality of opportunity merely in the sense of the fabled offer of milk to the stork and the fox. On the contrary, Congress has now required that the posture and condition of the job seeker be taken into account. It has to resort again to the fable – provided that the vessel in which the milk is proffered be one all seekers can use. The Act proscribes not only overt discrimination but also practices that are fair in form, but discriminatory in operation. The touch-stone is business necessity. If an employment practice which operates to exclude Negroes cannot be shown to be related to the job performance, the practice is prohibited.

The Griggs test was applied in Steel v The Union of Post Office Workers and the General Post Office [1977] IRLR 288 and Price v Civil Service Commission [1977] IRLR 291. It was held at p. 291 in Steel that,

...a practice which would otherwise be discriminatory – which is the case here – is not to be licensed unless it can be shown to be justifiable, and it cannot be justifiable unless its discriminatory effect is justified by the need – not the convenience – of the business or enterprise.

Both Price and Steel (each decided by Phillips J) were to the effect that the Tribunal should be satisfied that the stipulated requirement imposes a genuine rule. In Steel, Phillips J noted at p. 290:

The question is what considerations are relevant and proper to be taken into account when determining whether the requirement or condition was justifiable; in particular, is it sufficient merely to take into account the needs of the enterprise for the purpose of which the requirement or condition has been imposed, or is it necessary to look at all the circumstances including the discriminatory effect of the requirement or condition? We are satisfied that the latter is the case and that the industrial tribunal has to weigh up the needs of the enterprise against the discriminatory effect of the requirement or condition. Were it not so many acts prima facie discriminatory would be allowed when there was no overriding need.

Thus a condition which entails discriminatory effects cannot be accepted unless an employer can justify the need for such a condition. If such a need is shown, then the employer may introduce the discriminatory practice irrespective of colour, race or ethnicity. In the decisions of both Panesar and Singh v Rowntree MacKintosh, the mere business convenience of the employer was used to justify dismissals of employees.

The argument of the complainants in both Singh and Panesar that the test laid down as to 'can comply' and 'justifiable' by Steel and Price should be applied in determining whether the alleged condition was discriminatory was rejected. At p. 557 in Singh v Rowntree MacKintosh, rejecting the interpretation offered by Philips J in Steel, Lord MacDonald held that 'justifiable' means 'reasonably necessary in all the circumstances'. In his view, 'necessity' should not be rigidly construed to mean 'absolutely essential' as it was in Steel. While admitting that 'convenience' alone was not sufficient to prove the justification of a particular requirement, and that something more is required, he did not properly explain what this extra element was. However, a requirement should be applied, according to His Lordship, reasonably and with common-sense. In his finding Lord MacDonald admitted that the respondent company might have applied the requirement merely on convenience. Yet, the finding reflected only the perspectives of the respondent. It was held at p. 557:

> Here, however, we are dealing with an employer who is a manufacturer of foodstuff, who is in competition with other manufacturers, and who considers it important that the highest standards of hygiene are seen to apply to his products. In this context at least we feel that consideration has to be given to what is reasonable and that the industrial tribunal did not err in approaching their task on that basis. Moreover in this industry at least an employer must be allowed some independence of judgement as to what he deems to be commercially expedient in the conduct of his business.

This negative trend, begun by Lord MacDonald in Singh v. Rowntree MacKintosh, was continued by the Court of Appeal in Ojutiku and Oburoni v Manpower Services Commission [1982] IRLR 418 CA. Rejecting the appellants' request that the interpretation of 'justifiable' in Steel by Philips J be adopted, it was held that in order to prove that a requirement is justifiable, it is not essential for the employer to prove that the requirement is necessary for the good of his business. Lord MacDonald's approach was praised by Kerr LJ., referring to Steel at p. 422 of Ojutiku, where he said:

> The Employment Appeal Tribunal... in that case put something of a gloss on the word 'justifiable' by suggesting that it was equivalent, or close to having the same meaning as 'necessary'. But that gloss was rightly shaded, to put it no higher, by another decision of the Employment Appeal Tribunal in Singh v Rowntree MacKintosh Ltd. [1979] IRLR 199 at p. 200, in which the approach was in effect that 'justifiable' means 'reasonably necessary in all the circumstances'. In the same way as Lord Justice Eveleigh, I decline to put any gloss on the word 'justifiable', which is a perfectly easily understandable ordinary word, except that I would say that it clearly applies to a lower standard than the word 'necessary'.

Stephenson and Eveleigh LJJ agreed with Kerr LJ. The constructive approach taken in Steel by Phillips J continued when he discussed the onus of proof on an employer. He held that the onus of proof was a heavy one and laid down five criteria for establishing the onus of proof on an employer (p. 291):

> First, the onus of proof lies upon the party asserting this proposition ...Secondly, it is a heavy onus in the sense that at the end of the day the Industrial Tribunal must be satisfied that the case is a genuine one where it can be said that the requirement or condition is necessary. Thirdly, in deciding whether the employer has discharged the onus the Industrial Tribunal should take into account all the circumstances, including the discriminatory effect of the requirement or condition if it is permitted to continue. Fourthly, it is necessary to weigh the need for the requirement or condition against that effect. Fifthly, it is right to distinguish between the requirement or condition which is necessary and one which is merely convenient, and for this purpose it is relevant to consider whether the employer can find some other and non-discriminatory method of achieving his object.

Again Lord MacDonald in Singh v MacKintosh was less than constructive. In ignoring the purpose of the law designed to combat racial discrimination, and the possible higher duties in such cases owed by employers, he downgraded the comments on onus of proof in Steel by Philips J to a mere obiter (p. 556). At p. 557 he stated:

> The onus of proving that a requirement is justifiable is on the party who discriminates but it is not accurate to describe it as a heavy onus. It is the burden of proof applicable to a civil case viz, the balance of probabilities.

This approach was affirmed in Ojutiku. The negative impact of the lowering of the test becomes clear in Kuldip Singh, where at p. 26 Mr. Scouller commented:

> The onus is on the person seeking to justify the discriminatory requirement. That justification is one to prove on the balance of probabilities. An objective justification is called for: it is not enough that there is a genuine belief that the requirement is justified. But it is not necessary to go so far as to prove that the requirement is necessary: it is sufficient that the reasons are good or adequate.

The impact of the approach in Singh, Kuldip Singh and Ojutiku is that commercial expediency is prioritised over the cultural and religious values of an ethnic group. This seems so even if an employer can justify a condition to a lesser degree and on a subjective ground by deviating from the test laid down in Steel and Price as to the form and onus of proof. The danger is that the employer is not required to prove to the satisfaction of the tribunal or court that the particular practice is a genuine one and as such necessary. The business convenience of the employer, on the balance of probabilities, has been given priority. These judgments therefore reduced the onus on the respondent to a significantly lower level, allowing employers a considerable margin of discretion. The current law therefore encourages employers to breach the responsibilities imposed on them by the Race Relations Act, 1976.

In the cases discussed above, the applicants did not succeed in establishing their claims with regard to religion. The judiciary failed to find out whether the applicants would be able to comply with such employment conditions without being in breach of their religious requirements and whether the respondent employers failed to observe the statutory requirements imposed by s. 1(1)(b)(ii) of the Race Relations Act, 1976. The judges also did not check carefully enough, in our view, whether the employer had exploited other alternative non-discriminatory means to achieve the company's objective and whether the imposed requirements were justifiable as understood in Steel, Price and Hussein v Saints Complete House Furnishers [1979] IRLR 337.

These judicial opinions have influenced many other cases where non-Sikh ethnic minority workers were involved. Critically analysing this negative judicial trend, Jeanne Gregory (1987: 39) wrote:

> ...it begins to look as though the judiciary is particularly resistant to the concept of indirect discrimination when it is used on behalf of black applicants. The courts are sometimes able to recognise the structural impediments that arise from the sexual division of labour; they are less prepared to acknowledge the existence of institutionalised racism or take any effective remedies against it. It is no more of any imposition to require one employer to revise his rules on factory hygiene than it is to require another to revise the age limits for job applicants. Even so, the Steel and Price decisions did not open the flood-gates to the victims of either sex or race discrimination. Those two favourable judgments were destined to remain in splendid isola-

tion for some time to come, as the victims of indirect discrimination fought unsuccessfully to extend their application to other areas.

Most importantly, judges seem to be ignoring the underlying purpose of the Race Relations Act of 1976, the elimination of discriminatory practices in employment. The domestic law, therefore, does not appear to offer meaningful remedies. We explore in the final section below whether recourse to European law and human rights jurisprudence could offer some avenues for ethnic minorities like the Sikhs in this field.

7.5 The European Convention on Human Rights

After S. S. Dhanjal, the British Sikh Federation had seriously considered the possibility of challenging the 'no turban rule' in the European Court of Human Rights. A commonly held belief amongst Sikh activists was that the right to wear turbans and beards was protected by the rights guaranteed by the European Convention on Human Rights, 1950 (the ECHR).

Under European human rights law, an individual may canvas his or her rights given that those rights are within the confines of the ECHR. However, not all rights are covered by the ECHR nor even by international human rights jurisprudence. Article 1 of the ECHR postulates that the member countries are only responsible for securing the rights and freedoms which are contained in s. 1 of the ECHR, which concerns 17 rights. Later, the Convention's rights have gradually been extended in its subsequent Protocols. Nevertheless, the law relating to manifestation of religions or beliefs still remains as it stood when the ECHR was ratified.

The Sikhs may argue that the prohibition of beards and turbans violates Article 9 of the European Convention on Human Rights. The right to freedom of thought and conscience and religion is guaranteed by Article 9 of the ECHR which stipulates:

(1) Everyone has the right to freedom of thought, conscience and religion; this right includes freedom to change his religion or belief and freedom, either alone or in community with others and in public or private, to manifest his religion or belief, in worship, teaching, practice and observance.

(2) Freedom to manifest one's religion or beliefs shall be subject only to such limitations as are prescribed by law and are neces-

sary in a democratic society in the interests of public safety, for the protection of public order, health or morals, or for the protection of the rights and freedoms of others.

This Article clearly distinguishes between the right to freedom of religion and freedom to manifest one's religion or beliefs. The question here is whether the wearing of beards and turbans comes under Article 9 ECHR as a matter of freedom of religion. In R v Crown Court at Aylesbury, ex parte Chahal [1976] RTR 489, a Sikh motor-cyclist argued in the High Court that the conviction imposed on him by the Crown Court for not wearing a crash-helmet while riding a motor-cycle violated the rights guaranteed by the ECHR. The divisional court, dismissing his application, found that there was no substance in his argument. Wearing beards and turbans may be a manifestation of religion, as protected under Article 9 ECHR, but subject to the proviso in paragraph (2). This view was affirmed in Panesar v Nestlé Co Ltd [1980] IRLR 64, where Lord Denning commented at p. 65:

> I ought just to mention, as Mr. Harjit Singh has, Article 9 of the European Convention. It is not law here, but we have much regard to it. That assures to everyone the freedom to manifest his religion. No doubt the Sikhs are manifesting their religion in wearing their hair unshorn. But this article goes on to say: '...subject only to such limitations as are prescribed by law and are necessary in a democratic society in the interests of public safety, for the protection of public order, health or morals for the protection of the rights and freedom of others.' This rule is for the protection of public health – on the evidence. So there is no breach of that Article: even if it were regarded as law in this country.

A similar position is found in X v United Kingdom [1978] 14 Commission Report 234. Between 1973 and 1976, the petitioner, a Sikh living in the UK, had been convicted twenty times for not wearing a crash-helmet. He petitioned the European Commission of Human Rights, alleging that his convictions were in violation of Article 9 of the ECHR. Rejecting his claim, the Commission held that the alleged requirement imposed by the British government was justifiable, because it was necessary on the ground of public safety.

However the Commission has found that the manifestation of a belief may fall outside the protection of Article 9(1) where the act at issue is not a manifestation of the belief itself, but has only been motivated or influenced by it (Gomien, 1991: 69). The practice of wearing a turban is, it could be argued, a habit or a custom motivated by personal beliefs and as such is not a legal right guaranteed by the ECHR. The test to be applied, then, is whether Sikhs can follow their religion even without wearing turbans. It is evident that especially members of the younger generation of Sikhs do not strongly adhere to turbans and beards (Ballard 1994b: 113). Some remain sceptical, some younger Sikhs prefer American base-ball caps to turbans. Therefore it has become even more difficult to argue, against the background of increasing modernisation of Sikh youngsters, that removal of the 'no turban /no beard rule' is a sine qua non for Sikhs living in Britain.

The right to wear a turban or beard may be identified as a custom rather than a religious tenet of Sikhism. However, the customs or personal laws of ethnic minorities are not specifically protected by the ECHR. In that sense, wearing a turban is a right that can be enjoyed at the mercy of the respective state. Alternatively it may be viewed as a private decision, left to the individual, who then must bear the consequences of accidents or unemployment.

The views of the Human Rights Committee in Singh Binder v Canada [208/1986, Human Rights Committee Report 1990, Vol. II A/45/40 IX F], at pp. 50-54, can be considered as reflecting the current legal opinion in this sphere in international law and human rights jurisprudence. In Singh Binder, a naturalised Canadian citizen and Sikh by religion approached the Human Rights Committee, alleging that he had been discriminated against by the Canadian Railway Company on grounds of his religion and ethnicity. Being a Sikh, he believed that he was obliged to wear a turban, seeing this as a custom imposed by his religion. He was employed by the Canadian Railway Company as a maintenance electrician, but later this employment was terminated as a result of his refusal to wear safety headgear at work, instead of his turban.

Mr. Singh Binder argued his case relying mainly upon Article 18 of the International Covenant on Civil and Political Rights 1966. This Article stipulates that everyone shall have the right to freedom of thought, con-science and religion. This right shall include freedom to have or to adopt a religion or belief of one's choice and freedom, either individually or in community with others and in public or private, to manifest one's religion or belief in worship and to observe the manifestation of those rights enshrined in the International Covenant on Civil and Political Rights of 1966. Article 18(3) states that the freedom to manifest one's religion or beliefs may be limited on the grounds of public safety, order, health or morals. On the other hand, the right to freedom of thought, conscience and religion is a non-derogable one. Article 4 of the International Covenant on Civil and Political Rights 1966 states that no derogation from Article 6, 7, 8, (paras. 1 and 2) 11, 15, 16 and 18 may be made. This does not cover the right to manifestation of one's religion or beliefs. Therefore it is not an absolute right. The petitioner argued that since the rights guaranteed by Article 18 are non-derogable, termination of his employment by the Canadian Railway Company amounted to a violation of Article 18. The Committee held that such rights could be subjected to restrictions by the signatory parties if they thought it necessary to do so. However, the Committee concluded that interference with Mr. Singh Binder's religious practice was justified in the interest of public safety in accordance with Article 18(3) of the International Covenant on Civil and Political Rights. The Human Rights Committee found that Mr. Singh Binder's claim to wear a turban at work was merely a manifestation of religious beliefs.

It is likely that the European Court of Human Rights would rely on Singh Binder if a similar case were to come before it. It is now an established practice in international tribunals to consider on appropriate occasions the decisions of similar international tribunals. Article 9(2) of the ECHR is postulating the same legal principle as Article 18(3) of the International Covenant on Civil and Political Rights. Public safety and health is one of the grounds which can be used to restrict or limit particular customs of a racial group.

In conclusion, the above cases demonstrate the extent to which the refusal to recognise the right to wear beards and turbans continues to cause concerns for Sikhs in Britain today. Parliament has legislated specifically on this issue, but the legislation has been seen as either too limited or smacking of favouritism. Courts and tribunals have been inconsistent and seem to favour employers rather than employees. Sikhs are evidently frustrated that the loyalty shown by thousands of Sikh soldiers who fought shoulder to shoulder with white British soldiers, wearing turbans instead of helmets, demonstrating their allegiance both to the British

Empire and to Sikhism, has not been adequately recognised in today's society.

Sikhs have, in modern post-war Britain, been able to achieve a number of legal concessions not equalled by Muslims and Hindus. Yet many problems remain unresolved in this sensitive area. In this unfriendly socio-legal environment solutions cannot be found easily and the law seems unwilling to provide stable guarantees of non-discrimination, as even the supposedly privileged Sikhs continue to experience. A sustained strong campaign of lobbying, perhaps reminding the British public and politicians that they are still loyal allies with whom the British establishment can work with confidence, might offer a long-term solution to the Sikhs. At present, neither domestic law, nor European or international law, seem to go far enough in safeguarding the legal concerns of ethnic minorities like the Sikhs of Britain.

Chapter 8

Conclusions

The recent study by Ian Spencer (1997) confirms that large-scale immigration of new ethnic minorities into the UK since the 1950s has created the need for substantial adjustments on the part of the immigrants and their descendants as well as the 'host community' (as it used to be called), policy makers and the judiciary. Our study shows in different ways that members of the higher judiciary have been less than enthusiastic in recognising the presence of ethnic minorities in Britain and the difficulties people as individuals and members of communities face living in a country in which even the third- and fourth-generation descendants of earlier immigrants are not treated as equals.

The colour-blind, culture-blind approach continues to be preferred and English law is treated (and still perceives itself) as a legal system that applies to everybody equally. In other words, the ethnic minority status of millions of people to whom this law applies has been considered more or less totally irrelevant. As a result, the interpretation and application of law as it applies to ethnic minority groups has been quite restrictive, with little or no accommodation of the value systems of such groups and, to apply Chiba's illuminating term, their 'legal postulates'.

Some members of the judiciary assumed that immigration was something to fear, that it was an invasion of 'this dangerously overcrowded land', as envisioned in the Dockers' Labour Club case in 1974. Granting of resident status to migrants from Africa, Asia and the Caribbean islands was something to be resisted because it was giving precious rights to black and brown (earlier 'coloured') migrants whose differing cultural or religious values were likely to bring them into conflict with the 'host community' and its value system. New ethnic minorities were viewed not just as foreigners, but as foreigners who were likely to be antagonistic to the indigenous white community.

When legislation to prevent racial discrimination was introduced, it brought a hostile response from some members of the judiciary. Legislative initiatives to combat racial discrimination were therefore to some extent doomed to become ineffective. The consequent restrictive interpretation of the term 'racial group' has meant that of the many new ethnic groups now present in the United Kingdom, only Sikhs, Jews and Gypsies have been entitled to some recognition as a racial group within the provisions of the Race Relations Act, 1976. While the criteria of 'race', 'colour' and 'ethnic characteristics' have been written into the Act – but not religion – they have not been defined as clearly as could be. The entire system of recognition seems haphazard and contradictory: While the Sikhs, clearly a religious group, have won 'ethnic minority status' and a pole position as a 'racial group', Rastafarians, the larger religious groups of Muslims and Hindus, as well as many smaller groups, have been refused such recognition. Of the post-war migrants, therefore, only Sikhs have succeeded in obtaining official legal recognition of their ethnic minority status. One may question whether their historical relationship with, and allegiance to, the British Empire was instrumental in their success or whether this is a result of different lobbying tactics, as is often suggested.

The judiciary have been illogical and inconsistent in their application of the criteria developed to establish the ambit of 'racial group'. Despite the wide-ranging, culture-focused and liberal definition of 'racial group' by the House of Lords in Mandla v Dowell Lee, Muslims and Rastafarians, who regard themselves as separate ethnic minority communities, have subsequently not been granted such recognition. In some cases, the presence of a unifying religion was ignored, but discounting religion should have led to the refusal to recognise Sikhs and Jews. Muslims, who have continued to assert their separate identity based on religion rather than on geographical or biological differences, have constantly experienced rejection. The claims for recognition of Muslims as a racial group as argued in Yasin v Northern Home [1993]; Azam, Bhayat and others v J H Walker [1994] and Commission for Racial Equality v Precision Manufacturing Services [1991] (all cited in UK Action Committee on Islamic Affairs 1993: 12) all serve to enhance and assert Muslim ethnic identity. It is not surprising that British Muslims are becoming increasingly disappointed and bitter about the fact that their claims to a semblance of equal status are constantly being refused.

Mandla v Dowell Lee established seven criteria for the recognition of ethnic minority status, two major and five minor ones. We saw that the need for a long shared history as an essential criterion is not without difficulty. In denying the claim of Rastafarians in Crown Suppliers (Property Service Agency) v Dawkins, 60 years was treated as not long enough to obtain legal recognition as a separate ethnic or racial group. In Mandla, it was not disputed that the Sikhs had a tradition going back between 450 and 500 years, and in Commission for Racial Equality v Dutton, Gypsies could show a tradition going back over 700 years. No doubt the Jews, too, can trace their culture back thousands of years, but so can Muslims and Hindus. The refusal of the judiciary to recognise Muslims and Hindus as 'racial groups' while accepting the claims of Jews and Sikhs in this regard seems, at best, inconsistent.

The refusal to recognise Rastafarian claims to 'ethnic status' in Dawkins shows the complexity of the scenario especially well. The conclusion that Rastafarians are only part of a 'religious cult' or a movement with some political and religious tenets confirms the reluctance of the judiciary to move with the changing social structure of contemporary British society. Any ethnic or racial group has elements of political, religious and cultural identities which separate it from other racial or ethnic groups. Dawkins makes reference to Rastafarian reggae music, eating habits, religious beliefs and to some extent their own cultural traditions. They worship the former Emperor of Ethiopia, Haile Selassie, as the God of their religion. They trace their history back to King Solomon, and in that sense they clearly have a long history. We would suggest that when interpreting the term 'racial group' or 'ethnic group', reference should be made to the socio-cultural aspects associated with such terms and a more inclusive approach should be taken.

Existing jurisprudence suggests that there is still no clear-cut definition presented by the courts or given by an Act of Parliament to identify separate racial or ethnic groups. It seems that law makers are not interested in clarity, rather the race relations law is based on discretionary distinctions, which are kept in place. The judiciary has been given wide discretionary power to deal with issues as they arise, on a one-to-one or case-by-case basis. Lord Fraser's test in Mandla has not been able to produce an unambiguous definition of the key terms. The result of keeping such important matters in limbo has been a denial of rights to members of other groups, whether or not such rights are guaranteed by domestic or international human rights documents. Deprivation of such rights is no more than subjecting a particular group of people to degrading and inhuman treatment.

On the other hand, as the Sikh cases discussed in ch. 7 show with particular clarity, judicial recognition as a 'racial group' has not prevented racial and other discrimination, as the courts have tended to emphasise the concerns of employers and of business, rather than human rights. The case law involving Sikhs demonstrates the extent of the law's refusal to recognise the right to mark religious and ethnic differences in contemporary British society. Parliament may have legislated specifically on this issue, but the legislation has been seen as either too limited or smacking of favouritism. Current debates about including religion as a criterion in the Race Relations Act of 1976, driven by Muslim lobbying, have remained inconclusive, although there is increasing evidence of grudging recognition for the key role of religion. In view of legislative unwillingness to address questions of religion, courts and tribunals have remained inconsistent. In the field of employment law, the courts seem to have favoured employers and health and safety issues are regularly given priority over cultural and religious beliefs. British Sikhs are rightly frustrated about the limits placed upon their freedom to express and mark their cultural and religious identity.

Regarding application of the general law to issues that have impacted upon the ethnic minority communities, the courts have shown a narrowness of approach that has prevented the cultural values and norms of the new ethic minority groups to be recognised. In other words, English law has shown a marked reluctance to accept concepts of legal pluralism. In refusing to acknowledge the claims of those who wish to adopt different values, the courts have given a variety of explanations. We suggest that the cases fall into a number of categories.

Firstly, cases where the judiciary use a set of Christian values to vilify certain customs, classify them as repugnant and consequently refuse to recognise them. Included here are cases such as Hyde v Hyde, Harvey v Farnie, Warrender v Warrender and Mohamed v Knott. In Baindail v

Baindail common sense, some attention to reasonable policy and decency were applied when issues relating to the personal laws of immigrants were involved. In most cases, vague principles were applied in determining the legitimacy of foreign marriages and conferring titles and dignity arising out of such marriages. Lord Maugham LC in the Sinha Peerage Claim, while determining the hereditary title of Aroon Kumar Sinha, used 'English ideas' as one of the tests. In Brook v Brook [1861] 9 HL 756, the test applied was 'the general consent of Christendom which is normally identified with the civilised notions' (see Cheni v Cheni [1962] 1 All ER 873).

The second category of cases are those where the judiciary question the motives of the applicants, often assuming that the claimants merely wish to evade the rules of the domestic law. It appears that English judges have become increasingly nervous about this issue. There is no mandatory rule or developed theory in English law similar to French anti-evasion laws (see Fawcett, 1990). English law has developed ad hoc principles particularly in the area of family disputes, i.e. marriage and divorce (Shaw v Gould [1868] LR 3). In such cases, rather than viewing the claims of ethnic minorities as an attempt to gain limited recognition for their values, claims tend to be seen as attempts to deliberately flout the law. Domiciled subjects of the Crown were allowed only recourse to English law (see R v Secretary of State for the Home Department, ex parte Ghulam Fatima and others [1985] 1 QB 190; Chaudhary v Chaudhary [1984] 3 All ER 1017; R v Registrar General of Births, Deaths and Marriages and another, ex parte Minhas [1977] QB 1). Even recent legislation, particularly s. 46 of the Family Law Act 1986 further reinforces this message, which has led to many undesirable effects (see now Pearl and Menski 1998, ch. 4). English law has turned hostile to individuals from ethnic minority groups who, as members of trans-national communities, have been using the provisions of overseas legal systems. This approach is particularly clearly illustrated by the ban on so-called 'trans-national divorces'.

Finally there are cases in which the courts have justified their approach by employing public policy as a yardstick. Foreign customs or personal laws of ethnic minorities were assessed as inherently violative of supposedly dominant Western concepts of 'justice'. Earlier, too, some judgments of foreign courts were not recognised in cases said to be offensive to English notions of substantial justice. In Pemberton v Hughes [1899] 1 Ch 781, Lindley MR held that 'the courts of this country are not compelled to recognise the decree of the court of another country when it offends against our ideas of justice' (p. 790). A divorce obtained by way of a talaq in Malaysia was held contrary to ideas of 'substantial justice' in Viswalingham v Viswalingham. A similar position was taken in Salvesen v Austrian Property Administrator in terms of 'substantial justice according to our notions'. Many more recent judicial statements could be adduced here to show remarkably little change of perspective, for example Bush J's judgement in Zaal v Zaal (1982) 4 FLR 284, at p. 289, and Wood J's judgement in Sharif v Sharif (1980) 10 Fam Law 216.

The supposed supremacy of English or British concepts, and of the Christian religion and its values has impeded religious tolerance and understanding. This is most evident in the failure of the judiciary to take positive steps in enhancing the scope of blasphemy laws (ch. 6). The assumption that an unlimited right to freedom of expression is desirable faces difficulties in any conflict situation, more so in a multicultural context. We have argued that particularly in a multi-ethnic and multi-religious society, freedom of expression should be enjoyed with restraint. No one is advocating unlimited rights. Rights bring with them the duty to pay due regard to the effects of those rights on other members of the community. We have shown how the rights of freedom of thought, conscience and religion are guaranteed by Article 9 of the ECHR. Both Article 9 and 10 are subject to derogation, duties and responsibilities are subject to formalities, conditions, restrictions or penalties as prescribed by law and are necessary in a democratic society in the interest of, inter alia, morals and the reputation of others (see Article 10(2) ECHR). Freedom of expression is not an absolute right the individual can enjoy at his whim and pleasure. As such it is difficult to see why the modern common law, irrespective of what the traditional common law of blasphemy may be, should allow one section of the population or their religious faith to be attacked by an irresponsible person. Such a position cannot find any justification in the context of any human rights treaty laws and the existing form of blasphemy laws is hard to justify in a pluralist society such as Britain (Feldman, 1993: 690). Existing laws remain concerned only about the sensitivities of Anglican Christians.

There is much reason to be concerned about the effects of such insensitive refusal on the part of the law to reflect Britain's multicultural realities. If a section of the population feel that they are subjected to discrimination with the connivance of the judiciary and the law makers, hatred among various groups is bound to be exacerbated. The dangers of such a scenario are reflected in the horrendous recent events in former Yugoslavia. The current policy which legally allows one, as Lord Denning said, to discriminate even for or against Roman Catholics (Mandla v Dowell Lee [1982] 3 All ER 1108, at p. 1111) cannot be a proper guiding formula in today's multicultural and religiously plural British society. Such a policy leads communities and community relations nowhere and endangers internal peace and harmony between different religious communities. Lord Scarman stated in R v Lemon [1979] AC 617, at p. 658:

> In an increasingly plural society such as that of modern Britain it is necessary not only to respect the differing religious beliefs, feelings and practices of all but also to protect them from scurrility, vilification, ridicule and contempt.

There is a need to move away from Anglo-focused thinking and policies towards a broader recognition of plurality. In blasphemy law, as we argued in ch. 6, the better proposition would be extension of the scope of the law of blasphemy to protect all recognised religions with a view to strengthening the fundamental institutions of a modern pluralist society, thus creating better race relations. It is said that one of the objectives of this law is to 'protect the social fabric of the society' and to 'safeguard the tranquillity of the kingdom' (respectively Bowman v Secular Society [1917] AC 406 at pp. 466-467 and R v Lemon [1979] AC 617, at p. 658). Without supporting the faiths of the various religious groups, the social fabric in a modern multicultural society cannot be properly protected.

Now that Britain is a pluralist society, whether people like it or not, it is advisable for law makers and the judiciary to come to terms with the new demographic and religious developments. Britain has many mansions in which Anglican Christians, Roman Catholics, Muslims, Hindus, Sikhs, Jews, Moonies and many other groups are living. Accommodation to such diversity is necessary to develop better race relations. Outdated assimilationist assumptions – especially in terms of religion – are clearly not showing the way forward.

If we want better race relations and greater social harmony between major sections of society, the law should not allow people to ridicule and insult the feelings and faiths of religious minorities at their whim. For the above reasons we are of the view that:

- it is necessary to respect and honour the differing religious beliefs and practices of all religious groups;

- it should be social and public policy to protect the beliefs most sacred to those groups, from scurrility, vilification, ridicule and contempt;

- application of the law of blasphemy should extend to cover, at least, the recognised religions.

As we emphasised already, the English judiciary has very well been able to develop new legal principles to take account of new social conditions (see R v R [1991] 4 All ER 481), so the law contains within itself the mechanisms for flexibility, growth and reform. What is lacking is the political will to implement certain changes in the law and its application that would reflect the changing ethnic and religious composition of the British population today.

The imposition of the dominant value system is particularly evident in a series of cases involving children and the application of the concept of 'welfare'. The courts have considered the child's best interests in the light of good and common values of the majority, values that may not be shared by many members of ethnic minority communities. As a result many decisions concerning the placement and treatment of children have been made without considering the values and cultures in which such children are being raised. Decisions such as Re E (A Minor) (Wardship: Medical Treatment) [1993]1 FLR 386, where the courts are prepared to impose their own values rather than those of the child or parent are a high water mark in the arrogance of the courts when it comes to constructing concepts of 'welfare' and the imposition of values alien to the parties. Such an approach will lead to more questionable decisions, similar to Re N [1990] 1 FLR 58, where the needs of ethnic minority children to be part of their culture are ignored.

We are certainly not advocating the rejection of the values and norms of the dominant culture, but we are asking for a new balance within the emerging pluralist context, leading to a larger degree of acceptance that the values of ethnic minorities can and should form part of the reasoning process of the English judiciary today.

Table of cases

List of statutes

Bibliography

Adams, B., J. Okely, J. Morgans and D. Smith (eds.) [1975]: Gypsies and government policy in England. A study of the travellers' way of life. Heinemann: London

Ahmed, Akbar S. [1992]: Postmodernism and Islam: Predicament and promise. Routledge: London

Akers, S. [1994]: 'Female genital mutilation'.In: Vol. 6 Journal of Child Law, pp. 27-31

Akhtar, Shabbir [1989]: Be careful with Muhammad! The Salman Rushdie affair. Bellew Publishers: London

Akzin, B. [1970]: 'Who is a Jew? A hard case'. In: Vol. 5 No. 2 Israel Law Review, pp. 259-263

Ali, Abdullah Yusuf [1946]: The Holy Qur'an. Islamic Propagation Centre International: Birmingham

Allott, Antony N. [1980]: The limits of law. Butterworths: London

Alston, P. [1994]: 'The best interests principle: Towards a reconciliation of culture and human rights'. In: Vol. 8 No. 1 Journal of Law and the Family, pp. 1-25

Amin, Sayed Hassan [1985]: Islamic law in the contemporary world. Vahid: Teheran and Royston: Glasgow

Anwar, M. [1979]: The myth of return: Pakistanis in Britain. Heinemann: London

Appignanesi, Lisa and Sara Maitland (eds.) [1989]: The Rushdie file. Fourth Estate: London

Archer, J. C. [1946]: The Sikhs in relation to Hindus, Moslems, Christians and Ahmadiyyas: A study in comparative religion. Princeton University Press: Princeton

Aurora, G. S. [1967]: The new frontiersmen: A sociological study of Indian immigrants in the United Kingdom. Popular Prakashan: Bombay

Azzam, Salem (ed.) [1982]: Islam and contemporary society. Longman in association with Islamic Council of Europe: London and New York

Bainham, Andrew [1991]: 'Care after 1991 – a reply'. In: Vol. 3 No. 3 Journal of Child Law, pp. 99-104

Bainham, Andrew [1993]: Children. The modern law. Family Law: Bristol

Bainham, Andrew [1995]: 'Family law in a pluralistic society'. In: Vol. 22 No. 2 [June 1995] Journal of Law and Society, pp. 234-247

Ballard, Roger [1979]: 'Ethnic minorities and the social services'. In: Khan, Verity S. (ed.) Minority families in Britain: Support and stress. Macmillan: London and Basingstoke, pp. 147-164

Ballard, Roger (ed.) [1994a]: Desh pardesh: The South Asian presence in Britain. Hurst and Co.: London

Ballard, Roger [1994b]: 'Differentiation and disjunction among the Sikhs'. In: Ballard, R. (ed.) [1994a], pp. 88-116

Ballard, Roger [1996]: 'Negotiating race and ethnicity: Exploring the implications of the 1991 Census'. In: Vol. 30 No. 3 Patterns of Prejudice, pp. 3-33

Ballard, Roger [1997]: 'The construction of a conceptual vision: 'Ethnic groups' and the 1991 U. K. Census' (Review Article). In: Vol. 20 No. 1 [January] Ethnic and Racial Studies, pp. 182-194

Banton, Michael [1959]: White and coloured: The behaviour of British people towards coloured immigrants. Jonathan Cape: London

Banton, Michael [1972]: Racial minorities. Fontana: London

Banton, Michael [1985]: Promoting racial harmony. Cambridge University Press: Cambridge

Banton, Michael [1989]: 'Are Rastafarians an ethnic group?'. In: Vol. 16 No. 1 [October 1989] New Community, pp. 153-157

Banton, Michael and H. Harwood [1975]: The race concept. David and Charles: Newton Abbot

Barker, Anthony J. [1978]: The African link: British attitudes to the Negro in the era of the Atlantic slave trade, 1550-1807. Frank Cass: London

Barnet, H. [1995]: 'The end of the road for Gypsies'. In: Vol. 24 No. 2 Anglo-American Law Review, pp. 133-167

Barton, Chris and Gillian Douglas [1995]: Law and parenthood. Butterworths: London, Dublin and Edinburgh

Bates, P. [1992]: 'Minorities, multi-culturalism and parenthood in Australian family law'. In: Vol. 21 No. 2 Anglo-American Law Review, pp. 202-219

Berghahn, M. [1984]: German-Jewish refugees in England: The ambiguities of assimilation. Macmillan: London

Berkeley, Humphry [1977]: The odyssey of Enoch: A political memoir. Hamish Hamilton: London

Bevan, Vaughan [1986]: The development of British immigration law. Croom Helm: London

Bhachu, Parminder K. [1985]: Twice migrants: East African Sikh settlers in Britain. Tavistock Publications: London and New York

Bowlby, J. [1969]: Attachment. Hogarth Press: London

Bowlby, J. [1972]: Child care and the growth of love. Penguin: Harmondsworth

Bowlby, J. [1980]: Attachment and loss. Vol. 3: Loss, sadness and depression. Hogarth: London

Bradney, Anthony [1993]: Religions, rights and laws. Leicester University Press: Leicester et al.

Braham, Peter, Ali Rattansi and Richard Skellington (eds.) [1992]: Racism and antiracism: Inequalities, opportunities and policies. Sage and Open University: Milton Keynes

Brohi, Allabukhsh K. [1982]: 'Islam, its politics and legal principles. A prolegomena to the theory and practice of politics and law'. In: Azzam, S. (ed.), pp. 62-100

Brown, Colin [1984]: Black and white Britain. The third PSI survey. Policy Studies Institute and Heinemann: London

Cain, M. and S. Sadigh [1982]: 'Racism, police and community policing: A comment on the Scarman Report'. In: Vol. 9 No. 1 [Summer 1982] The Journal of Law and Society, pp. 87-102

Caportorti, F. [1967]: Protection of minorities: Special protective measures of an international character for ethnic, religious or linguistic groups. United Nations: New York

Campaign Against Racism and Fascism (CARF) [1992]: 'Racial violence: Taking stock'. No. 10 [September 1992], p. 3

Carroll, Lucy [1997]: 'Muslim women and 'Islamic divorce' in England'. In: Vol. 17 No. 1 Journal of Muslim Minority Affairs, pp. 97-115

Carter, B., C. Harris and S. Joshi [1987]: The 1951-55 Conservative government and the racialisation of black immigration. [Policy Papers in Ethnic Relations, No. 11]. University of Warwick, Centre for Research in Ethnic Relations, Warwick

Cashmore, Ernest Ellis [1979]: Rastaman: The Rastafarian movement in England. Allen and Unwin: London

Cashmore, Ernest Ellis [1984a]: Dictionary of race and ethnic relations. Routledge and Kegan Paul: London

Cashmore, Ernest Ellis [1984b]: The Rastafarians. Minority Rights Group: London

Cashmore, Ernest Ellis [1989]: 'The Dawkins case: Official ethnic status for Rastas'. In: Vol. 16 No. 1 [October 1989] New Community, pp. 158-160

Cashmore, Ernest Ellis and Barry Troyna [1990]: Introduction to race relations. 2nd ed. Falmer Press: London

Centre for Contemporary Cultural Studies (ed.) [1982]: The Empire strikes back: Race and racism in 70s Britain. Routledge: London and New York

Chiba, Masaji (ed.) [1986]: Asian indigenous law in interaction with received law. KPI: London and New York

Claydon, J. [1975]: 'The transnational protection of ethnic minorities: A tentative framework for inquiry'. In: Vol. 13 Canadian Year Book of International Law, pp. 25-60

Cohen, P. [1988a]: 'Introduction: Perspective on the present'. In: Cohen, P. (ed.) [1988b], pp. 1-6

Cohen, Philip and Harwant S. Bains (eds.) [1988b]: Multi-racist Britain. Macmillan: London

Cole, W. Owen and Piara Singh Sambhi [1978]: The Sikhs: Their religious beliefs and practices. Routledge and Kegan Paul: London

Cox, B. [1975]: Civil liberties in Britain. Penguin: Harmondsworth

CRE [1987]: Living in terror. [Report of the Independent Commission of Inquiry, Leeds Community Relations Council, Leeds]. Commission for Racial Equality: London

CRE [1994]: Code of practice for the elimination of racial discrimination and the promotion of equal opportunity in employment. 3rd ed. Commission for Racial Equality: London

Cretney, Stephen M. [1997]: Family law. 3rd ed. Sweet and Maxwell: London

Cretney, Stephen M. and Judith Masson [1997]: Principles of family law. 6th ed. Sweet and Maxwell: London

Crick, Bernard [1995]: 'The sense of identity of the indigenous British'. In: Vol. 21 No. 2 [April 1995] New Community, pp. 167-182

Crossman, R. H. J. [1976]: The diaries of a Cabinet Minister, Vol. II. Hamish Hamilton: London

Cruz, Antonio [1995]: Shifting responsibility. Carriers' liability in the member states of the European Union and North America. Trentham Books and SOAS: Stoke-on-Trent: [GEMS No. 4]

Denning, Lord Alfred Thompson [1982]: What next in the law. Butterworths: London

Department of Health [1992a]: Manual of practice guidance for guardians ad litem and reporting officers. HMSO: London

Department of Health [1992b]: Review of adoption law: Report to ministers of an interdepartmental working group. HMSO: London

Department of Health [1993]: Adoption: The future. [Cmnd 2288]. HMSO: London

Diamond, Stanley [1992]: 'The rule of law versus the order of custom'. In: Varga, Csaba (ed.): Comparative legal cultures. Dartmouth: Aldershot et al., pp. 193-223

Dickens, B. M. [1981]: 'Functions and limits of parental rights'. In: Vol. 97 Law Quarterly Review, pp. 462-485

Dijk, P. Van den and G. J. H. Van Hoof [1990]: Theory and practice of the European Convention on Human Rights. 2nd ed. Kluwer Law and Taxation Publishers: Deventer and Boston

Drzemczewski, A. Z. [1983]: European Human Rights Convention in domestic law: A comparative study. Clarendon Press: Oxford

Dummett, Ann [1973]: A portrait of English racism. Penguin: Harmondsworth

Dummett, Ann [1994]: 'Immigration and nationality'. In: C. McCrudden and G. Chambers (eds.): Individual rights and the law in Britain. Clarendon Press: Oxford, pp. 335-362

Dummett, Ann and Andrew Nicol [1990]: Subjects, citizens, aliens and others: Nationality and immigration law. Weidenfeld and Nicolson: London

Dummett, Michael and Ann Dummett [1982]: 'The role of government in Britain's racial crisis'. In: Husband, Charles (ed.), pp. 97-127

Dunn, L. C. (ed.) [1950]: Race and biology: The significance of racial differences. UNESCO: Paris

Eade, John [1990]: 'Nationalism and the quest for authenticity: The Bangladeshis in Tower Hamlets'. In: Vol. 16 No. 4 [July 1990] New Community, pp. 493-503

Eekelaar, John [1973]: 'What are parental rights?' In: Vol. 89 Law Quarterly Review, pp. 210-234

Eekelaar, John [1984]: Family law and social policy. 2nd ed. Weidenfeld and Nicolson: London

Elton, Lord Godfrey [1965]: The unarmed invasion: A survey of Afro-Asian immigration. Geoffrey Bles: London

Esposito, John L. (ed.) [1983]: Voices of resurgent Islam. Oxford University Press: New York and Oxford

Evans, J. M [1983]: Immigration law. 2nd ed. Sweet and Maxwell: London

Faruqi, M. H. [1988]: 'Publishing sacrileges is not acceptable'. In: [28 October-10 November] Impact International. Reprinted in Appignanesi, L. and S. Maitland (eds.) [1989], pp. 60-61

Fawcett, J. J. [1990]: 'Evasion of law and mandatory rules in private international law'. In: Vol. 49 No. 1 [March 1990] Cambridge Law Journal, pp. 44-62

Feldman, David [1993]: Civil liberties and human rights in England and Wales. Clarendon Press: Oxford

Fentiman, R. [1992]: 'Foreign law in English courts'. In: Vol. 108 The Law Quarterly Review, pp. 142-156

Fielding, N. [1981]: The National Front. Routledge and Kegan Paul: London

Fischer, Michael M. J. [1983]: 'Imam Khomeini: Four levels of understanding'. In: Esposito, J. L. (ed.), pp. 150-174

Fischer, Michael M. J. and M. Abedi (eds.) [1990]: Debating Muslims: Cultural dialogues in postmodernity and traditions. The University of Wisconsin Press: Madison, Wisconsin

Fitzpatrick, Peter [1987]: 'Racism and the innocence of law'. In: Vol. 14 No. 1 Journal of Law and Society, pp. 114-132

Foot, Paul [1969]: The rise of Enoch Powell: an examination of Enoch Powell's attitude to immigration and race. Cornmarket Press: London

Ford, G. [1992]: Fascist Europe: The rise of racism and xenophobia. Pluto Press: London

Freeman, Michael D. A. [1983]: The rights and wrongs of children. Pinter: London

Fryer, Peter [1984]: Staying power. The history of black people in Britain. Pluto Press: London

Galanter, Marc [1981]: 'Justice in many rooms: Courts, private ordering, and indigenous law'. In: Vol. 19 Journal of Legal Pluralism and Unofficial Law, pp. 1-25

Gartner, L. P. [1973]: The Jewish immigrants in England 1870-1914. Simon Publishers: London

Gerils, S. [1995]: 'Racial awareness for judges'. In: Vol. 25 [May 1995] Family Law, p. 260

Gibson, B. [1994]: 'Black people and Magistrates' Courts'. In: Vol. 158 No. 18 [30 April 1994] Justice of the Peace and Local Government Law, pp. 282-283

Gilroy, Paul [1987]: There ain't no black in the Union Jack. The cultural politics of race and nation. Unwin Hyman: London

Goldstein, Joseph, Anna Freud and Albert J. Solnit [1979]: Beyond the best interests of the child. Free Press: New York

Gomien, D. [1991]: Short guide to the European Convention on Human Rights. Council of Europe: Strasbourg

Goonesekere, S. [1994]: 'The best interests of a child: A South Asian perspective'. In: Vol. 8 No. 1 International Journal of Law and the Family, pp. 117-149

Gordon, Milton Myron [1964]: Assimilation in American life: The role of race, religion and national origins. Oxford University Press: New York

Gordon, Paul [1983]: White law: Racism in the police, courts and prisons. Pluto Press: London

Gordon, Paul [1989]: Fortress Europe? The meaning of 1992. Runnymede Trust: London

Gordon, Paul and A. Newnham [1986]: Different worlds: Racism and discrimination in Britain. 2nd ed. Runnymede Trust: London

Gordon, Paul and D. Rosenberg [1983]: Daily racism: The press and black people in Britain. Runnymede Trust: London

Goulbourne, Harry [1991]: Ethnicity and nationalism in post-imperial Britain. Cambridge University Press: Cambridge

Gregory, Jeanne [1987]: Sex, race and the law. Legislating for equality. Sage: London

Griffith, J. A. G. [1985]: The politics of the judiciary. 3rd ed. Fontana Press: London

Griffiths, John [1985]: 'Introduction'. In: Allott, Antony and Gordon Woodman (eds.): Peoples' law and state law. The Bellagio Papers. Foris: Dordrecht, pp. 13-20

Griffiths, John [1986]: 'What is legal pluralism?'. In: Vol. 24 Journal of Legal Pluralism and Unofficial Law, pp. 1-56

Hall, J. C. [1972]: 'The waning of parental rights'. In: Vol. 31 No. 1 Cambridge Law Journal, pp. 248-265

Hall, S. [1991]: 'Old and new identities: Old and new ethnicities'. In: King, A. D. (ed.): Culture, globalization and the world system. Macmillan: London, pp. 41-68

Hallaq, Wael B. [1984]: 'Was the gate of ijtihad closed?'. In: Vol. 16 No. 1 [March 1984] International Journal of Middle East Studies, pp. 3-41

Hamilton, Carolyn [1995]: Family, law and religion. Sweet and Maxwell: London

Hamilton, Carolyn and K. Standley (eds.) [1995]: Family law in Europe. Butterworths: London

Harris, G. [1994]: The dark side of Europe. The extreme right today. Edinburgh University Press: Edinburgh

Harris, N. S. [1995]: The law relating to schools. 2nd ed. Tolley: Croydon

Hayes, P. C. [1995]: 'Transracial attitudes to adoption'. In: Vol. 9 International Journal of Law and the Family, pp. 1-27

Haymass, C., C. Lloyd and S. Wavell [1993]: 'Immigration: The false behind Churchill's outburst'. In: The Sunday Times, 30 May 1993

Henderson, R. [1995]: 'Is it in the blood?'. In: Wisden Cricket Magazine. Guildford, Surrey, pp. 9-10

Herbert, Peter [1995]: 'Racism, impartiality and juries'. In: Vol. 146 No. 6706 New Law Journal, pp. 1138-1139

Hiro, Dilip [1971]: Black British, white British. A history of race relations in Britain. Eyre and Spottiswoode: London

HMSO [1994]: Racial attacks and harassment: The government reply to the third report from the Home Affairs Committee Session, 1993-4. [House of Commons 71]. HMSO Publications: London

HMSO [1998]: Social Trends 28. Central Statistical Office, HMSO: London

Hodkinson, Keith [1984-85]: 'Legal decisions affecting ethnic minorities and discrimination – No. 22'. In: Vol. 12 No. 1 [Winter 1984-85] New Community, pp. 179-187

Hoggett, Brenda [1993]: Parents and children: The law of parental responsibility. 4th ed. Sweet and Maxwell: London

Hoggett, Brenda, David Pearl, Elizabeth J. Cooke and Philip D. Bates [1996]: The family, law and society. Cases and materials. 4th ed. Butterworths: London et al.

Holgate, C. [1991]: 'McKenzie friends: Commonsense prevails in the Court of Appeal'. In: Vol. 155 No. 39 Justice of the Peace, pp. 617-618

Holland, Brian [1995]: 'Kicking racism out of football': An assessment of racial harassment in and around football grounds'. In: Vol. 21 No. 4 [October 1995] New Community, pp. 567-586

Hooker, M. B. [1975]: Legal pluralism: An introduction to colonial and neo-colonial laws. Clarendon Press: Oxford

Hughes, T. P. [1935]: A dictionary of Islam. W. H. Allen and Company: London

Humphrey, J. P. [1989]: No distant millennium: The international law of human rights. UNESCO: Paris

Husband, Charles (ed.) [1982]: 'Race' in Britain: Continuity and change. Hutchinson: London et al.

Hutley, Rebecca [1998]: 'Privileged minority? The social and legal position of Japanese migrants in Britain'. In: Vol. 12 No. 1 [January 1998] Immigration & Nationality Law & Practice, pp. 3-7

Ingman, Terence [1994]: The English legal process. 5th ed. Blackstone: London

Jain, Madhu [1988]: 'Interviews with Salman Rushdie'. In: [15 September 1988] India Today. Reprinted in Appignanesi and Maitland (eds.) [1989], pp. 38-40

James, A.G. [1974]: Sikh children in Britain. Oxford University Press: London, New York and Delhi

James, W. [1989]: 'The making of black identities'. In: Samuel, R. (ed.): Patriotism: The making and unmaking of British national identity. Vol. 2. Routledge: London, pp. 230-255

Jeffery, Patricia [1972]: Migrants and refugees: Muslim and Christian Pakistani families in Bristol. Cambridge University Press: Cambridge et al.

Jewish Women in London Group [1989]: Generations of memories: Voices of Jewish women. The Women's Press: London

Joly, Danièle [1995]: Britannia's crescent: Making a place for Muslims in British society. Avebury: Aldershot

Jones, Richard and Gnanapala Welhengama [1996]: 'Child marriages in contemporary Britain'. In: Vol. 18 Liverpool Law Review, pp. 197-203

Jones, Trevor [1993]: Britain's ethnic minorities. Policy Studies Institute: London

Jordan, Winthrop D. [1982]: 'First impressions: Initial English confrontation with Africans'. In: Husband, C. (ed.), pp. 42-58

Juss, Satvinder S. [1995]: 'The Constitution and Sikhs in Britain'. In: [1995] Brigham Young University Law Review, pp. 481- 533

Khadduri, Majid [1955]: War and peace in the law of Islam. The Johns Hopkins Press: Baltimore and London

King, M. [1978]: 'Mad dances and magistrates'. In: Vol. 45 New Society, pp. 564-566

King, Michael (ed.) [1995]: God's law versus state law. The construction of an Islamic identity in Western Europe. Grey Seal: London

Krausz, Ernest [1972]: Ethnic minorities in Britain. Paladin: London

Kureishi, H. [1989]: 'London and Karachi'. In: Samuel, R. (ed.), pp. 271-287

Lane, David [1987]: 'The Commission for Racial Equality: the first five years'. In: Vol. 14 Nos. 1-2 [Autumn 1987] New Community, pp. 12-16

Law Commission [1970]: Report on nullity of marriage. [No. 30]. HMSO: London

Lee, Trevor R. [1973]: 'Immigrants in London: Trends in distribution and concentration 1961-71'. In: Vol. 2 No. 2 [Spring 1973] New Community, pp.145-158

Lester, Anthony [1993]: 'English judges as law makers'. In: Public Law, pp. 269-290

Lester, Anthony and Geoffrey Bindman [1972]: Race and law. Penguin: London

Lewis, Bernard [1994]: 'Legal and historical reflections on the position of Muslim populations under non-Muslim rule'. In: Lewis, Bernard and D. Schnapper (eds.) [1994]: Muslims in Europe. Pinter Publishers, London and New York, pp.1-18

Lewis, P. [1994]: Islamic Britain: Religion, politics and identity among British Muslims. Bradford in the 1990s. I. B. Tauris: London and New York

Liégeois, Jean-Pierre [1985]: Gypsies : An illustrated history. AI Saqui Books: London

Liégeois, Jean-Pierre [1987]: Gypsies and travellers. Council for Cultural Co-operation: Strasbourg

Lipman, Vivian D. [1954]: Social history of the Jews in England 1850-1950. Watts and Company: London

Lynch, James [1989]: 'Cultural pluralism, structural pluralism and the United Kingdom'. In: Britain: A plural society. [Report of a seminar organised by the Commission for Racial Equality and The Runnymede Trust]. CRE: London, pp. 29-43

Macdonald, Ian A. [1969]: Race relations and immigration law. Butterworths: London

Macdonald, Ian A. and Nicholas J. Blake [1991]: Immigration law and practice in the United Kingdom. 3rd ed. Butterworths: London et al.

McLeod, W. H. [1968]: Guru Nanak and the Sikh religion. Clarendon Press: Oxford.

Maidment, Susan [1981]: 'The fragmentation of parental rights'. In: Vol. 40 Cambridge Law Journal, p. 135-158

Maidment, Susan [1984]: Child custody and divorce: the law in social context. Croom Helm: London and Sydney

Marquand, David [1995]: 'After Whig imperialism: Can there be a new British identity?' In: Vol. 21 No. 2 [April 1995] New Community, pp. 183-193

Maududi, M. A. A. [1993]: Laws of marriage and divorce in Islam. Islamic Book Publishers: Safat, Kuwait

Mazzel, C. and J. Frewin [1992]: 'Realities of divided kingdom'. In: November [1992] London Students, p. 17

McCrudden, C. and G. Chambers (eds.) [1994]: Individual rights and the law in Britain. Clarendon Press: Oxford

McLennan, Gregor [1995]: Pluralism. Open University Press: Buckingham

Menski, Werner F. [1987]: 'Legal pluralism in the Hindu marriage'. In: Burghart, Richard (ed.): Hinduism in Great Britain. Tavistock: London, pp. 180-200

Menski, Werner F. [1988]: 'English family law and ethnic laws in Britain'. In: 1988(1) Kerala Law Times, Journal section, pp. 55-66

Menski, Werner F. [1993]: 'Asians in Britain and the question of adaptation to a new legal order: Asian laws in Britain'. In: Israel, Milton and N. K. Wagle (eds.): Ethnicity, identity, migration: The South Asian context. University of Toronto: Toronto, pp. 238-268

Menski, Werner (ed.) [1998]: South Asians and the dowry problem. Trentham Books: Stoke-on-Trent.

Mercer, K. [1990]: 'Welcome to the jungle: Identity and diversity in post-modern politics'. In: Rutherford, Jonathan (ed.): Identity: Community, culture, difference. Lawrence and Wisehart: London, pp. 43-71

Merry, S .E. [1988]: 'Legal pluralism'. In: Vol. 22 Part 5 Law and Society, pp. 869-896

Miles, R. [1993]: Racism after race relations. Routledge: London

Miller, David [1995]: 'Reflections on British national identity'. In: Vol. 21 No. 2 [April 1995] New Community, pp. 153-166

Mnookin, R. H. [1975]: 'Child-custody adjudication: Judicial functions in the face of indeterminacy'. In: Vol. 39 Law and Contemporary Problems, pp. 226-293

Mnookin, R. H. [1984]: 'Divorce bargaining: The limits on private ordering', In: Eekelaar, J. M. and S. N. Katz (eds.): The resolution of family conflict: Comparative legal perspectives. Butterworths: Toronto et al., pp. 364-383

Modood, Tariq [1990]: 'British Asian Muslims and the Rushdie affair'. In: Vol. 61 No. 2 [April 1990] Political Quarterly, pp. 143-160

Modood, Tariq [1992]: Not easy being British: Colour, culture and citizenship. Trentham Books: Stoke-on-Trent

Modood, Tariq [1993]: 'Muslims, incitement to hatred and the law'. In: The UK Action Committee on Islamic Affairs (UKACIA) (ed.): Muslims and the law in multi-faith Britain. Need for reform. UKACIA: London, pp. 65-81

Morris, H. [1968]: 'Ethnic groups'. In: International Encyclopaedia of Social Science, McMillan, New York

Mortimore, Claudia [1994]: Immigration and adoption. Trentham Books: Stoke-on-Trent

Munroe, M. [1985]: 'The Prestige case: Putting the lid on the Commission for Racial Equality'. In: Vol. 14 No. 3 Anglo-American Law Review, pp.187-203

Nielsen, Jørgen S. [1987]: 'Muslims in Britain: Searching for an identity?'. In: Vol. 13 No. 3 [Spring 1987] New Community, pp. 384-394

Nielsen, Jørgen S. [1991]: A Muslim agenda for Britain: Some reflections'. In: Vol. 17 No. 3 [April 1991] New Community, pp. 467-475

Nielsen, Jørgen S. [1992]: Muslims in Western Europe. Edinburgh University Press: Edinburgh

Noonan, J. J. Jr. [1976]: Persons and masks of the law: Cardozo, Holmes, Jefferson and Whythe as makers of the masks. Farrar, Straw and Giroux: New York

Pannick, David [1987]: Judges. Oxford University Press: Oxford

Parekh, Bhikhu [1995]: 'The concept of national identity'. In: Vol. 21 No. 2 [April 1995] New Community, pp. 255-268

Parker-Jenkins, Marie (July, 1991): 'Muslim matters: The educational needs of the Muslim child'. In: Vol. 17 No. 4 [July 1991] New Community, pp. 569-582

Parry, C. [1957]: Nationality and citizenship laws of the Commonwealth and of the Republic of Ireland. Stevens: London

Patterson, Sheila [1984-85]: 'Usage and abusage: Notes on the term 'nig-nog''. In: Vol. 12 No. 1 [Winter 1984-85] New Community, pp. 155-161

Pearl, David [1972]: 'Muslim marriages in English law'. In: Vol. 30 Cambridge Law Journal, pp. 120-143

Pearl, David [1981]: 'Islam in English family law', in Nielsen, Joergen S. (ed.): Muslims in Europe. CSIC: Birmingham, pp. 6-10

Pearl, David [1983]: 'Legal decisions affecting ethnic minorities and discrimination – No. 19'. In: Vol. 10 No. 3 [Spring 1983] New Community, pp. 496-501

Pearl, David [1986]: Family law and the immigrant communities. Jordan: Bristol

Pearl, David [1987]: A textbook on Muslim personal law. 2nd ed. Croom Helm: London

Pospisil, L. [1971]: Anthropology of law: A comparative theory. Harper and Row: New York

Poulter, Sebastian M. [1986]: English law and ethnic minority customs. Butterworths: London

Poulter, Sebastian M. [1987]: 'Ethnic minority customs, English law and human rights'. In: Vol. 36 International and Comparative Law Quarterly, pp. 589-615

Poulter, Sebastian M. [1989]: 'The significance of ethnic minority customs and traditions in English criminal law'. In: Vol. 16 No. 1 [October 1989] New Community, pp. 121-128

Poulter, Sebastian M. [1990a]: Asian traditions and English law: A handbook. The Runnymede Trust with Trentham Books: Stoke-on-Trent

Poulter, Sebastian M. [1990b]: 'The claim to a separate Islamic system of personal law for British Muslims'. In: Mallat, Chibli and Jane Connors (eds.): Islamic family law. Graham and Trotman: London, pp. 147-166

Poulter, Sebastian [1995]: 'Multiculturalism and human rights for Muslim families in English law'. In: King, Michael (ed.): God's law versus state law. The construction of an Islamic identity in Western Europe. Grey Seal: London, pp. 81-87

Poulter, Sebastian M. [1998]: Ethnicity, law and human rights. Clarendon Press: Oxford

Powell, Enoch [1965]: A nation not afraid. Hodder and Stoughton: London

Qureshi, S. and J. Khan (eds.) [1989]: The politics of Satanic Verses: Unmasking Western attitudes. Muslim Community Studies Institute: Leicester

Radcliffe, The Rt. Hon. Viscount Lord [1969]: 'Immigration and settlement: Some general considerations'. In: Vol. 11 Race, pp. 35-51

Ramdin, R. [1987]: The making of the black working class in Britain. Gower: London

Rath, Jan, Kees Groenendijk and Rinos Penninx [1995]: 'The recognition and institutionalisation of Islam in Belgium, Great Britain and the Netherlands'. In: Vol. 18 No. 1 [October 1991] New Community, pp. 101-114

Raz, J. [1974]: 'Multi-culturalism: A liberal perspective'. In: [1974] Dissent, pp. 67-70

Raza, Mohammad S. [1991]: Islam in Britain. Past, present and future. Volcano Press: Leicester

Reed, A. [1996]: 'Extra-judicial divorces since Berkovits'. In: Vol. 26 Family Law, pp. 100-103

Rex, John and Sally Tomlinson [1979]: Colonial immigrants in a British city: A class analysis. Routledge and Kegan Paul: London

Rich, P. B. [1990]: Race and empire in British politics. 2nd ed. Cambridge University Press: Cambridge

Richardson, J. and J. Lambert [1985]: The sociology of race. Causeway Press: London

Rippin, Andrew [1990]: Muslims: Their religious beliefs and practices. Vol. 1: The formative period. Routledge: London and New York

Robilliard, St. John A. [1983]: 'Sikhs, religion and the Race Relations Act 1976'. In: [1983] Public Law, pp. 348-351

Roosens, Eugeen E. [1989]: Creating ethnicity: The process of ethnogenesis. Sage: London

Ruthven, Malise [1991]: A satanic affair: Salman Rushdie and the wrath of Islam. The Hogarth Press: London

Sachdeva, Sanjiv [1993]: The primary purpose rule in British immigration law. Trentham Books and SOAS: Stoke-on-Trent and London. [GEMS No. 1]

Saggar, Shamit [1992]: Race and politics in Britain. Harvester Wheatsheaf: New York et al.

Saifullah-Khan, Verity [1976]: 'Pakistanis in Britain: Perception of a population'. In: Vol. 5 No. 3 [Autumn 1976] New Community, pp. 222-229

Salkey, A. (ed.) [1973]: Caribbean essays: An anthology. Evans: London

Samad, Yunas [1992]: 'Bookburning and race relations: Political mobilisation of Bradford Muslims'. In: Vol. 18 No. 4 [July 1992] New Community, pp. 507-519

Samuel, R. (ed.) [1989]: Patriots: The making and unmaking of British national identity. Vol. 2. Routledge: London

Scantlebury, Elizabeth [1995]: 'Muslims in Manchester: The depiction of a religious community'. In: Vol. 21 No. 3 [July 1995] New Community, pp. 425-435

Searle, C. [1989]: Your daily dose: Racism and the Sun. Campaign for Press and Broadcasting Freedom:London

Seligman, E. R. A. [1949]: 'Ethnic communities'. In: Vol. 5 Encyclopaedia of Social Science, p. 607

Shackle, Christopher [1986]: The Sikhs. Rev. ed. Minority Rights Group: London

Shah, Prakash [1994]: 'Legal pluralism – British law and possibilities with Muslim ethnic minorities'. In: Vol. 17 Nos. 3-4 Retfærd, pp. 18-33.

Shah, S. [1979]: 'Asian marriages: A case of white propaganda'. In: Vol. 15 No. 1 [11 October] New Society, pp. 132-133

Shaikh, Farzana (ed.) [1992]: Islam and Islamic groups: A worldwide reference guide. Longman: Harlow

Shaw, Alison [1988]: A Pakistani community in Britain. Basil Blackwell: Oxford

Sikh Missionary Centre [1990]: Sikh Religion. Sikh Missionary Centre: Detroit, Michigan

Singh, H. [1969]: Guru Nanak and the origin of the Sikh faith. Asia Publishing House: Bombay

Singh, K. [1963]: A history of the Sikhs. Vol. 1. Asia Publishing House: Bombay

Singh, Pritam and Shinder S. Thandi [1996]: Globalisation and the region. Explorations in Punjabi identity. Association for Punjab Studies (UK): Coventry

Singh, T. [1939]: Sikhism: Its ideals and institutions. Longmans Green and Co: Calcutta

Sivanandan, A. [1991]: A different hunger: Writings on black resistance. Pluto Press: London

Skellington, R. and P. Morris [1992]: Race in Britain today. Sage in Association with the Open University: London

Skolnik, A. [1975]: 'The limits of childhood: Conceptions of child development and social context'. In: Vol. 39 Law and Contemporary Problems, pp. 38-77

Smith, J. C. and B. Hogan [1983]: Criminal law. 5th ed. Butterworths: London

Smith, J. and B. Hogan [1996]: Criminal law. 8th ed. Butterworths: London

Solomos, John [1989]: Race and racism in contemporary Britain. Macmillan: London

Solomos, John [1992]: 'The politics of immigration since 1945'. In: Braham, Rattansi and Skellington (eds.), pp. 7-29

Solomos, John, B. Findlay, S. Jones and P. Gilroy [1982]: 'The organic crisis of British capitalism and race: The experience of the seventies'. In: Centre for Contemporary Cultural Studies (ed.), pp. 9-46

Sondhi, Ranjit [1987]: Divided families: British immigration control in the Indian subcontinent. Runnymede Trust: London

Spencer, Ian R. G. [1997]: British immigration policy since 1939. The making of multiracial Britain. Routledge: London and New York

Stone, Richard [1994]: Textbook on civil liberties. Blackstone: London

Taheri, Amir [1989]: 'Khomeini's scape-goat'. In: [13 February 1989] The Times

Tajfel, Henri and John L. Dawson (eds.) [1965]: Disappointed guests: Essays by African, Asian and West Indian students. Oxford University Press: London

Taylor, S. [1982]: The National Front in English politics. Macmillan: London

The UK Action Committee on Islamic Affairs [1993]: Muslims and the law in multifaith Britain. Need for reform. UKACIA Publications: London

Tizard, B. and A. Phoenix [1993]: Black, white or mixed race: Race and racism in the lives of young people of mixed parentage. Routledge: London

Troyna, Barry [1981]: Public awareness and the media: A study of reporting on race. Commission for Racial Equality: London

Van den Bergh, G. C. J. J. [1992]: 'Legal pluralism in Roman law'. In: Varga, Csaba (ed.): Comparative legal cultures. Dartmouth: Aldershot et al., pp. 451-463

Walker, M. [1971]: The National Front. Fontana: London

Walvin, James [1982]: 'Black caricature: The roots of racialism'. In: Husband (ed.), pp. 59-72

Webster, Richard [1990]: A brief history of blasphemy: Liberalism, censorship and 'The Satanic Verses'. The Orwell Press: Southwold

Welhengama, Gnanapala [1994]: 'Sikhs and industrial tribunals'. In: Vol. 144 No. 6648 New Law Journal, pp. 671-672

Welhengama, Gnanapala [1995]: 'Race and rejection'. In: Vol. 145 No. 6699 New Law Journal, pp. 863-864

Wilkinson, J. P. [1985-86]: 'Why magistrates need race relations training'. In: Vol. 12 No. 3 [Winter 1985-86] New Community, pp. 476-484

Wirsing, Robert C. [1981]: 'Dimensions of minority protection'. In: Wirsing, Robert C. (ed.): Protection of ethnic minorities: Comparative perspectives. Pergamon Press: New York et al., pp. 3-17

Yapp, Malcolm [1989]: 'The hubris of the hidden Imam'. The Independent, 22 February 1989. In: Appignanesi, L. and S. Maitland (eds.): The Rushdie file. Fourth Estate Ltd: London, pp. 95-98

Index